Intimate Spirituality

Intimate Spirituality

The Catholic Way of Love and Sex

Gordon J. Hilsman, D. Min.

A Sheed & Ward Book

ROWMAN & LITTLEFIELD PUBLISHERS, INC.
Lanham • Boulder • New York • Toronto • Plymouth, UK

Excerpt from THE FOUR LOVES, copyright © 1960 by C.S. Lewis, renewed 1988 by
Arthur Owen Barfield, reprinted by permission of Harcourt, Inc.

A SHEED & WARD BOOK

ROWMAN & LITTLEFIELD PUBLISHERS, INC.

Published in the United States of America
by Rowman & Littlefield Publishers, Inc.
A wholly owned subsidary of The Rowman & Littlefield Publishing Group, Inc.
4501 Forbes Boulevard, Suite 200, Lanham, Maryland 20706
www.rowmanlittlefield.com

Estover Road
Plymouth PL6 7PY
United Kingdom

Copyright © 2007 by Gordon J. Hilsman

British Library Cataloguing in Publication Information Available

Library of Congress Cataloging-in-Publication Data

Hilsman, Gordon J., 1941–
 Intimate spirituality : the Catholic way of love and sex / Gordon J. Hilsman.
   p. cm.
 "A Sheed & Ward Book."
 Includes bibliographical references and index.
 ISBN-13: 978-1-58051-211-4 (cloth : alk. paper)
 ISBN-10: 1-58051-211-9 (cloth : alk. paper)
 1. Sex—Religious aspects—Catholic Church. 2. Love—Religious aspects—Catholic
Church. 3. Intimacy (Psychology)—Religious aspects—Catholic Church. 4. Catholic
Church—Doctrines. I. Title.
 BX1795.S48H55 2007
 261.8'357--dc22

                                                                        2006038383

Printed in the United States of America

∞™ The paper used in this publication meets the minimum requirements of
American National Standard for Information Sciences—Permanence of Paper
for Printed Library Materials, ANSI/NISO Z39.48-1992.

Dedicated to Nancy,
who I finally found and with whom I've learned
the most about intimate love

~

Contents

Foreword, *by Eugene C. Kennedy*   ix

Introduction   xiii

Part I: Eros and Individual Spirituality   1

Chapter 1   The Natural Mystery of the Loving Spirit   3

Chapter 2   Nine Fruits of Romantic Love   15

Chapter 3   Seven Enduring Gifts of Maturing Love   29

Chapter 4   Death, Resurrection, and the Ending of Love   47

Chapter 5   Lust or Lusty Love—The Moral and the Spiritual   53

Chapter 6   Six Other Styles of Intimate Failure   69

Chapter 7   Four Cardinal Virtues of Love's Foundation   87

Part II: Eros and Community   101

Chapter 8   Sacramental Enhancement: Can Agape Learn from Eros?   103

Chapter 9   The Evangelical Counsels for All   129

Chapter 10   Eros and Social Spirituality   139

Chapter 11   Eros and Catholic Social Teaching   153

Chapter 12   Intimate Love and the Leader's Own Spirituality   165

              Index   181

              About the Author   187

~

Foreword

Eugene C. Kennedy

Only men with a large sense of their destiny and a well-practiced gift for self-dramatization make bold claims about the timing of their arrivals in history. Such figures are usually bigger than life and hardly bashful about their self-promotion. Pope John Paul II, as large a figure as ever stepped onto the world stage, reputedly felt providentially chosen to take on communism in his native Poland as a prelude to his becoming pope to return the Vatican II Church to the ways of Vatican I. General George S. Patton Jr. felt just as privileged a role in history when, knowing that the tank had changed the nature of battle, he claimed to be the right man with the right weapon at exactly the right moment to break Allied forces out during their invasion in World War II. Such great men may be secretly humble before their God, but they are never modest before their fellow man.

Beyond these towering figures, however, stand men and women who, without laying claim to entitlement or hungering for applause, are just the right persons with just the right understanding of human affairs at exactly the right moment in history. Because they do not seek even ten minutes of celebrity acclaim, they place their gifts quietly at our common altar. They think about bringing light to our experience rather than fame to themselves.

Gordon Hilsman enters our age with the right book at exactly the right moment in our history. History, of course, chronicles everything that makes us human, from our sexuality to our spirituality. In his understanding of these elements and their unity in personality, Hilsman bears gifts as simple as those of which the Quakers sing and for which, drained by the vampire narcissists all around us, we so deeply long. He preaches as gently as St. Francis not about the glory of elected poverty but of the neglected glory of our profoundly interwoven sexual and spiritual lives.

Hilsman's goal is to restore a sense of integrity to the human personality that for so long has been stratified, often by church leaders, including Pope John Paul II, into spirit that is good and the flesh that is the usual suspect in every fall from grace. Pope John Paul II went so far as to make the renunciation of sexual experience superior to its expression between man and wife. The only couple he ever canonized had, in fact, stopped having sexual relations when they were not yet into middle age.

Answering Parzival's Question

In writing *The Unhealed Wound*, I realized that many of the great mythic figures—their stories seemingly of long ago are really about us now—suffered serious sexual wounds that would not heal. Tristan's leads to the *Love Death* and the Fisher King can find ease only if he is rowed out into the lulling deep. Von Eschenbach's version of *Parzival* re-creates the tale of the Knight of the West, the symbol of Spirit, setting out for the East just as the Knight of the East, the symbol of Nature, sets out for the West. They meet and do battle and the Knight of the West, symbol of Spirit, slays the Knight of the East, symbol of Nature. He suffers, however, a sexual wound—a spear thrust through his testicles—that will not heal, and he lives, unable to find a place to sit or stand or lie down with comfort in his Grail castle. The members of his court remain silent in his presence out of fear that they may say something that would incur the wounded king's wrath.

Parzival sets out to find and heal this king, but on arriving at his castle he is inhibited by the court protocol and departs without speaking to the king. After other adventures and the maturing love of a woman, Conduamirs, he returns to the castle in which the king still suffers, and his fearful court still remains silent. Horrifying its members, Parzival puts a simple human question to the king: "What is it that ails you?" By the very asking of the question, the king is healed, and Parzival become the inheritor of the Grail castle without the wound.

For centuries, believers have been told that their essential spiritual struggle—that will win or lose eternal life for them—depends on Spirit's slaying Nature, on our overcoming, silencing, or numbing altogether what is natural and healthy about us by invoking means that are unnatural and unhealthy for us. Readers of this book will awaken to what is natural and healthy and therefore spiritually healthy and good in themselves.

Hilsman gives his thoughtful answers to young Parzival's question. This question is asked of all of us—and who of us has not felt this wound often in the presence of members of Church courts who remain silent lest they incur the wrath of the pope? Shakespeare writes in *Romeo and Juliet*, "He jests at scars that never felt the wound." Because we feel it in greater or lesser ways still, Hilsman's preaching is to our own wounded experience. He does not excoriate Church courts that have remained silent while their people suffered but offers strong, gospel-based meditations not from the viewpoint of an academician's lofty desk but from the bedroom in which our sexuality should be expressed and experienced in a healthy and integrating fashion.

These reflections will, therefore, strike readers, especially those whose sexual wounding by church personnel has not healed, as a relief from the sermons and instructions that make them feel guilty just because they are human and therefore sexual beings. Hilsman's words, based on what is old, will seem as fresh and new as they are comforting to such readers. The latter will be surprised by his openness and encouraged by his rich and unstrained reflections on the fundamentally healthy nature of human sexual experience. He addresses what ailed the Grail king and still ails so many good people who, for all the culture's supposed sophistication with sex, cannot easily find a comfortable place to sit or stand or lie down with their own human natures. These reflections will wash over readers as the healing waters in biblical pools did. They will emerge with an appreciation that the words *hale*, *whole*, and *holy* all derive from the same root, *hal*, and all refer to the same freeing and affirming experience that is the energizing subtext of this remarkable book.

~

Introduction

Growing up as an inward, disciplined, and mostly well-behaved German-American Catholic boy in the midwestern 1950s, I came to love the stability and mystical beauty of the Catholic Church's teaching and liturgical practice. One of my first memories includes the doting smiles of my Grandma Hilsman and Aunt Louise as I shared childhood versions of Bible stories I'd no doubt heard in church. Mostly a well-motivated and cooperative student, I was first to recite the Ten Commandments in a catechism class of sixty-one and to memorize the altar boy Latin at the age of ten.

Fitting the blast of sexual pleasure into that calming and inspiring spiritual life framework during adolescence, however, wasn't so easy. As a better-than-average athlete, I heard plenty of locker room sex and girl talk. But my introversion impeded my participation in the scary endeavor of romance while I listened intently, trying to make some morsel of sense out of that almost irresistible fascination with penis pleasure. Was "impurity by myself" really a sin that could damn me to hell forever?

Combining the reality of sexual ecstasy with intimate love took me thirty-seven years, and I now believe it may be the grandest achievement of most lives. As we seek to employ the pure gift of sexuality in loving mutuality, we are engaging a profound mystery that continues forever to deepen and unfold in complexity. Built into humanity as a fundamental aspect of creation, sexual loving stands along with prayer, meditation, communal worship, and social action as spiritual modalities capable of deeply feeding the soul. The chasm that has grown between intimate loving and Catholic practice is now finding a bridge.

Spirituality and Morality

There has been good reason for that separation. Sex is dangerous. We are, in the present era, finding out more and more just how destructive it can be, in rape, incest, pedophilia, molestation, and otherwise sexualizing a person too soon or by force at any age. This peril inherent in sexuality's combination of intense pleasure and enormous vulnerability has overshadowed the beauty of intimate love and its potential to enhance life's richness and prod spiritual maturity. Over the centuries, ecclesiastical leaders and theological thinkers, in striving to protect us—and particularly our daughters—from the damage of sex-without-love, have never been ready to recognize the spiritual potential of its beauty. Catholic culture has almost totally neglected the spiritual power of sexual loving beyond mentioning it relative to the sacrament of matrimony.

All religious traditions develop writings that teach what is considered to be beautiful and virtuous in human behavior and what is ugly or evil—their spiritual theology and their moral theology. In Catholic tradition, the moral view has long overshadowed the spiritual regarding the sexual aspect of life.

But a youth doesn't learn baseball from reading the rulebook, nor fishing from an instruction manual. They need coaching, envisioning excellence, daydreaming, emulating heroes, and especially experience at playing the game, with all its performance mistakes, mental blunders, and necessary early ineptness. Similarly, intimate loving needs perspectives of human engagement beyond regulation, awkward silence, and moral cautions.

This book is intended to begin filling a significant gap in Catholic culture between its well-developed individual and communal spiritualities. Beliefs and practices to enhance the individual relationship between God and oneself have characterized every Christian age. Likewise, encountering of the living Christ in small and large groups has been well developed as communal spirituality. Both continue to feed a half billion gathering Catholics worldwide.

What could be called intimate spirituality, however, the partnering between lovers inherent in a race of people physically capable of easily pleasuring one another, has largely been overlooked by eight hundred years of celibate theological and organizational Church leadership. This remains true even though sexual loving continues to be a significant factor in shaping and maintaining the spiritual lives of most people, century after century. A perspective that emphasizes what sexual intimacy contributes to a spiritual life has long awaited evolution's readiness.

Only in the twentieth century has the distinction between religion and spirituality been widely developed. Many factors have contributed to making the differentiation between them useful. Freud, psychology, and the self-help movement have made us more reflective on our internal reverie and its impact on our level of happiness. The Twelve Step and hospice movements have prompted practical addressing of spiritual issues for the sake of crucial life projects—dying and addiction recovery—by large numbers of people, many of whom are disenchanted with religious leadership yet desperate for spiritual meaning and purpose. Women finding their voices have insisted that the inward experience of the heart take a prominent place in spirituality amidst intellectual perspectives that have often eclipsed it. The pragmatism of U.S. society has prompted us to seek spiritual modalities that are observably effective with richness of experience, increasingly bypassing divided Christianity's incessant, subtle competitiveness about which denomination's theology is closer to absolute truth. The human endeavor of seeking spiritual fulfillment in a wide variety of ways, inside and outside of established religious practices and traditional beliefs, has mushroomed in the past half hundred years.

The "Catholic Way" Reflected in Intimate Love

In the midst of the spiritual renaissance taking place worldwide, many of us continue to treasure the Catholic religious traditions that have lived for centuries because they have more or less successfully guided millions of spiritual lives in diverse cultures all over the world. The meaning and purpose of Catholic ways of living and believing that inspire care of one another, frequent openness to sacramental mystery, individual devotional practices, fostering closeness with the incarnate Transcendent, and investment in the mission of improving world living conditions for all people are treasures for which many of us would die as history's martyrs have done and others still do today. But we need to see sexual loving as an integral part of Catholic practice as well. It is time to recognize that the natural human mystery of intimate love can shine light on virtually every aspect of Catholic tradition.

You will find no debunking of Catholic authority in this book, though later chapters contain observations and suggestions about the personal spirituality of any spiritual leader. There is no scandal for the young here either, though the book's openness about how sexual love seeking can influence the human spirit for either well or ill challenges both the imagination and the self-responsibility of those new to intimate relationships. Metaphorically, there is no trashing of an old house or effort to build a new one. There are presented here suggestions for significant renovation and augmentation of a house that is already cherished. How might Catholic culture look if intimate love were taken seriously as primary data for theology and ecclesiastical policy? Beginning to develop answers to that question is this book's chief aim.

Neither is this book a marriage manual or self-help treatment of how to inject richness into a love life, find a great lover, or make marriage work. Instead, it uses the common experiences of virtually all people as we engage the loving mystery, to bring deeper insight into the age-old traditions of Catholic spiritual practice.

Sexuality and Love

Intimate Spirituality is based on a conviction that relationships that combine sex and love are a primary mode of conveyance of the gospel. The kernel of the kerygma, or core meaning of the New Testament, is a profoundly personal message that "God loves you—and all humans—deeply, abundantly, freely, gloriously, and unconditionally." We come to experience this love of God as real in our lives through being loved, although imperfectly, by others—parents, siblings, teachers, uncles, cousins, catechists, coaches, godparents, friends, mentors, and strangers who notice the best in us—and richly, earthily, and bodily through our lovers. The erotic energy that begins commanding our attention during early adolescence relentlessly compels intimate partnering during adulthood and continues to enrich and complicate life into aging is a major font of experiencing the gospel. Romantic loving, built into humanity by the Creator, is actually a rich and underpreached model of relating with the Divine.

Some of the historic separation between eros (sexual love) and agape (selfless communal love) is practical and absolutely necessary. I remember one church history class that revealed how the early Christian practice of the "kiss of peace" had been transformed into a handshake and then phased out altogether in liturgical worship because of the disruptive jockeying for position of young men and women in the sacred space. Eros and agape do not easily coexist in place and time. One focuses on community celebration and altruistic care of all humanity, while the other needs privacy for passionate bodily expression. They are distinct forms of love. Like cars speeding in opposite directions on a two-lane highway, they are similar and parallel but for the most part must remain separate.

Yet both are experiences of the living God. Taking the old-age musings of the Evangelist John seriously when he wrote that "God is love and he who abides in love abides in God and God in him" indicates that "love" is the major criterion of spiritual health. Granted, the Greek word for love in New Testament writing referred to the "selfless love" called agape rather than the earlier, more basic love termed eros. But intimate loving has clearly been built into creation by the two-person, intimacy-fed, pleasure-energized configuration in which human beings continue to be born. Even after the great agape outpouring of the early Christian centuries, eros persisted and continues to develop into a more partnering style of loving as we evolve.

Partnership Spirituality

Whatever or whoever is energizing creative evolution clearly uses partnering as one major model of people relating to each other and to the Divine. Taking that observation seriously constitutes partnership spirituality, that is, looking at humans less as autonomous individuals and more as collaborative partners in facing and fashioning their lives, their relationships, and the human community itself.

Psychoanalyst Alfred Adler once noted that little formal education prepares one for living in partnership. Thinking for yourself, seeking autonomy, pursuing individual excellence, being "the best that you can be," pulling your weight, winning races, paying your own way, earning your best academic grades, competing for awards, becoming a saint, and going to heaven all imply that individually getting ahead is preferred over deeply partnering with an "other." Adler advocated the early teaching of dancing as a lifelong metaphor for the partnering attempts that can either enrich or devastate a life.

What happens in bed and all through the day in prologue and appreciation is a life arena that constantly compels and virtually forces humans to learn how to partner. Being educated by our stubborn striving for loving companionship is highly suitable to our current age. We have been awakened by the sexual revolution, instructed by the feminist movement, and bombarded by incessant technologically promoted sexual images in the last half of the twentieth century. The twenty-first century will be the age for learning to combine sex with love for life enrichment and maturity, as taught in the biblical love themes of the Song of Songs, Hosea, and the Epistles of John.

There are global implications for this evolutionary movement. As the human race becomes denser on the planet, the capacity to collaborate, cooperate, and flourish in communal partnerships becomes ever more crucial. A partnering paradigm is prescriptive to the developing world community that can be promoted by exploring the basic essentials of intimate partnering at home and in bed.

For purposes of clarity and respecting limitations, some practical definitions of essentially undefinable realities are needed. I distinguish between "romantic love" and "maturing love" to honor the difference between the high-emotion, largely blind, early stage of intimate loving and the deeply fulfilling long-term committed love that evolves over time.

The term "eros" is used to mean "the powerful and mysterious sexual energy that naturally compels the uniting of people in romantic love." The term "spirituality" is used from a functional perspective, referring to the array of ways a given individual meets the uncontrollable mysteries of human living in augmenting and nurturing his or her own unique human core, or soul.

What is meant here by "Catholic Way" is not a particular set of unchangeable principles, teachings, or regulations enshrined somewhere as eternally true. It refers rather more broadly to that entire diverse body of belief, concept, and spiritual practice that developed through discussion and conflict over Hebrew revelation and the Christ events, was molded and shaped by history, and eventually was summarized in "catechisms" to perpetuate its use in assisting the development and enhancement of the spiritual lives of people. For practical purposes, the reader could consider the Catholic Way to mean what spiritual language found its way into standard Catholic teaching during the twentieth century.

Catholics honor and practice their beliefs with enormous diversity across the globe, within a local church, and indeed even within a single pew. Yet there is a Catholic Way that characterizes our tradition that goes far beyond regulatory, moral, and procedural correctness. Major elements of the Way include deep sentiment for Eucharistic celebration, a sacramental view of creation, a movement toward universal communal fulfillment, and an honoring of all persons as of equal and enormous dignity and value. This book intends to show that these and other Catholic traditions are vividly reflected in the natural mystery of intimate sexual love.

Paul Tillich once taught about a "Protestant Principle," essentially meaning that the Protestant movement seeks to remove all barriers between people and God—including priests, statues, and prayer aids such as the rosary. The opposite conviction could be called the "Catholic Principle"—the conviction that all of creation is capable of helping bridge the gap between the human and the Transcendent. Sacraments and sacramentals fill the world, combining symbol and word to enhance natural meanings of human living. Included in that natural world is the inherent partnering energized by the intense pleasure of sexual arousal and attraction.

When post-Reformation Catholic leaders retained matrimony as a sacrament, they preserved a reverence for intimate love as sacred. The minister of that sacrament is not a priest or a bishop but the couple themselves who administer it to one another. While the spirituality of intimate partnering has not been significantly developed over the past five centuries since, the seed is indeed there to do so now that humanity has readied itself.

This is not a book about marriage, however. It is about loving sexuality, an arena of human living that spans a toddler's first infatuation with his kindergarten teacher to the flirting of disoriented nursing home residents in their nineties. A wedding can be a major event in a person's love life, but the spirituality of intimate loving in no way begins with that public event. Lovers of all ages and life situations are accosted, shaken, warmed, and challenged to grow by the inexplicable mystery of falling in love and seeking to keep that love alive. As they do so, they experience an opportunity to see the primary elements of the Catholic Way unfolding and enhancing themselves before their very eyes.

PART I

EROS AND
INDIVIDUAL SPIRITUALITY

Individual spiritual excellence in Catholic culture has been defined largely by clusters of virtues memorized in childhood and pursued throughout one's life. These characteristics of human beauty, developed from biblical texts and distilled over the first twenty centuries of Christian preaching, have become standards for marking growth in the spiritual life. Commonly accepted as developed capacities that promote richness of a person's relationships with other people and with the Divine, the fruits and gifts of the Spirit, and the cardinal and theological virtues, have found their way into literature and other arenas of society as common aspects of simple goodness.

Intimate love helps shape these virtues. Swept into engagement by the natural mystery of falling in love and then challenged by love's changes and inevitable conflicts, we find ourselves wafting and flailing in a crucible of human pleasure-driven partnering that both feeds and tries our souls on at least a daily basis. Just as we have fashioned our personalities in the context of nuclear family relationships in childhood, so we continue our adult spiritual development with love partners in intimate dialogues that affect us to the core.

Part I connects the established wisdom of Christian virtues and the styles of personal ugliness known as the seven deadly sins, with the always mysterious spiritual arena made up of seeking and feeding our natural thirst for intimate love. What would the basic aspects of Christian spirituality look like if viewed through lovers' eyes? How does the personally shaking romantic love aspect of life continually energize us to spiritually mature? How is eros, that inscrutable power moving us to bodily, pleasure-sharing passion, a central aspect of Christian spirituality and a source of encounters with the living God?

CHAPTER ONE

~

The Natural Mystery
of the Loving Spirit

Out beyond ideas of wrongdoing and rightdoing
There is a field. I'll meet you there.
When the soul lies down in that grass,
The world is too full to talk about.
Ideas, language, even the phrase each other
Doesn't make any sense.

—Rumi

Near the end of the 2005 romantic comedy *Hitch*, Will Smith's character is writhing on the street after leaping onto a moving car to keep the love of his life from leaving in it. An incredulous bystander hurls him the obvious question, "Why did you jump onto that speeding car?!!" "Because it's what people do," he answers passionately. "We all just leap and hope to God we can fly."

A spirituality of intimate loving begins with acknowledging that the romantic loving spirit between human beings is an absolutely mysterious reality, never to be completely comprehended. Keeping a sense of wonder at its refusal to be controlled, analyzed, captured, pinned down, or regulated will be basic to appreciating its spiritual depth and value.

Sexuality itself remains one of the great mysteries of human living. Mysteries have been distinguished from problems in that their enormous complexity perpetually defies solutions. Mysteries are *aspects of reality that must be entered into in order to be realized and endlessly unfold without ever being completely mastered.* Even those who write books about sex are mostly mystified by it in their own lives.

Sexual *loving*, however, is far more complex than sex itself. Two people energetically engaged in emotionally treasuring and physically pleasuring one another, compelled by a vigor from nowhere that can disappear willy-nilly, has no equal in human mystery. Books, articles, movie story lines, cultural mores, religious teachings, legal structures, and research studies of all kinds never scratch the surface of bringing intimate loving into some kind of assurance or certitude. It defies understanding. As Masha, one of the "Three Sisters" in Chekhov's play by that name, protests in midlife, "but when you fall in love yourself then it becomes obvious to you that nobody knows anything and each person must make their [sic] own decisions."[1]

This perpetually ambiguous phenomenon of intimate loving serves as a universal model for the spiritual life. Spirituality itself, though always beyond being captured in a definition, can be seen functionally as *what individuals believe and do to cope with and enjoy what they cannot control.* It is the entire array of beliefs, practices, values, attitudes, and decisions we learn to employ in facing the inherent mysteries of everyday living. Primary among those uncontrollable elements are our personal relationships, and among those, our romantic love life stands tall.

Hitch's response above, "we all just leap and hope to God we can fly," contains unintended reference to the three theological virtues of Catholic tradition—faith, hope, and charity—fundamental personal characteristics that orient us to the Divine. In romance we leap in *faith*, which feeds our *hope*, motivated by the "greatest of these," our *love*. Gathered together in a phrase from St. Paul (1 Cor 13:13), these fundamental virtues were traditionally considered to be "infused," as different from other virtues that were gained through a combination of grace and human effort. Faith, hope, and charity are gifts, unable to be obtained on our own.

The universal "bigger than both of us" quality of early romance, as one of life's most vivid experiences of genuine love, thrusts us into engagement with the living God. It solves nothing about life and religion, explains nothing, and proves nothing. But we cannot ignore it. Reflecting on one's own love life ought to convince any one of us that, in that otherworldly path of finding an exquisite partner, manifesting love to her, engaging her intimately, and being transformed by the experience, we are dancing with a Power greater than ourselves. We can merely influence but never control the outcome and are often astounded at the magnificence of the love with which we find ourselves blessed. Faith, hope, and charity, as traditional virtues that orient us to the Divine, all take on new meaning when seen through lover's eyes.

Faith in Love's Mystery

The myriad ways in which romantic love takes us beyond our former selves can be illustrated by any good love story. Aren't we all invited to make fools of ourselves at some time or another in that aspect of life? From the very beginning, dancing with eros requires a kind of constant openness to "the now," a dynamic responsiveness in the moment when we aren't sure of anything. Even flirting requires some basic belief that human existence is fundamentally trustable so that a positive future may result. In theological language, romantic loving invariably requires a functional level of *faith* since only a "leap of faith" allows one to "fall" in love and actively pursue a promising intimate relationship.

At every stage of its path loving engagement renders us hurtable. When two people begin to rely on each other to consistently partner for fulfillment of their bodies' thirst for pleasure and their hearts' hunger for companionship, they allow themselves an awesome vulnerability. If I feel you loving me beautifully, I know that you will someday—maybe today—stop doing so. Life and love are always temporary. Reflective lovers ask themselves, "Will I hurt more seeing her turn away, seeing her dying, or seeing her watch me die?"

Even while it lasts, the fulfillment of intense mutual pleasuring has potential to hurt as deeply as any other pain a human can endure. When you come to know what fulfills and pleasures me most, you possess a power over me that can be allowed only by the fact that I possess the same power over you. The fundamental mutuality created by that basic arrangement of creation challenges all lovers who want long-term relationship, to find and maintain "faithfulness." And all who have seriously engaged the loving mystery know the depth of hurt that eats at the heart or gut when love is lost.

Lovers share vulnerability, or they are not actually lovers. As individuals, we all become utterly vulnerable about every eighteen hours in our need for sleep. We rely on communal collaboration in order to keep our bodies warm and to eat a few times a day. Lovers' soulful communion eventually centers on eating and sleeping together as well as sharing the nesting, work, and transportation that support life. Verbal and emotional soul flow between lovers emerges daily from sharing these basic human vulnerabilities.

Thus intimate lovers live day to day in the midst of creation's primary model of faith—the capacity to live in the vulnerability of mystery's ambiguity. Romantic loving is a human relationship that mirrors the partnering between people and their God. The biblical minor prophet Hosea wrote from the crucible of sexual love as he repeatedly used his gnarly relationship with Gomer, an adulterous woman he loved, married, and persistently pined for, to illustrate Yahweh's yearning for and pursuing of human responsive love. Hosea's words entreat readers to use what they know of loving and being loved carnally to acknowledge and return the love Yahweh has consistently shown them. "I will espouse you to me forever: I will espouse you in right and in justice, in love and in mercy; I will espouse you in fidelity and you shall know the Lord" (Hos 2:16–17, 21–22).

Like Hosea, for many lovers maintaining faithfulness in sexual loving becomes one of the greatest challenges of all. The most difficult project is not merely staying together through the inevitable "hard times" but doing what we can to keep the love alive. When couples lose faith in one another, stop believing that the loving response will continue to be there "in good times and in bad," then only faith in something beyond them will provide hope. Poetic singers like Paul Stookey ("Wedding Song") and the country music world remind listeners that loving eventually requires effort to stay faithful and that there is a Power Beyond us available to assist that persistence.[2]

The faith needed to let oneself get "carried away" in early romance is a mere shadow of the faithfulness that challenges and sustains lovers as they continue to engage one another and mature. That perennial challenge to stable relationship has prompted cultures worldwide to evolve practices and laws intended to help meet it. Wedding traditions and marriage mores can't remove the need for faith in facing the daunting and delicious mystery of intimate loving, but they have been developed over time in order to help successfully engage it.

Faith involves truly relying on something or someone outside oneself for assistance on things one can't handle alone. In romance, profound reliance on one another forms one of the best manifestations of faith humans ever encounter. Finding that even that partnership is not enough, both are invited to rely on a "Higher Power" to assist them in the complex struggles that characterize any maturing relationship.

Faith is not something you can simply "have" because you want it or need it, however. In Christian tradition it has always been considered to be a gift, unable to be obtained on one's own effort. It can grow and be cultivated as it is employed in relationship, "stirred up" as the early sermons of St. Paul indicate. His listeners were reminded about their faith by examples from previous behavior and by stories of heroic faith of their ancestors. Romantic faith in one another is similarly a combination of faith that seems magically born by falling in love and the intentional development of that faith as intimacy grows. As relationships mature, faith tends to grow as a product of actively relying on one another in the nitty-gritty aspects of intimacy.

It can be amusing to ponder the effects romantic faith might have had on the historical development of theology. The Protestant Reformation was largely about faith. That decades-long battle that vastly accelerated the incessant denominational dividing of Christianity, in which thousands have been misunderstood, persecuted, tortured, and executed, was begun largely with the question, "Is it by faith in God or is it in doing good works that people are 'saved' or can 'go to heaven'?" In essence, "Is it God's grace or is it our efforts that make the spiritual life succeed?"

Now, five hundred years later, it seems apparent that a few simple questions might have brought dawn to the night of their conflict: "Is it your efforts or your wife's that makes your marriage relationship flourish?" "Is it your internal loving or your decisive, outward actions that manifest the love and make intimate partnering possible?" Without applying perspectives from intimate partnering relationships in bed, it has taken centuries to shape theological agreement that faith and works go together. People and God are partners in the spiritual life, collaborative spouses whose love is both from beyond and needing of their investment. Religious faith is more than a list of dogmas to which one assents; it is a rich, evolving, maturing relationship of intimacy with the Divine.

As in romance, so with God—if you love, then you rely on the one you love, and your actions naturally show it. A partnering theology would have served both the reformers and the establishment well and might have prevented entire wars. But evolution wasn't yet ready for a partnering view of faith.

The Hope That Partnering Breeds and Feeds

As a young chaplain in a small hospital in Ashland, Wisconsin, I stopped to see a fifty-five-year-old cancer patient who, in a few moments, unintentionally taught me a great deal about hope. What I learned that day I've since seen confirmed hundreds of times. This lady looked relaxed as I entered the room, and in the first few minutes of our conversation she directly mentioned her newly diagnosed cancer. When I asked her how she was feeling about it, she said,

> Pretty good now. You know, my sister just left here. I've been in the hospital three days now, and many of my friends and relatives have come to see me. We all chatted and reminisced and everything. But underneath I kept feeling really lonely and sad about my situation. Then my sister arrived from Minneapolis. She pulled up a chair right close to my bed, looked straight into my face and asked, "Helen, where is your cancer?" We had such a good talk after that. And I feel so much better now.

When souls commune, directly and in depth, hope grows. The flow between souls is mysteriously and powerfully nourishing of the human spirit. The feeding of hope is often that simple.

The most visible I've ever seen *new hope* being born was in the eyes of people in the early stages of treatment for chemical addiction. After being admitted to the treatment center in failure, followed by a few days of detoxification and encounter of the starkly sharing openness of treatment groups, they would then attend a first meeting of Alcoholics Anonymous in town. When they would return from that meeting, a careful observer could visibly see on the faces and in the excitement of their communicational demeanor the ones who had talked in some authentic depth at that meeting. As they returned, they were observably more hopeful. Hope actually showed in their eyes. It had grown because rather than whining about the pain of their lives, blaming others, or sitting in self-pity, for the first time in a long time, maybe ever, they had shared with similarly defeated peers, deeply and directly from the soul.

Since human hope is somewhat mysteriously fed by personal sharing in depth, lovers possess countless opportunities to augment one another's hope— in small ways on a daily basis and in big ways during crisis times. "Sharing about your day," for many couples, is fundamental to love's resilience. And on catastrophic days, at the accident scene or in the hospital, for example, yearning for the lover's presence quickly becomes an ache until that unique beloved arrives. In fact, it seems clear that love partners are given to one another to help keep life hopeful, beginning with early romance and ending at the deathbed of one or the other.

When people are "in love," they clearly are more hopeful than when they are not. A lighthearted mood naturally buoys lovers is a sense that all obstacles can be overcome. When in love, it seems like today is bright and tomorrow will be brighter. Later, as love matures, hope serves as a buffer to the stings and disappointments of everyday life. As Eddie Arnold and Elvis Presley wrote and sang about, coming home at the end of some days one wants the beloved to "Make the World Go Away."[3] And he or she can.

The hopeful glow of feeling loved just for being yourself and for actively contributing to a treasured "we" tends to spill over into virtually all aspects of one's life. Intimate loving gives more promise of a positive tomorrow than do solitary efforts—even if work, money, leisure, and all other aspects of existence aren't going so well. In fact, even while a romantic relationship is slowly sinking, life can feel more hopeful than it does after the breakup when that bed is so, so empty.

Hope as the *expectation of a positive future* grounds human functioning. When it persists into habit, we call it *optimism*. When it is exaggerated, we call it *idealism*. When it grows thin, we face *discouragement*, and when it gets skeletal, we fight *depression*. When it is nearly gone, we call it *despair*, we may be called suicidal, and those who care about us legitimately fear for our very lives.

All lovers eventually confront dark times that test the capacity to remain positive about what is ahead. How individuals and couples deal with those times either tempers their hope into more optimistic aging or steers them into discouragement or even depression. A key concept of the therapy of Alfred Adler was the question, "What has discouraged this person?"[4] Early family relationships, failures at finding meaningful work, and one's love life were some likely possibilities.

In Christian tradition there were two opposite failures of hope—*despair* on one side and *presumption* on the other. Although hope was catechistically defined in terms of relationship with God, it can easily be adapted to the intimate loving relationship. Despair meant giving up on one's relationship with God, believing that there was no longer any hope of salvation. Presumption meant exaggerating either a person's own power to save him- or herself or overrelying on God to grant that salvation regardless of his or her own significant efforts. Both despair and presumption find useful parallels in the intimate loving partnership.

Despair may often be what is called clinical depression today, a condition that needs professional assistance, suffered by 2 to 4 percent of the U.S. population in any given year. Science and medicine now know a bit more about despair and its chemical component than during the centuries when that word was first evolving. Many professionals and even knowledgeable people in general now recognize depression as it is growing. Medications can help depression immensely—both acute and chronic varieties—and, combined with excellent personal therapeutic care, can usually bring a measure of healing. No one ought to be ashamed of seeking help for depression. As despair, it was once called a "sin" against hope but is now recognized as a more complex condition for which those who suffer it carry little if any responsibility. There is often unresolved grief involved in depression and sometimes other deeply personal issues that could possibly benefit from professional help as a component of the healing. Learning how to get help for depression by employing humility and an attitude of partnering rather than victimization evidences significant spiritual growth.

More of what used to be called despair as a spiritual condition may now be seen as simply giving up on a relationship before investing seriously in its success. Who knows the percentage of divorces that result from giving up by those who abandon the challenge of finding and nurturing love when things get tough and one is not getting what one needs? Seeking divorce too soon, acquiescing to food or alcohol, deferring to rigid habits, settling for the overarching pursuit of comfort, and a thousand other flavors of excessive self-indulgence get in the way of some of the best life has to offer.

Presumption is the other failure of hope. If despair is the losing of hope, presumption is unrealistically exaggerating it. In partnership language, it blithely expects either oneself or one's partner to take an excessive proportion of the shared responsibility. These may now be called, respectively, codependence and dependence. "Taking" responsibilities rather than sharing them can grow slowly and insidiously in some of us who are prone to overfunctioning. And most of us fail on one side of these hope issues or the other on our way to finding out experientially what partnering really entails.

Maturing lovers possess an incredible font of hope, one that is intricately built into the immediate accessibility of one another's souls. Songs like Billy Joel's "Tell Her About It"[5] advise guys to make decisions to simply talk, like we've never talked before, trusting that we won't get misunderstood. If we talk, we are likely to begin sharing, that is, combining our feelings with our words, which is what almost magically touches the soul. If we do get misunderstood in our efforts, we're to try it again and again because that's the food that partnerships need. It constitutes "soul flow," communication in depth between people, the primary nurturance of intimacy. Risking verbal vulnerability repeatedly requires a measure of hope that can grow in the sharing.

The sharing that takes place on reuniting after a day apart is responsible to a great degree for enduring hopefulness among lovers. Indeed, when that sharing wanes, "wondering" about the relationship increases. The soul flow between lovers feeds the "we" like nothing else and may be as crucial to hope in the relationship as food is to their bodies.

The Primacy of Love Evolving

I happened to be standing in my office glancing at the Olympic Mountains when the earth began to convulse violently beneath me in the Puget Sound in February 2001. The first major earthquake jolt ever felt by this aging philosophical Iowan shook new and lively respect into my soul for a Transcendent Power capable of rocking an entire county. The word "respect" is derived from the two Latin words: *re*, meaning "again," and *spectare* meaning "to look." It implies "look again" because what you see is worthy of closer scrutiny. Respect is one response to the emotion of awe, which includes an element of a fear that can't be ignored.

Fear and respect can be powerful, but they generally aren't very affectionate. They are, in the end, poor substitutes for love.

The movement from fearful respect to affectionate loving in relating to the Transcendent parallels an adolescent boy's awe at flashy girls that eventually transforms into the simple joy of fledgling romance. Nature itself can still quickly inspire fear through volcanoes, tsunamis, hurricanes, and tornadoes that defy any influence by the combined power of the entire human race. Learning to love such an obviously powerful Transcendence closely and affectionately seems to be what the Jesus events were all about. "Fear of the Lord is the beginning of wisdom," (Prov 9:10), but eventually "perfect love casts out fear" (1 Jn 4:18). As the Catechism taught, we were made not to fear but to know, love, and serve God here and be happy in a beatific vision of the Divine after we die.[6]

Intimate human love as a criterion for social decisions has always had a difficult time finding its way into organizational structures such as law, politics, and even studies of theology. Likely it always will. Eros is simply too ethereal, too unpredictable, too absolutely uncontrollable for it to be relied on in the political and legal processes for managing people. Even psychology has found no consistently effective way of including it in the study of human behavior.

Freud, for example, named love and work as the two primary human endeavors, yet he wrote entirely about sex rather than love. Kinsey scientifically studied sexual behavior and reportedly remained rather unfamiliar with the power of love itself during his entire life. Even marriage psychologist John Gottman, who has scientifically studied marriage relationships at the University of Washington for decades, uses as a criterion for success whether couples stay together for at least fifteen year, rather than what would be much more difficult to study, that is, how deeply they actually love each other.[7]

Yet human loving is the centerpiece of all spiritual experience. Words attributed to Pedro Arrupe, S.J., former superior general of the Jesuit order, capture the view that loving another human being and loving God flow together:

> Nothing is more practical than finding God, that is, than falling in love in a quite absolute, final way.
>
> What you are in love with, what seizes your imagination, will affect everything. It will decide what will get you out of bed in the morning, what you will do with your evenings, how you will spend your weekends, what you read, who you know, what breaks your heart, and what amazes you with joy and gratitude.
>
> Fall in love, stay in love and it will decide everything.[8]

The ways in which intimate lovers experience God in the love between them depends in part on what they *believe* and in turn influences the level of their *hope*. In early romance, feeling the excitement and warmth of being loved by a person who attracts you is a pure gift. Like the wind, it comes from nowhere you can identify, yet it compels you like nothing else you've known. You can't say you deserve it, you can't control it, you can't make it happen, yet it feeds your soul so deeply that it clearly is essentially good. If such love is a gift, *from whom* is it given?

A colleague once sent me the following anonymous quote stolen from an Internet chat room on love relationships:

> I was actually floored when Don and I first starting making love, because it felt so very spiritual to me, and although I'd had sex before (obviously) the feeling I had when I looked into his eyes when he was inside me felt like being close to God. Like I was praying. He felt the same. Like . . . on a higher plane.
>
> We still feel that way. Well, some of the time . . . other times, we're just outright too *nasty* to pay attention to it.

Sadly the connection between sexual loving and loving a Transcendent power is not often made. Yet possibly the most compelling manifestation of the love of God in adulthood is to be found in the obvious way the Creator continually configures humanity to enjoy and learn from erotic partnering. She continues to send us girl and boy babies that become sexual men and women. She constantly promotes not only personal magnificence worthy of awe, respect, and fear but carnally penetrating experiences of tenderness, gentleness, freely mutual pleasuring, conveyed understanding, courageous interpersonal loyalty, and the beauty of shared vulnerability that mingles intimately with power. Sexual loving in partnership is a rich model of a living and loving God, comparable only to child raising and the miracles of the natural world.

St. Paul put loving God at the very top of the virtue list with, "There are in the end, these three—faith, hope and charity. And the greatest of these is charity" (1Cor 13:13). Without it, there is only clanging and tinkling, he wrote (1Cor 13:1). Human love and the love of God need to be taken seriously and comprehensively in any regulation, teaching, or dogmatic formulations made about sex and religion.

How might tortuous current ecclesiastical issues be seen differently if the element of actual human love were comprehensively taken seriously in considering them? Is mutual loving a factor in thinking about gay and lesbian spirituality, artificial birth regulation, remarriage after divorce, and sex outside of marriage? Including it would without a doubt even further "complexify" these already perpetually confounding issues. We would need to reduce our reliance on regulation and find ways to care rather than condemn, focus on nurturing spirituality rather than remain preoccupied with morality, stand in awe at unmanageable reality rather than imply that human experience can and ought to be controlled.

When the early members of Alcoholics Anonymous were clarifying their observations of "steps" to describe the new lifestyle they eventually called recovery, they found they needed to include a few about *maintaining* that life. Step 11 simply states, "We sought through prayer and meditation to improve our conscious contact with God as we understood Him [sic], praying only for knowledge of His [sic] will for us and the power to carry that out."[9] *Improve our conscious contact with God.* Persistently seeking and developing ways to know and love God surely includes serious reflection on how sexual loving manifests God's great love for humanity in general and each of us in particular.

Notes

1. Anton Pavlovich Chekhov, *The Three Sisters*, act 3, trans. Randall Jarrell (London: Macmillan, 1969), 70.

2. Paul Stookey, "Wedding Song," on *Paul And* album (Public Domain Foundation, 1971).

3. Eddy Arnold, "Make the World Go Away" (RCA 1967).

4. Alfred Adler. *Cooperation between the Sexes: Writings on Women, Love and Marriage, Sexuality and Its Disorders,* trans. and ed. Heinz L. Ansbacher and Rowena R. Ansbacher (New York: Jason Aronson, 1980), 398 ff.

5. Billy Joel, "Tell Her About It," on *Innocent Man* album (Columbia, 1983)

6. Bennet Kelly, C.P., *The New St. Joseph Baltimore Catechism, Official Revised Edition* (New York: Catholic Book Publishing, 1964), 6.

7. John Gottman, *Why Marriages Succeed or Fail and What You Can Learn from Breakthrough Research to Make Your Marriage Last* (New York: Simon & Schuster, 1994).

8. Origin uncertain, attributed to Pedro Arrupe, S.J. (1907–1991), former superior general of the Society of Jesus, 1961–1984 (www2.bc.edu/~anderso/sr/arrupe.html).

9. *Alcoholics Anonymous*, 4th ed. (New York: Alcoholics Anonymous World Services, 2001), 59.

CHAPTER TWO

~

Nine Fruits of Romantic Love

I tell you love is Nature's second sun,
Causing a spring of virtues where he shines.

—George Chapman

Intimate loving offers enormous spiritual benefits. While most romantic relationships fail to endure, spiritually they almost always succeed. They help to shape the love histories, the adult personalities, the basis of future love-seeking, and the personal virtues of both lovers. As Goethe wrote in the eighteenth century, "We are shaped and fashioned by what we love."[1]

A language for the ways in which the early stages of romance enrich life can be found in the oldest book of the New Testament. Never intended to refer to intimate or erotic love, the fruits of the Spirit found in the fifth chapter of St. Paul's Letter to the Galatians nevertheless reflect the presence of God as partially visible in people who are in love. He saw early Christians deeply changed by the Spirit of Christ within them and described what he saw in terms of nine partially observable characteristics—*charity, joy, peace, patience, kindness, goodness, trustfulness, gentleness,* and *self-control* (Gal 5:22–23). They describe the best of what happens to souls immersed in the wonders of romance.

What distinguishes intimate loving from all other two-person relationships is the phenomenon of intense sexual pleasure. Friends can be emotionally intimate, parents forever devoted, and mentors incredibly healing. Lovers can be all of these too, but in addition they agree in some unique way that fits them, to *indulge* one another in bodily pleasuring as well.

That simple covenant, to persistently attend to one another both carnally and personally, defines intimate loving. Personal attentiveness begins as spontaneous and informal flirting, expands with increasing presence to one another as the love grows, may eventually be formalized in a wedding commitment, and continues all through enthusiastic early love. The sensual pleasures lovers naturally bring to each other's lives—in the sights of faces and bodies, smiles, laughter, feelings of emotional connection, caresses, voice inflections, gentle words, aromas, and orgasmic ecstasy—are life transforming and become pieces of a solid agreement between them to consistently express loving devotion. Freud and Matthew Fox are two who drew our attention to how people are changed more by pleasure than by anything else.[2]

Romantic loving is essentially indefinable. But for purposes of providing a basis for discussion, a working definition might be *that profoundly mysterious aspect of life in which two people seek to be energized by emotional exchange as mutually treasured partners in a relationship that includes bodily attraction and remains open to passionate sexual expression.* Despite major personal differences between them, which are either seen as enchanting or completely ignored in early romance, lovers agree on some level to indulge one another with the expectation of also being indulged.

Indulge, from the Latin *indulgere,* originally meant to "give free rein to," especially the human passions for food, drink, and sexual pleasure. Lovers agree to make pleasuring easy for one another, on a consistent basis, whatever unique forms and rhythms that may take in the unfolding "we" of their partnering. They are essentially agreeing, from first flirt to "death do us part," to enhance one another's joy of living.

The resultant mix of intense pleasure and equally powerful pain thrusts lovers into a whirlwind of emotional, relational upheaval that changes them one way or another. St. Paul, who apparently never married, probably didn't intend that the nine characteristics now called the fruits of the Spirit would describe the presence of erotic (sexual) love as well as agape (selfless) love. In fact, he may never have married. Yet today he may be pleased to see how they usefully reflect both kinds of love.

Resonant Joy

My wife and I were in our thirties and had been married six months when we were able to buy our first house. Perched on a hill in a small town of northern Wisconsin, it included a large yard with nineteen good-sized trees. On the night we took possession of that house, she led me merrily from tree to tree as we gleefully hugged them all. In those days, gaiety captured and pervaded our every day.

Lovers laugh. Those who are in love laugh twice as much as those who aren't. Abundant giggles, smiles, smirks, and grins signal the presence of budding romance in any culture. Can anything as naturally joyful and universal as the physically bursting happiness of young love not be intended by the Creator?

The physics concept of "resonance" fits the way in which the joy of two multiplies as it reverberates between them. Resonance as used in engineering acoustics refers to the process of sounds being intensified and prolonged through sympathetic vibration. Boys learn that humming a certain note in a bathroom stall, for example, curiously amplifies the sound waves in a small space as they reinforce one another. Similarly, when one lover laughs, it injects energy into the laugh of the other, which in turn evokes more laughter in the first. One common response of women asked why they fell in love with a specific man is that "he made me laugh." The childhood experience of uncontrollably "getting the giggles" with a chum is revisited on lovers who multiply one another's "enjoy-ment" of life.

This most obvious sign of being in love is a joy so striking that it borders on pain. Burned into our souls, memories from the days of love's intoxication shape our incessant search for happiness, pulling us into lifelong pursuit of heartwarming relationships of bodily pleasing and being pleased. What we learn about ourselves, human relationships, and humanity in general, through the utter glee of foolhardy love decisions, can enhance our understanding of the traditions that form the structure of most Christians' spiritual lives.

Christianity has never accomplished what the *Kama Sutra* partly achieved for the Hindus. That fourth-century Indian compilation of sexual lore related to religious traditions by "editor" Vatsyayana sought to enrich people's sexual loving by seeing it from a spiritual rather than merely moral point of view. The underlying beliefs of that work claim that the joy of intimate relating can be enriched by knowledge and technique (*Kama Sutra* means "rules of love"[3]) and that it is a primary influence in the happiness and spiritual richness of any human life. Married theologians and spiritual leaders would do well to begin the formulation of a "Catholic Kama Sutra." Perhaps it would now take less time than the eight hundred years of wisdom-gathering the Hindu version required.

Our own experience confirms the power of sexual love's joy as a body of intensely spiritual nurture and challenge. Current conventional wisdom or "common knowledge" is that the woman of any age who is "getting enough" romantic affection—which is spontaneously emotional, personally meaningful, gently physical, visually aesthetic, verbally tender, leisurely attentive, lightly humorous, fairly consistent, creatively expressed, and sometimes passionate—simply goes through the day with more joy in her heart. A man who is "getting enough," sexual loving that includes a fairly regular vigorous bodily response from a partner he treasures, negotiates all the other aspects of his life with more courage, peacefulness, and a lighter disposition. Romantic loving brings with it into every other aspect of life a deep and delightful joy.

Laughing emerges from the soul. Laughing *together* connects people at the core, however briefly. Certainly enjoying one another can be faked but not for long. Charles Schulz used Snoopy to proclaim that "joy is the most infallible sign of the presence of God." Frequent genuine and hearty laughter between lovers doesn't absolutely signify the beginnings of long-term love. But that infectious mirth in its many forms is an indicator that God is present in that early partnering. Even romance that is merely fledgling already deserves respect and reflective care.

Integrating the intense pleasure of erotic passion into the learned principles and practices of religious tradition, as a major project for any life, starts with embracing the joy of sexual loving as sacred.

Sexual Generosity

We who were taught Christian principles and stories as children remember the notion of "charity" that we received in catechism class. Great for healthily formative childhood, it implored us to love God, be nice to friends, and cheerfully offer food and shelter to the homeless and to starving, distant children.

When sex came alive in us during early adolescence, however, that view of charity got severely, if inwardly, challenged. Even the early adventures of falling in love began to teach us a new meaning to giving—"give in" for congeniality and "give out" for shared pleasure—even in fantasy before the kissing and hugging stage. In romantic fantasy you dream of having the capacity to make your partner feel great any day you choose. When you're in love with one another, indeed both of you have that ability.

One thing that romantic love tends to teach all heterosexual lovers is that intimate love is something quite different for most men than for most women. Males and females generally emphasize different aspects of the relationship. While these differences do not rigidly follow gender lines and can be temporarily blurred in one's first love, there are patterns among us that tend to distinguish men from women in the ways we experience love. For each to *feel* loved repeatedly by a treasured someone requires two utterly different kinds of response. This is of course not new to most experienced lovers, but it is simply never learned by others, even through years and numerous attempts to make love succeed.

Men with normal levels of testosterone simply will not feel loved without fairly regular sex. If one were to describe men's traditional fantasy, it would generally include a sex partner who is enthusiastic about him as a lover and who never tires of pleasuring him sexually. While that fantasy is rarely met, it can be an impression profitably tucked away in the mind of a woman who loves him. Affection and companionship are absolutely essential to men's loving appetite as well, and that fact must never be lost. But men will generally feel misunderstood and discouraged without loving sex a few times a week. For most women, sex that often will require a new kind of generosity—partnering bodily with willingness and generating whatever enthusiasm she can, often when she doesn't feel much like it.

Women, on the other hand, generally see genital sex as a secondary loving need. As Clarissa Pinkola-Estes (author of *Women Who Run with the Wolves*) has said, "The eroticism of women is an endless search for meaning and beauty."[4] Orgasmic sex is a component of women's pleasure but far down the list for most of them, below intimate emotional connection, spontaneous fun, tasteful ambiance, prolonged leisurely caresses, humorous perspectives, aesthetic surprises, luxuriating in the sun, and almost anything joyfully shared. Loving a woman will require making constant contributions to that natural search for beauty and meaning, a far more difficult task than men imagine at first. A new kind of "giving" will be called for, even in early romance.

During the twentieth century, drastic new discoveries were made that improved the appreciation of both sexes for the physical pleasuring aspect of women's intimate loving. The discovery of the hormone oxytocin confirmed scientifically what many couples have always known—that women's pleasure through extended leisurely caress exceeds that of men and for many women compares to orgasmic ecstasy in men.[5] The 1940s discovery of the Grafenberg spot, colloquially called the "G spot," allowed greater possibility of women's orgasm for at least some couples. And the realization that many women simply do not become aroused nearly as often as others do promises less blame of themselves or of their men for lower frequency of orgasmic experience. Only in the past century did it become clear among the general population that sexual makeup is unique in every person and every couple. Early love invites people into a compelling relationship in which they can learn that only generosity in the here and now of intimate interaction transcends the barriers to lasting relationships of shared mutual pleasuring in the uniqueness of each couple.

Leisurely caressing his lover's back for twenty or thirty minutes several times a week may not be a man's first inclination, for example, but he can easily engage in and highly enjoy it for someone that he cherishes. Engendering enthusiasm in orgasmic intercourse a few times a week might not be a woman's preference, but she may be able to offer it with some level of joy for one she loves and by whom she feels treasured.

The term *making love* as opposed to *having sex* emphasizes soulful investment and intentional energy rather than riding a mutual free train to ecstasy. In sexual loving, "spontaneity" must be augmented by "responsibility." Both words are rooted in the Latin *pons*, or "bridge." Loving sex bridges gaps between the bodies and souls of very different kinds of people. Ironically, "eros" forms the heart of the word "gen-*eros*-ity."

Cuddling Peace

Many men and women have woken up cuddling and realized that quietly sharing the warmth of a lover's body after passionate intercourse is the calmest time they've ever known. Engulfed in a peace that passes all previous understanding, we find that life urgencies have receded to their proper perspective. In those moments it is easy to believe that the profound relaxation that follows shared orgasm does as much to calm the soul as any traditional spiritual practice— including such classic individual religious stalwarts as meditation, contemplation, spiritual reading, yoga, and personal prayer.

Besides seizing the schedule of your day, sometimes in chaotic excitement, romance is also mysteriously calming. When romantic love is flourishing, it bestows a quieting effect on a day and to one's entire life. Responding both spontaneously and strategically to a lover who is in love with you is far more peaceful than actively seeking romance knowing that it might not happen. Even the quiet pining of lovers temporarily separated from one another is more peaceful than the emptiness of persistent unwanted aloneness.

God is in the peace brought by eros. That peace is indeed a heavenly gift. It is a wonder like the sunset that cannot be engineered, explained, or comprehended. It is a mystery and a beauty, a spark of God Herself. Science does no more to explain such peace than it does to enhance the smile of a daughter or the antics of a son. Only poetry and song come close to adequately expressed appreciation of that peace as one of the true high points of human living.

Erotic peacefulness emerges from soulfully and bodily *partnering* with another human being. Its quality is not something attained alone in masturbation or to any significant degree in "recreational sex." The peaceful cuddling of intimate loving arises from a combination of sensitive, empathic emotional exchange; spontaneous bodily freedom; rhythms of both mindful and mindless responsiveness; and an inscrutable power beyond us. When it is found, it etches increased capacities for partnering into our souls. *Only a combination of efforts on the level of body and soul together* contributes to experiencing this peace even once in a lifetime, let alone with any enduring and fulfilling frequency.

It is a matter of faith for some of us that shared partnership love also promotes the mission of global peace. While feeding our souls in the moment, shared bodily peacefulness also is preparing humanity ever so slowly for relationships of global harmony. One of the ways peace-seeking societies are already evolving is through the partnership flavor of romantic loving that grew like a mutation in some countries during the twentieth century. No longer settling for exploitation, oppression, manipulation, or passivity in their beds, people are increasingly requiring in their leaders a partnering spirit of peacefulness—along with the thoughtful fortitude commonly expected. Evolution has not yet progressed far enough to allow an end to all military conflicts, but as the concentration of people vociferously clamoring for peaceful leadership increases, more serenity-oriented leaders with globally sharing attitudes will emerge.

Complementary Patience

A high school teacher of mine once silently drew two mountains on the blackboard, obviously indicating he wanted to illustrate something important. They were of equal height but opposite width, one a sharp, narrow peak and the other a wide, squat ridge. He called one the rapidly rising, quickly falling sexual response of a man and the other the long, gradual arousal and gentle lingering decline of a woman's passion. That diagram is still a useful illustration of why men need patience in order to partner with women. On the other hand, the egos of men, both large and fragile, show themselves often enough to challenge and stretch the patience of any woman invested in loving one of us.

Personal pace is indeed a deep and unique feature of every human being. We all operate best in certain gears. Changing that pace for the sake of another requires willingness to endure tiny bits of "suffering," which is the root of the word *patience*. Ironically, partners of distinctly different personal paces seem to attract one another. Learning to share those opposite (or complementary) paces in the service of intimate closeness and mutual pleasuring, as well as in the practicality of daily living, requires both partners to either generate patience or fail in the loving.

In men, seeking to coalesce "how I want it" with "how she likes it" can produce either the increased patience of mature masculine restraint or deep frustrated bitterness from overpersonalized hurt. A recently married nineteen-year-old junior high dropout seemed to have grasped this quickly as he told me, "Slow hands is the key—twenty minutes of slow hands on her back can usually get her in the mood."

For many women, growing patience is more likely to involve tolerating her man's process of learning to share his heart in words. He evolved as a hunter, mostly far from the cave fires where verbal sharing developed. If he has emerged from a strain of ancestors that lags behind in learning to fertilize flow from his soul, that learning won't come quickly or easily. Helping him learn to touch his heart and his experience and to mix them with his words can require the "patience of Job" in a woman who longs to hear just what is going on inside him.

Patience isn't natural in most lives. It has to be learned. While there may be many arenas in which to incorporate patience into our lives, it is in the context of erotic partnerships with lovers we treasure that patience grows best. How we experiment with and learn from the stark differences in relational and sexual pace offers a powerful arena in which to develop sensitivity and restraint. If the "we" of a relationship is significant enough, partners undergo the necessary "focus on the other" that breeds patience as a flourishing characteristic of our personalities.

Simple Goodness

When the electricity went out for days from Detroit to New York in the summer of 2003, many were amazed at how little looting or violence occurred, even in Manhattan. A few months later, as my wife and I explored that city in our first extended vacation there, we noted how stories abounded among residents that testified to how there is a "simply good" core to most people. Despite media emphasis on the breakdowns in societal structures during crises, among ordinary people one easily finds just below the surface what Catholic tradition called *benignity*.

While on ordinary days we can remain clueless to the hurts, grief, losses, and predicaments of strangers, when disaster creates acute needs, most human beings naturally empathize and extend themselves to aid however they can. Is this guilt motivation, as the cynic would claim? Or is it a down-deep simple goodness, born, at least in part, of being personally and physically loved—clearly, thoroughly, and often—by parents, neighbors, teachers, and lovers with whom we have encountered the essential goodness of life and of ourselves?

Forever mysterious, the slip into a "climb any mountain, cross any sea" sentiment of romance is "simply good." Love songs, as perhaps the oldest form of verbal music, emerge from the souls of those who have once wafted in the breezes and braced for the gales of romance. A man in love surprises himself at how easily he leaves behind the sexual searching and experimenting phase of his life—even promiscuity, pornography, and prostitution—for the intense and seizing jolt of sex-entwined-with-love.

Movie portrayals of love stories characteristically include a benignity component that has prompted the "chick flick" label. In *The Graduate* (United Artists, 1967), for example, Dustin Hoffman's character is seduced into a sexual relationship with a much older woman just as he graduates from high school. The sex soon becomes disturbing, boring, and tedious, until he finds himself truly in love with the woman's daughter. Quickly transformed by the "simple goodness" of romance, he moves to action that is more effective and masculine than he had ever previously achieved.

I still can't see the final scene of *An Officer and a Gentleman* (Paramount Pictures, 1982) without a tear. Having grown up on the streets of an Asian city, Zach Mayo, played by Richard Gere, attempts to achieve success as a U.S. Navy aviator recruit, believing he has nowhere else meaningful to go. While in training, he meets a local girl who has been enjoying life romancing sailors in short-term *liaisons*. The love that is enkindled between these two faces major problems. But in the end it transforms both of them as expressed in the climactic scene, arguably the most romantic in movie history. In full white U.S. Navy dress uniform, he marches with class and masculine boldness into the textile mill where she works, sweeps her off her feet, and carries her out and away to the cheers of her coworkers and the background tune, "Love Lifts Us Up Where We Belong."

Simple goodness means habitually not allowing yourself to miss the clear, obvious beauty of life through cynical humor, taciturn attitudes, stubborn resentments, remorseful guilt, or stubbornly held regrets. The freshness of romance continually endeavors to assuage the negative.

The polar opposites of benignity are *terminal naïveté* on one side and *entrenched cynicism* on the other. Benignity encounters the passionate romp, with its spontaneous frolicking exchange of embracing caress, moans, fluids, and aromas, and incorporates them quickly into all that is good. It spurns guilt and shame for the sake of this newfound experience of exhilarating love, awed at its power and simplicity. Benignity welcomes this end to the developmental sexual naïveté of childhood.

Part of Christians' spiritual responsibility in the twenty-first century is to resist the wide torrent of semihumorous cynicism rampant in our age. *Eros* can help. Despite intimacy's dangers, its mysterious, powerful, relentless, and exhilarating energy incessantly beckons us back into what the cynical call the "chick flick" theme—the simple goodness of romantic love.

Extraordinary Kindness

We parents naturally attempt to teach our children kindness as a way of relating harmoniously to other kids. Our own parents and religion teachers wanted us as children to notice how other people feel and be willing to do things that make life a little easier for them. Childhood stories of animals in trouble, feeble old folks, fearful children, sad poor people, and suffering martyrs helped us develop human empathy with which to recognize and respond to the needs of others. The effort intends to counteract innate human selfishness and nurture the inclination to respond to others' needs with acts that help.

When eros awakens in the hormone-rich eruption of puberty, however, human kindness can take on a deeper dimension. Adolescence yanks us almost overnight into enormous self-preoccupation and an irresistible "urge to merge" with the beauty of some guy or girl we only recently found odious. It pulls open our hearts into a new vulnerability to pain that we could not previously imagine. A simple smile or act of kindness from the lad or lass who has unpredictably become the object of our affection yields a bliss that literally warms the chest for hours.

Early romance becomes a brand-new school for learning to value kindness. It is no longer just obediently "doing the right thing" or "being a good boy/girl." Boys find out rather quickly that the days of "spiders and snakes" are over in impressing girls. And a girl can learn quickly that despite their gawky haughtiness, when boys are alone, they melt with kind words, dare she risk them.

Once you have touched another person's soul in this new way that you simply couldn't imagine before, you find that for a time, his or her deep pain is in your hands. You could easily hurt his or her feelings or manipulate, betray, punish, or even devastate him or her. In that realization you find a chance to develop new sensitivity to the heart life of another. You have an opportunity to take your kindness, your actively seeking to increase the joy of another person, to the next level—or not.

Being a good guy in general just isn't enough. Having good intentions or *wanting* to please her won't cut it. *Doing things* is required. And on a global level, kindness will be an absolute essential to contribute to the active and sensitive empathy that is an aspect of humanity's growing universal acceptance of one another's cultural, ethnic, sexual orientation, gender, religious, and personality style differences.

Expressed Gentleness

If there is a "vital sign" for the health of romance, comparable to body temperature, blood pressure, and respiration rate in nursing, it is the observable reality of *expressed gentleness* in the relationship. In intimate loving, gentleness has no substitute. Early romance pulls gentleness out of every male lover and fans the flames of gentleness in every woman. Expressed gentleness must show its face frequently between lovers, even fairly soon after spats and major disagreements. While "tough love" assertiveness is indispensable in some situations, expressed gentleness is to the spirits of lovers as water is to their bodies.

In the movie *Dinner with Friends* (HBO, 2001), based on a Pulitzer Prize–winning play, a divorcing man attempts to explain to his long-term buddy why he has decided to end what both he and his friend have known as a fairly happy marriage relationship. He says, in paraphrase, "I began to notice that she never touched me. All of the touching was started by me. I stopped touching her just to see what would happen. She didn't even seem to notice. I began to realize that it was already over."

Gentle touching is so vital to intimacy that its absence is more than an indicator of troubled romance. It is a diagnostic certitude that when expressed gentleness is absent for a long period of time, the relationship needs major assistance, is dying, or is already dead. Unless and until it returns, there will be little if any love. As a body three days without food changes its physiology to adapt, a love relationship shifts into survival mode without some form of expressed gentleness about every three days.

There are three kinds of gentleness—touch, word, and sentiment—corresponding to the sharing of body, mind, and soul. They are distinct yet similar. In relationship to a cherished person, all three are composed of warm softness— the first in caress, carus (from Latin meaning "dear"), the second in speech, and the third carried inside the heart. All three serve as indicators of intimate love's beginnings. They can be faked but not for long. The character Mayme in Lynn Nottage's play Intimate Apparel compares gentle touch to "gold in any country."6

Trustfulness

A dramatic moment immediately following the birth of most every child is that instant of first sight in the initial embrace by mom or dad. Swiftly searching each centimeter of the newborn's pristine body to see that everything is "as it should be," parents seek to identify all tiny attributes and anomalies that trumpet this new person's uniqueness. Most all of us were thus carefully scrutinized and enjoyed in our first few moments of life, basking in the absolute delight of at least one parent.

In the months that followed, however, we each began to develop the responsible charge of our own bodies, gradually in preadolescence, excluding even our parents from the close-up view of our physique.

Years or decades later, in the midst of the exhilarating adventure of romantic love, the energy of our self-guarding modesty begins to change. A major component of the getting-to-know-you elation of falling in love is the gentle and close exploration of one another's bodies. Piecemeal at first—face, torso, arms, and legs—the exploration proceeds more comprehensively in the bedroom. Once again our physical makeup, mediocre as it may be, becomes the subject of someone's joyous delight in the seeing, sensing, and caressing celebration of every round inch of our carnal makeup. The protectiveness of our modesty melts away immersed in the responding presence of our mutual fascination with one another's body-connected-to-soul. A trust in the "we" of us grows quickly as we rely on one another's positive regard in ways we never planned on trusting. We surprise even ourselves with our openness.

Thus is the healing power of romantic loving unleashed on the self-doubts and self-esteem ambivalence left over from our imperfect infancy, childhood, adolescence, and previous romantic relationships. All of us have been loved imperfectly and thus harbor pockets of self-doubt, feel occasionally reticent, and sometimes cope with excessive shame about ourselves. It takes the adoring gaze and endearing intimacy of flourishing romance to finish what parental doting started and hasn't yet been confirmed through friendship and other positive relationships in the first third of life. Erotic loving wields a powerful healing effect on bits of basic trust that didn't "take" as infants, and it propels us beyond self-doubt to eventually treasuring our own person.

Trust-*fullness* goes beyond mere trust. It is a pervasive confidence that persists through the natural failures, hurts, and binds that make up much of life. Less than a year after I had met my wife, I reconnected with a close colleague at a professional conference. Not knowing about my recent history, he immediately noted that I seemed more mature, more settled, and more self-confident and asked about it. I said nothing as he scrutinized my smiling face. "You met a good woman, didn't you!" he said.

It is the sharing of souls not merely of bodies that contributes the most to intimacy and abundant trustfulness. In ancient Hebrew there were two words that developed from initial observation that air moving through the body was essential for life. The word *soul* evolved from the Hebrew *nefesh,* which initially referred to the throat, where a life was most vulnerable. It came to mean the essence of a person, her core that was obviously gone when she died. *Ruah,* on the other hand, was used to communicate how differences in breathing signaled specific dispositions or "feelings," such as anger and sadness, indicators of what we now call the "spirit" of a person at any given time. In these terms sharing both spirit and soul constitute intimacy.

The delicate "soul flow" between people combines with carnal engagement in intimate love. The mutual sharing of souls—airing what is most dear to each of you, what renders you extremely vulnerable to disclose, what you guard most preciously—confirms your goodness despite the regrets, resentments, and particles of shame that have gathered in you in the early shaping of your person. Some of the most tender of this flow is made up of victories, great moments, events of which you are proud but that have never been verbally appreciated by anyone, or at least not enough. The spontaneous exchange of these "secrets" doubles the self-confidence of lovers everywhere.

Trustfulness could be defined as *abundant ease and persistence in meeting the world with an enduring positive attitude.* Such was the likely meaning Paul the Apostle saw in new Christians full of life and optimism, expecting the best of a day and meeting all events with the hope of relying on something solid, as a boy holding his father's hand faces virtually any situation with little fear. As Paul wrote in 1 Corinthians 13:6–7, "Love . . . is always ready to excuse, to trust, to hope and to endure whatever comes."

One cannot generate that kind of trustfulness out of intention, wisdom, or manufactured excitement alone. One of the chief ways it grows is through love partnering, under the warm, earthy, and radically accepting regard of another who is deeply in love with you.

The Beginnings of Adult Self-Control

When the apostle Paul first wrote about the fruits of the Spirit in the letter to the Galatians, he juxtaposed them with several specific signs of excessive self-indulgence. He named them "fornication, gross indecency and sexual irresponsibility; idolatry and sorcery; feuds and wrangling; jealousy, bad temper and quarrels; disagreements, factions, envy, drunkenness, orgies and similar things" (Gal 5:19). Every one of them bespeaks lack of *self-control*. The fruits of the Spirit were seen as the presence of God fostering a measure of control over one's natural impulses to excessive self-indulgence.

Early, high-emotion romance has a "carried away" quality about it, necessary for the love to take root. But that spontaneity-with-abandon needs to wait for its proper time. Woe to those who ignore the relationship-building aspect of intimate love in favor of wild passion. Such is the stuff of unwanted pregnancy, sexually transmitted diseases, persistent feelings of having been exploited, and worse. This is the subject of moral theology and civil law perspectives on intimate love to help minimize the destructive potential of violent or sexually motivated behavior that damages self, other people, and/or society itself.

Adolescent boys are known to get into much less behavioral trouble when they are accompanied by girls. The mere presence of the feminine as vague promise of romance prompts greater restraint on one's self-absorbed, rascally, and inconsiderate impulses. It is not as clear that girls act more like women with boys around than when they cluster only with one another, but one can guess that is true as well. As another person, outside oneself, becomes important, mutual indulgence becomes a bit more interesting and valued than self-indulgence. Actively combining the two is a major characteristic of mutual intimate loving.

Thus is born in boys the masculine restraint of men and in girls the poise and class of women. Romances feed the natural impetus to grow up, to use oneself in relationship, with responsible self-possession rather than youthful, high-risk abandon. Budding self-control is a benefit of the Spirit of romantic love. It helps all lovers face the subject of the next four chapters.

Notes

1. Johann Wolfgang von Goethe, *The Encyclopedia of Religious Quotations*, ed. Frank Mead (Westwood N.J.: Fleming H. Revell, 1985), 279.

2. Matthew Fox, *Original Blessing* (New York: HarperCollins, 1991), 288.

3. Alain Danielou, trans., *The Complete Kama Sutra* (Rochester, Vt.: Park Street Press, 1994), 3.

4. Clarissa Pinkola-Estes, *How to Love a Woman* (Boulder, Colo.: Sounds True, 1993), audiotape.

5. Nigel Barber, *The Science of Romance: Secrets of the Sexual Brain* (Amherst, N.Y.: Prometheus Books, 2002), 38.

6. Lynn Nottage, *Intimate Apparel* (New York: Dramatist's Play Service, 2005).

~

CHAPTER THREE

Seven Enduring Gifts
of Maturing Love

Marriages are people growing machines.

—Marriage theorist and therapist David Schnarch

While the spiritual benefits of *early* passionate romance gloriously transform the soul, those of *maturing* sexual love far surpass them. Relatively few lovers ever find their way to long-term loving bliss, but those who do so enter into a unique dimension of life that is enormously fulfilling despite and because of the decades of trials and conflict that emerge while engaging its mystery.

Maturing eros can be defined as *love partners evolving a relationship of openness to actively engage one another in mutual soul connection and bodily pleasuring through major and minor conflicts from differing sexual preferences, changing erotic rhythms, diverging personalities, trying financial challenges, diverse career energies, competing friendships, intimate misunderstandings, child-raising pressures, acute and chronic illnesses, aging bodies, menopausal aggravations, major losses, and deep personal hurts.* For a couple in their seventies who are still talking intimately and leisurely pleasuring one another for thirty to sixty minutes frequently enough to satisfy them both, exotic excitement has largely given way to comfort and depth, and the path has not been smooth.

Apparently created for the physical purpose of propagating humanity, sexual energy seems spiritually intended to compel us toward efforts at intimate connections in which we can be challenged to etch out virtues needed for communal collaboration.

The Christian tradition of the "Seven Gifts of the Holy Spirit" can be used to illustrate the spiritual benefits of maturing sexual love. *Gifts* last longer than fruits. While fruits are sweet and can be precisely what one needs for hunger, they are also short lived. If you eat fruits they are gone and if you don't they rot. Gifts on the other hand, can be well chosen to last, and to feed the soul over time.

Adapted from the Old Testament prophet Isaiah (Is 11:1–3), the gifts of the Spirit that many Catholics memorized in catechism class are named *wisdom*, *understanding*, *counsel*, *knowledge*, *fortitude*, *piety*, and *fear of the Lord (awe)*. For intimate partners they take on fresh meaning as human characteristics that tend to grow in the crucible of maturing intimate love.

Understanding: Never Stop Listening

About two years after my wife and I had moved our family from northern Wisconsin to the West Coast for adventure and a new job, I was told one day during a "downsizing" of the hospital that I had lost my job. "The layoff had no relationship to my job performance or productivity," they said. But I would be gone in a month.

On my way home that day, my mind was racing—from cluster to cluster of thought fractions and biting emotions about the future—things to do, directions to ponder, fears to moderate, and the tears of everyone I needed to tell. My children had been ages six, eight, and ten when we pulled them from their familiarity with small-town midwestern lake and forest to the midsized city complexity of South Puget Sound. Now they were eight, ten, and twelve. When I told them, two cried immediately, and the youngest quickly exited, slamming the front door.

But the worry was mostly about my wife. We had uprooted our entire life for the West Coast adventure. We'd found a house she loved, and she'd made it a home. She had a new job as a detox nurse that suited her fairly well. She had mostly loved the move from her hometown to the panoply of interesting opportunities and new friends of the Seattle area. How would she react? How would I bear the bitter mixture of her anger, her tears, and her eyes of hurt betrayal. I told her immediately, in the kitchen, describing the scene of the "bad news" day as best I could, scanning her eyes for the pain. Outwardly she reacted little as she listened, and I retreated to our bedroom downstairs, using my strong introversion to sulk, ponder, resent, and strategize.

A few minutes later Nancy appeared at the bedroom door, a glass of wine in each hand, swinging around the edge of the bed with a lightly devilish grin, quipping firmly with a ring in her voice, "Let's blow this place." Four words of serendipitous balm. A fresh breeze in the hotbox of my oppressive stewing. Every word perfect, she soothed my soul like nothing else could have. Four words.

"Let's"—meaning, "We're in this together forever. As long as we have each other's love we'll be fine and life will be rich. We can take this next step together too."

"Blow"—meaning, "Moving isn't disaster. We can minimize the pain and drudgery of it all. We're young yet (fifty-one and forty-six), and we can relocate, even if it is strenuous and disappointing."

"This place"—meaning, "This is just a place. Despite how we've liked it, there are other places we can like and even love. It's not heaven, it's just a place. We are the heaven together. We will find another beautiful place for our family and our love."

She understood. Despite her own disappointment and reluctance to face all the life-upsetting complications and downright work of moving an entire family and two developed professions, she caught the tortuous fears and anger of my heart and found the salve to soothe them. That is the "understanding" that one yearns to develop in romance. It exists only in shadow early in erotic loving, but in the maturing of love it grows from attentiveness to the content of one another's everyday emotions to this kind of deep comprehension of soul.

Understanding is truly a gift. We all seem to walk around being only partially understood most of the time, with a level of *mis*understanding just below the surface. When we experience exceptional understanding, for even a few minutes, we don't soon forget it.

When we humans are *receiving* understanding, we open like a flower. Our hearts seem to feed on the unspoken impression that "somebody knows what it's like to be me just now and cares actively about what I feel." When being deeply understood, even the reticent tend to talk spontaneously, disclosing more than we decide to, verbally and emotionally rushing ahead of our best judgment.

When we find ourselves able to *give* understanding, we may be able to see the other person actually creating herself before our eyes, through the freshness in the face born of the confluence of her sharing with our empathic listening. Feeling deeply understood is all too rare, and communicating that understanding to others is both an art and a gift.

Classic complaints of teenagers and love partners are "You don't listen to me" and "You don't understand me." When we're trying to find a new identity that fits a major life change like adolescence and romantic love, the needs of finding a listener and being one come together.

Knowledge—Getting to *Really* Know You

That lilting ballad *Getting to Know You* from Rogers and Hammerstein's 1956 Broadway musical *The King and I* illustrates so well the exhilarating "finding out all about you" aspect of early romance. New lovers find the most inane facts about their crush to be fascinating. The upheaval of early romance is due not only to the magnitude of the feelings that sweep new lovers around but also to the fact that those feelings are overshadowing the stability of what they already "know." New lovers are not only getting to know a new person but learning to know in a totally different way, sometimes in a brand-new arena of life. Knowing will never be the same again. In time that new way of knowing will mature them.

Five years after a new love, both partners may be surprised to feel that they barely know each other at all. And they also seem to know less than they thought about loving relationships. Several experts vie in any age for imparting the latest information and concepts on intimate loving. John Gray and Clarissa Pinkola-Estes were popular writers in the 1990s, David Deida and David Schnarch early in this millennium. Knowledge about intimate loving continues to unfold while never comprehending the relationship.

In the Spanish language there are two words for the English term "know." *Ser* means to "know cognitively," to comprehend. The meaning of the other one, *conoser*, is closer to the English phrase "be familiar with." You *ser* geographical facts about Seattle, but you only *conoser* that city if you have been there, tasted its primary features, and experienced its ambiance.

Similarly, there is a complex meaning of *jada* in Hebrew. It can be translated "know" in English but actually refers to "knowing through the heart," "knowing through feeling," and is even used to mean "knowing through intimate loving." When Abram "*knew* his wife Sarah," he did more than chat with her! When Jesus responds in his example of those people who would be saying "Lord, Lord" after death, "I don't know where you come from," or in the companion text in Matthew, "I never knew you," he was referring not only to a mere recognition of face or familiarity with personality but also to a deeper knowing of heart and soul. The knowledge gained from maturing romance is likewise a knowing of the total person, not only the mind.

Romantic experience invites people to make decisions about coping with, living with, and loving another person using both mind and heart. Most of us grow up with our personalities emphasizing one or the other. The Myers-Briggs Personality Inventory, for example, treats the T, or *thinking*, function of a person's character as clearly distinct from the F, or *feeling*, function. Pulling the two together is one of the projects of maturing. Being wrenched emotionally into *eros*, allowing yourself to be jostled and even bashed by it, getting deeply hurt a few times, pondering how that happened, and facing what all the confusing mass of ecstasy and sharp hurt yields, is a natural part of maturing. It can help us consolidate what we know from head and heart, in our love relationships and in many other aspects of life as well.

Three of the seven gifts of the Holy Spirit taken together refer to what one comprehends of reality. They are *knowledge, understanding*, and *wisdom*. Each of the three emphasizes different characteristics that are, in combination, instructive of how one benefits from what is learned through maturing romantic love.

Knowledge is the basis for deep personal *understanding*, which makes possible eventual *wisdom*.

The new *knowledge* that romance begins to offer takes frequent looks through both the window of the mind and the window of one's feelings. Doing so as a way of living is more difficult than it sounds, is learned only over time, and often proceeds only because the exhilaration of intimacy is so highly motivating. What you might have known technically or academically about sex, bodies, emotions, and personality theory—perhaps as a nurse, a physician, a scientist, a psychologist, or a social worker—is helpful but inadequate. If you've not been previously immersed in eros, if eros has not actually touched your soul and compelled your body over an extended period of time, you may only think you know humanity with any depth at all.

You may "know" from "girl talk" and reading novels and magazines that men are basically shallow animals who like to play with big toys and want sex way too often. But when you come to love one special man and find out through trial and painful error that he craves companionship just like you do and that sex to him is an integral part of love, then you know more deeply what women can't teach one another and men can't get across in writing. Most men eventually won't feel loved unless a woman cares about them enough to respond sexually with either genuine or well-feigned enthusiasm, probably more often than she is able to become aroused herself.

In the same way, a man may "know" from locker room jabber that women are capricious, flighty, self-absorbed, hyperverbal, and fickle. But when he comes to love one specific girl, he someday knows that the loving through slow hands, gentle caressing, sensuous ambiance, emotional connecting, and intentional signs of actual care cannot be faked for long, and then he knows more deeply what men can't teach one another. Leisurely presence and generating actual love in the caress have no substitute. Even fantastic, youthfully passionate sexual encounters will only go so far along the way that the specific knowledge of this particular lover from years of loving will lead.

When cooking recipes written in Spanish want to require "stirring," they use the word *envolver*, "to fold together until blended thoroughly." It seems that one of the few ways humans learn to integrate, bring together into one, their heart and their head is through loving intimate *involvement*, thorough folding together, over a long period of time. Those who lose themselves in maturing love's folds of disagreement, conflict, misunderstanding, and ecstasy of mutual pleasure indulgence, applying newfound flexibility, curiosity, forgiveness, and humor, reap the fruits of an improved facility to use both of the aspects of "knowing" in many other areas of life.

The transforming knowledge from loving a specific other person up close also helps teach us how to increasingly love the stranger. As Howard Thurman once wrote, "Community cannot long feed on itself, it can only flourish with the coming of others from beyond: their unknown and undiscovered sisters and brothers."[1] Our habits of stereotyping one another by culture, race, sexual orientation, and ethnic heritage will slowly dissolve in the deeper knowing of one particular human being in intimate love. Prejudice survives only outside of the persistent radical honesty of lasting and truly intimate relationships.

Wisdom—The Making of Guru and Crone

At bedtime after a tiring day in our twenty-sixth year of marriage, I began whining to my wife about the busyness of my next day schedule. She quickly asked, "Well, why do you do that to yourself?" No sympathy. Seeing the conversation was over, I retreated, slightly stung, into sleep. About 2:00 A.M., I woke up and lay in quiet for a few minutes. Then I felt the covers rustle and realized she too was awake. She gently leaned toward me and whispered, "Wanna dance?"

How easily resentments and self-pity begin and how simple is the wisdom that could heal them. At our age the signals of lovemaking between my wife and I, while never devoid of ambiguity, are quite well established and mostly graceful. But they still require wisdom born of experience, knowledge of one another, and intentional understanding.

In the above situation, for example, my wife was thinking, "That quick interchange last night hurt both of us. His pouting hurt me and my quick judgment hurt him. We've been here before. I know he grew up being treated special and at the same time being criticized for whatever he thought and felt that was truly his own. He easily feels judgment. My dad, on the other hand, was mostly silent, and though I loved him dearly, I still easily feel rejected when ignored. Gordy's pouting felt like I was being punished. We've talked about this 'interface' of his early background with mine many times. I know there's no lasting pain here. It wouldn't take much to restore the soul flow. He likes sex, especially when I invite it. I think I'll do that. He's waking up now." "Wanna dance?"

Wisdom could be defined as *"the uncanny capacity to put together all you know, with what you deeply understand, to form a perspective that fits a new and present situation in a way that is imaginative, practical, and aesthetic."*[2] It is facing "the new" by finding a gracious point of view that both works and edifies, that is both practically effective and situationally beautiful.

A huge part of what needs to be "put together" by maturing lovers is awareness of the emotional "hot buttons" established in all of us during our childhood and how they relate to our present relationship. Not in *some* of us, not in *other unfortunate people*, but in *all of us*. There is no question whether overly emotional reactions will eventually occur between all lovers. How both partners deal with those events virtually always makes or breaks the loving bond. Knowing what those buttons are takes careful attention and insight. Understanding the unique ways in which they affect each of us and how they intensify in reaction to each other allows wisdom to be born in the relating, though it can never ensure it.

Freud called it transference. In the context of his carefully attentive and impassive listening to people talk about themselves, he noticed a fascinating phenomenon. Sometimes the patient would abruptly begin acting with emotion toward him that seemed to have no reason related to how he'd acted toward that patient. The depth of emotional content seemed to come out of nowhere. In closely observing this phenomenon he eventually noted patterns and then was able to relate these relational events to the patient's father. The patient was suddenly beginning to act toward him as if he was that patient's dad. Because the patient seemed to be "transferring" emotions generated in the patient by the relationship he or she had with his or her father in childhood, he coined the term "transference."

Many other personality theorists have observed the same, almost universal phenomenon, broadening the perspective on it to include other significant childhood figures in their lives besides the father and calling it by different names. Astute lovers notice a similar dynamic in the conflicted intimacy of their relationship. Emotion from one partner at times seems to come at the other with excessive energy, distorted perception, and skewed intent.

Freud further learned, however, that in carefully observing his own emotions, at unpredictable times he would notice distorted feelings in himself that were generated by the natural expressions of the patient. Wondering why, he could often identify aspects of his own childhood relationships that became operant in his relationship with the patient. Because this "countertransference" was complicating the therapy, he sought to gradually "analyze" his own personality to minimize that effect.

Again, astute lovers can notice a similar phenomenon in their own surprising intimate responses to their partners. They see themselves "fly off the handle" in certain situations or get quiet in response to specific phrases from their partner. Highly reflective spouses are able to see such patterns in themselves, particularly after a fight. Often not noticed in the high-emotion newness of early romance, they can become powerful emotional barriers in a moment. Many spouses become beleaguered about their own behavior and that of their best lover in the nitty-gritty, normal disagreements of living closely with another human being.

In spiritual terms "wisdom" is often what a lover learns from intimate conflict. Allowing insight into how each other's childhood relationships with parents affects the here and now of their intimate loving and takes a maturity that new lovers almost never have. It is mostly from the hurts and failures of love's challenges—and even of love gone bad—that we garner the wisdom needed to navigate the puzzling waters of each other's naturally distorted emotional makeup.

Wisdom can grow from such small events that the change can't even be seen. And the decisions from which it grows are often bad ones. They are mistakes. They are things we wish we'd never done, said, decided, or allowed. We probably learn from the painful aspects of our "screwups" more often than from what we think were our great and glorious successes.

Near the end of the movie *Shall We Dance?* (Miramax, 2004), Richard Gere's character, a divorce attorney named John, is struggling to explain to his wife why, in his fifties, after many years of marriage, he has hidden from her that he has been taking dancing lessons for months. Their souls touch again as he confesses that he didn't tell her because he was ashamed of wanting more in their relationship when they already had so much. As they finally began to dance *together*, John and his wife both grew in wisdom through his creative "breaking out" of a comfortable mode that had begun to lose the liveliness of eros. Perhaps he learned to include her more often in his most treasured, inward musings. And maybe she learned to take less for granted in how stable their happiness seemed when, in reality, he was becoming restless.

Erotic relationships seize our attention and compel our schedule precisely because they so fiercely energize body, mind, and soul together in ways that are intense and focused on a single other individual. We are challenged to "pull ourselves together" when we feel like we are either falling apart or being created anew. *Eros* makes us feel things we don't feel in any other area of our lives, moves us to accomplishing what made little sense previously, and eventually we are able to think strategically about how to feed this new world. The process pulls together all aspects of our person and contributes to the eventual growing of wisdom.

The biblical "wisdom literature" is a major collection of ancient segments of the Old Testament, from Job through Ecclesiasticus, that lauds the beauty of wisdom as if it were a fine woman. Found there are some stories about Solomon that are widely considered to be wisdom classics. As children we heard the one story that started them all, launched his reputation as wise, and initiated the phrase "the wisdom of Solomon" (2 Chron 1:7–12). God was so pleased with Solomon that He told him he could have any gift he wanted, from the entire realm of the universe. Instead of "winning the lottery" or becoming "President of the World," Solomon asked for an understanding heart and *wisdom with which to govern the people*. Both the ecclesiastical and the political realms cry out today for such leaders.

Partnering Piety

Paul van Pernis was the young physician who initiated medical care of our first child after she was born in small-town Ashland, Wisconsin. As we left the hospital with Ashley, he offered a bit of advice we never forgot. It was simple. At least once a month, make sure we have a date, out of the house, just for ourselves, without any friends or children. We have followed his advice fairly well for twenty-five years, sometimes needing to overcome the illusion that we don't have time or money amidst the myriad involvements of work and family. Thank you Paul wherever you are.

It is difficult to know how or even whether that doctor knew the depth of wisdom in his advice, but Nancy and I found it to be astute indeed. Erotic love needs a party atmosphere—open hearts, free sharing talk, small excesses of food and drink, copious laughter, and some physically engaging fun like dancing or a frivolous game—on a fairly frequent basis. It often takes ingenuity to create that atmosphere regularly enough. But along with soul flow and some consistency in sexual engagement, romance needs an intimate party just as religion needs devotion and bodies need food.

Early romance makes partnering feel easy. The dedicated devotion of maturing love, however, requires a level of effort that surprises all young lovers. The 2004 romantic comedy *Fifty First Dates* (Sony Pictures Entertainment, 2004) featured a young woman played by Drew Barrymore whose unique brain-damage disability didn't allow her to remember anything beyond one day. Her charm made every date go well. The next day, however, when she would meet that man again, for her it was always the first time. Any man who would succeed in loving her would have to woo her every day of the rest of her life. That would require so much devotion that few men would ever be game for the challenge. In a sense the gift of knowledge would never materialize for her, understanding would be superficial, and depth of intimate wisdom nearly impossible.

On one hand, continuously repeating the high-emotion experience of meeting a treasured lover for the first time would become burdensome in its superficiality. On the other hand, there is a way in which lovers all need to become dedicated to *repeatedly investing in romantic experiences* in order for one another to *feel* the emotional impact of actually being loved rather than being content with merely *knowing* it.

The traditional Catholic term for how a person relates to the Divine or God, with deep sentiment, fervent expression, and devoted practice, is *piety*. For many of us the term "piety" evokes images of monks or nuns, people who are "holy" in an "otherworldly" sense. We fantasize that they meditate and fast for long periods of time, keep silence, do penance, maybe even flagellate themselves. Those images are of people vigorously relating to the Divine with a Transcendent image of God as committed mystics and aesthetics. Being called "pious" has now generally fallen into disfavor because it has referred to an exaggerated version of that view, a kind of obsessive energy spent on a "me-and-God spirituality" that doesn't fit a relationally oriented society.

Piety, in its best sense, refers to soulful sentiment and devoted intimacy with a personal God—one who feels, knows, and loves you deeply, intimately, and jealously throughout your life. The words of old sentimental hymns and some contemporary country gospel music capture the flavor of such intimate God-and-me relationships quite well:

> Just a closer walk with thee,
> Grant it Jesus if you please.
> Daily walking by your side,
> Let it be, dear Lord, let it be.
>
> —Christian hymn
> (words by unknown author)

The old monastic models of piety have served history well in providing a structure with which to understand and enhance experiences of God deep within. But today one could consider other models as well, ones that might carry significantly more appeal for the erotically involved. One such model would feature "partnering" rather than individual sainthood.

As one old saying goes, "We are all like angels with only one wing, unable to fly without clinging to another." While Catholic thinking has emphasized that each of us dies alone and will be judged uniquely for ourselves, what if the key question in that final judgment turns out to be "Who have you truly loved?" Rather than queries about your material, organizational, and ministry accomplishments, maybe only one question will be asked: "How have you invested in human loving of any kind?"

People continue to be created with two hands, allowing them to work together to complete tasks difficult for one. Our two eyes partner to offer depth perception, two ears to improve directional hearing. Two feet cooperating with one another allow walking. We're gloriously constructed to impress on us that partnering is fundamental to creation.

As romantic partnering increasingly became the theme of human relationships during the twentieth century, the parallel between traditional piety in relating intimately with God on the one hand and intentional nurturing of the joyful soul flow between loving partners on the other became more noticeable. The "Word was made flesh," and so we have a sense that spirituality has more to do with deeply engaging other people than traditional piety ever suggested. An "incarnational" way of looking at spiritual experience better fits lovers than monastic rigor does, and it powerfully augments our preparation for the broader communal partnering to come.

The parallel between the God–human relationship and romantic partnerships was clearly appreciated by biblical authors of the Song of Solomon and

Hosea. A rich example is found in Yahweh's promise in Hosea 2:19–22: "I will *espouse* you to me forever, I will *espouse* you in right and in justice, in love and in mercy; I will *espouse* you in fidelity, and you shall know the Lord." Verse 16 proclaims, "You shall no longer call me master, but husband."

Pope Benedict XVI, in his first encyclical promulgated on Christmas Day 2005, chose the topic of love and in it recognized the power and significance of romance. While his overall content was primarily love of God, he acknowledged that sexual relationship is indeed love and a major aspect of the spiritual life:

> Amid this multiplicity of meanings [of love], however, one in particular stands out: love between man and woman, where body and soul are inseparably joined and human beings glimpse an apparently irresistible promise of happiness. This would seem to be the very epitome of love; all other kinds of love immediately seem to fade in comparison.[3]

The Judeo-Christian tradition of the Deity's attitude toward humanity, first offered to the Hebrews at the call of Moses (Ex 6:7), "I will adopt you as my own people and I will be your God," is a genuine invitation to partner. Extended to all of humanity in the early Christian movement (e.g., Acts 10 and 11, Rom 3:29 and 9:24), the Transcendent seals this partnering with humanity by becoming a human infant and living a life among us. The incarnation confirms God's intention to neither seek mere compliance from us nor be satisfied with our living in isolation from Her jealous care. As a lover, She wants a partner as a spouse who cherishes, endures, contends, responds, adventures, and grieves wholeheartedly as "a part *of*" as well as "apart *from*" Herself.

The Catholic tradition that distinguishes four different classes of prayer is reflected in the intimate interaction that characterizes loving partners' days:

- Words of appreciation of one lover by another never lose their power to warm the heart. While that is not exactly parallel with *prayer of adoration*, which acknowledges the Divine as eternally on a higher plane than the praying person, the expression of love is always new if it includes intentional, authentic demonstration rather than mere ritual.
- Expressed gratefulness between lovers similarly parallels *prayers of thanksgiving*. The eight hundred and fifty-ninth time you bring your lover breakfast or even coffee in bed, "thank you," in either minimal or creative form, feeds the spirit of your day as much as the first time. The slowly growing feeling of being taken for granted results from neglect of expressed gratefulness for the ordinary contributions a lover makes to the partnering. It

may be logically true as some would claim that "I shouldn't have to tell him (or her) over and over." But feelings aren't necessarily logical. Noticing and complimenting what housework has been done, what income has been garnered, what plans imaginatively fashioned, and any other ordinary or extraordinary contribution has been made recently does for lovers what authentic Eucharistic worship does for the Catholic soul.

- *Prayers of supplication* or petition find their intimate parallel in earnest requests of one lover to do something that would please the other, something that one needs, or something one would like him or her to consider seriously about the relationship. Asking twice carries more power, and asking repeatedly, while it can become nagging, invests more in conveying the need for understanding. My wife must have hinted at being taken to the ballet *Swan Lake* fifteen times before I finally purchased tickets.

  Heartfelt apologies between lovers may be some of the most difficult interaction we ever hazard with one another. They parallel *prayers of atonement* in relationship with the Divine. Lovers inevitably hurt one another and sometimes more deeply than we ever intend. Apologies provide balm. Just as "cleaning house" of regrets in "what we have done and what we have failed to do" in relationship with God and with ourselves, so can apologies almost magically inject love energy into a partnership that has been limping under the burden of unspoken resentments and regrets.

The primary characteristics of true partnering—*mutual involvement, refusal to dominate or be dominated, sharing of responsibility, combining of efforts*, and *open, soulful communication*—seen between lovers and in God–human interaction, must also eventually become aspects of broader relationships among people seeking world community. They are all indispensable characteristics growing among the rich diversity of humanity for eventual global partnering.

Counsel—"Heart Seeking Help"

I met Jimmy while I was a counseling trainee at an alcoholism treatment program in Chicago in the mid-1970s. This smallish, perpetually disheveled and bent African-American man whose fifty-four years looked like seventy would stand up at Alcoholics Anonymous (AA) meetings, pull a scrap of paper from his right-hand pants pocket, and read off how many treatment centers he'd been in to no avail, so far in his life—at the time, seventeen—and then sit down. His brain appeared to be "fried," rendering him unable to actually carry on a conversation as he stumbled through his day absorbed entirely with feeding his obsession. He'd been drinking alcohol since he was four years old, having started on the corn liquor his daddy made in the mountains of Kentucky.

I happened to become Jimmy's counselor in his eighteenth treatment hospitalization. Almost a year after that, I saw him on the street, and he recognized me. He hurried over to greet me, looking a bit proud in a clean, cheap suit. I suggested he looked sober, and he said gleaming, "You bet. Six months now, longest of my life."

"Hey! Congratulations," I said. "How in the world are you doin' that?"

"I's in AA," he said.

"Jimmy," I said thoroughly surprised, "you've been in and out of AA dozens of times in the past thirty years. What do you mean you're in AA?"

"Well," he said with eyes gleaming, "those days I'd go to meetins sometimes but I was always '*above* it all,' or '*out in front* leadin' it, or way *behind* it tryin' to catch up, or *underneath* supportin' it, or *alongside* it lookin' like I was fine. But I couldn't get *in* it. Now I's *in* it!"

Somehow, through an unforeseeable set of circumstances, he'd "gotten with" what he needed beyond himself to live a day at a time without alcohol. He was in recovery. He was engaged in that cafeteria of mutual counsel, where members respond with grace to one another's naked vulnerability that constitutes actual help for one of the most gnarly of human quagmires—addiction. In a flourishing AA atmosphere, the experience-based, heart-level spiritual suggestions are always there, free for either the receiving or the "passing." One could call that atmosphere a free display of rich, warm, and basic "help soups," there for the taking, beginning only with your own genuine vulnerability and need expressed from the heart.

That atmosphere is a place full of the Roman Catholic traditional gift of *counsel*, one of the seven gifts of the Holy Spirit. It is the *capacity, courage, and initiative it takes to make effective use of heart level give-and-take from others regarding your actual major and minor difficulties in living.* It is the ability to engage others through a mixture of your own strength and vulnerability, your best thinking and your honest emotions—and listen openly for your own good.

Long-term lovers are repeatedly invited to learn counsel through the frequent sharing of their vulnerabilities and a growing trust born of their intimacy. A man needs help with his sexual urges, with his relationships, with finding self-expression, with appreciation of his endeavors in the world, and with companionship. A woman needs help with her loneliness, her sharing, her understanding of her life, her skin hunger, and her affection appetite. Both need one another's ideas and feelings about parenting, financial decisions, nesting options, work relationships, and fashioning our best appearance in public. We need each other—clearly and deeply. Perhaps it is only this need that prompts our facing one another and falling in love. It is the vulnerability of our need that goads us into intimacy and passionate loving and eventually to learn how to receive counsel humbly and gracefully, often and freely, in other areas of life as well.

Leaders of all kinds desperately need this capacity to open their vulnerability in counsel to give direction to their power. Is it so preposterous to imagine world diplomats as well as national policymaking leaders of professional associations, congresspersons, and military officials openly consulting with opposing leaders regarding decisions that affect us all? Could they come to know one another on a level of personal vulnerability as backdrop to decisions that affect the human race as a global community seeking to equitably share a planet?

Fortitude—The Courage and Savvy for "Going Against"

What contemporary culture calls "momma bear," that protective and violent rage that emerges from mothers when their offspring are seriously threatened, in Catholic tradition was called fortitude. Colloquially defined as *strength of mind that enables a person to encounter danger with courage*,[4] it combines bravery, activity, power, savvy, and persistence at those times when effectiveness is essential. It is what makes a mother formidable when her child is threatened, a man stand to protect his home or homeland, and a nation mobilize for war. It is the backbone that keeps a person erect against gravity and the fire that burns inside to keep one engaged when withdrawing from danger would be safer.

The word *fortitude* is a multicomposite word, combining the Italian *attitudine* (from the Latin *aptus*, or "fit") meaning "a fit posture" with the Latin *fors*, meaning "strength." An attitude today is understood to mean a *habitual emotional stance a person takes to another person, event, situation, or the world in general*. Fortitude is a strong attitude toward something that threatens.

No romance endures without fortitude. In fact, it takes at least a little fortitude even to flirt—make that first phone call and try (or respond to) that first "pickup line"—to get the relationship started. But fortitude has several functions during the entire life of a romance and is absolutely indispensable to maintain it into maturity. Fortitude alone is not enough, but only with it is there any hope of success. As the Broadway play *Aida* song title advises, "Fortune Favors the Brave."[5]

In Catholic tradition, fortitude is found on two lists of virtues. It is one of the Gifts of the Holy Spirit and is also one of the cardinal virtues from which all other virtues flow. Only "charity" is also found on more than one major list. That is how important fortitude was considered to be in the development of these spiritual traditions.

"Going against" pervades nature as one of its themes. Grazers kill plants, predators kill animals, winds move weather, and thumbs became "opposable" as a breakthrough in utility. Indeed, even the physical aspect of sexual loving requires a pushing against one another for ecstasy. Passivity mostly fails in intimate love.

Jesus himself died early for standing up to entrenched religious leaders of his time (e.g., Mt 3:7, 12:34, 23:33). He castigated Peter for so quickly trying to avoid the dangerous return to Jerusalem (Mk 8:33). Some phrases of Jesus' preaching urged the necessity of taking up his cross (Mt 16:24, Lk 14:27), and later apocalyptic writings warned severely about being lukewarm (Rev 3:15–16).

Like the other gifts of the Spirit, fortitude is necessary for the persistence of long-term mutual-pleasuring commitment and also grows through its use in the partnering relationship. When that first courageous flirting venture is rewarded with the warmth of a smile that feels genuine and uniquely targeted to you, the fortitude grows just a bit. Feeling that unpredictable and perhaps undeserved response, the hopeful lover gets encouraged, energized, and motivated. Thereafter, whenever the budding fortitude is used, it grows again and fairly soon becomes enough to "climb any mountain, cross any sea," and even fight and die for your lover.

In romance, fortitude can be focused in any of three different directions in service of the relationship: *against* your partner, *for* your partner, or *with* your partner. Depending on what is threatening, fortitude aims its strength in service of the loving *we*. While romance is largely the story of relating through the *vulnerability* of oneself with that of a lover, *strength* is required as well. *Laying together* symbolizes and feeds the loving, but the time for *standing together* will inevitably arrive as well.

Sometimes fortitude is required *with* your partner. The two of you need to form a united front against "the world," the neighbor, the boss, the in-laws, or the errant child. The adolescent slang phrase "I've got your back" inspires the feeling of support partners need from one another in most any conflict that involves them both.

Sometimes fortitude is required *for* your partner. You need to stand up for her, support her, protect her, and speak publicly in her behalf. Facing your gossipy friends, his coworkers, the customer service representative, and maybe even the police and the media, in support of your partner or in place of his or her when he or she is unable, may call forth fortitude you didn't know you had.

Sometimes fortitude is required *against* your partner. The illusion that two lovers will always agree disappears on the honeymoon or soon after, if not even before, in the early "cooking" of the relationship. Courage to raise a serious issue with your lover verbally—remind, assert, confront, refuse, persist, and stand your ground in issues of principle such as addiction, mental illness, and self-neglect—requires a serious measure of fortitude. Eventually seeking help for the relationship or for yourself if your partner persistently refuses requires a lot of it. When you discover that you are nagging, then getting that help *for yourself* is probably overdue.

Traditionally, fortitude refers to the strength needed to maintain Christian belief and practice in the face of persecution and even martyrdom. More broadly it is the personal power needed to assert oneself and stand up for the deep values that constitute your own soul. Once you are quite certain of what is important to you, the values for which you would spend money, time, and even your life, then you are ready for the unpredictable arrival of the "show-time" of fortitude that, it is hoped, has grown through the previous challenges that your life and your love have endured.

Fortitude is also indispensable in true leaders. All kinds of influential ecclesiastic, academic, and government people will fail to stand firmly for the human values of the good of all on the planet—amidst nationalism, greed, power thirst, and image enhancement—without solid fortitude.

Awe (Fear of the Lord)

All passionate lovers know awe, even if they never name it so. From the first realization of a potential lover's exquisite being to the wrenching pain of seeing her placed in the grave, awe visits often, the home and the bed of maturing lovers. The depth of mystery that captures the soul during prolonged eye contact, the delightful warmth of quiet presence, the frequent repetition of ecstatic mutual pleasuring, and the ever-deepening appreciation of the uniqueness of this soul who loves you through two-thirds of the life cycle all inspire indescribable awe many times in the course of a maturing love partnership.

When the early Christians and later theologians used the term "Fear of the Lord," they were actually referring to the notion of "awe," as when Moses removed his shoes and covered his face before Yahweh's presence in the burning bush (Ex 3). The Old Testament phrase "Fear of the Lord is the beginning of wisdom" (Ps 11:10, Prov 9:10) meant that until you stand in awe at creation and Creator as so far beyond human power that it is incomprehensible, your depth of understanding and wisdom about anything is questionable. Until you recognize the chasm between the finite and the Infinite, you are not experiencing the world deeply. When you stand profoundly shaken by the storm, speechless at the ocean, or reduced to tears by the birth of your own child, then you know awe and have begun to touch the meaning of life. Being loved sexually to luxurious bliss or uncontrollable orgasm is in the same sense awesome.

Experientially, awe is a curious mixture of profound *joy*, silencing *fear*, and often a touch of *shame*:

- The *joy* is a natural human response of delight at unspeakable beauty. It is the difference between awesome and awful, that is, the cold fear one sometimes feels regarding joyless stories of the devil or when meeting specific dark and scary people.

- The *fear* aspect of awe is response to sensing enormous power, which reveals one's own relative insignificance, as when paddling a canoe near an oceangoing freighter.
- The touch of *shame* emerges from awareness of one's own imperfections when standing in a profound and shaking presence of deep goodness. You simply feel unworthy to be there.

All these feelings compel one to acknowledge the awe in some appropriately sacred way—to "take off your shoes."

Young lovers may touch a hint of awe at the intense pleasure of shared passion and orgasm or the personal beauty, wonder, and depth of one another. Mature lovers, however, are gifted with awe they embrace regularly as they realize all that has transpired through the love that has guided and energized their intimate partnering through countless challenges and demands. Bold awareness of how it has shaped them, both individually and as a uniquely graced couple, at unpredictable times inspires grateful awe.

Awe is also the "stuff" of worship. In fact, worship activity without awe may be mere compliance to uniformity rather than actual relating closely with the Beyond. Sometimes a maturing churchgoer can get the impression that much of religion is obsessive attempts to insulate people from the unsettling awe that characterizes the best of human living and any authentic relating to the Divine. Traditionally, Catholics, for example, genuflect in reverence of the presence of the Eucharist, responding to the awe inside. Perfunctory, thoughtless, ritualized gestures may actually be fending off awe rather than expressing it.

Indeed, remaining open to and even nurturing continuing awareness of awe in one's life is the project of both religion and maturing romantic love. The Trinitarian tradition of Transcendence lends itself well to identifying the three kinds of experience of the Divine as all present in the romantic loving relationship: awe at "God above us" (the Father tradition), awe at "God among us" (the Son tradition), and awe at "God within us" (the Holy Spirit tradition).

For example, as we age, my wife and I sometimes fantasize about how we'd like to live after retirement, and the three primary ways of encountering the Divine are all there in those dreams. Sharing all this with one another would double its glory.

First, we envision a place overlooking Puget Sound, in full view of either the sunset or the sunrise, and perhaps even the magnificence of Mt. Rainier. The changing winds, waves, storms, clouds and tides, and the people weathering them in boats and planes could constantly astound us. There would be forest around us, a garden close by, some good-sized dogs to accompany in the woods each day, and a powerful telescope with which to maintain the impression of greater closeness to all this. Grand experiences of the *Creator God* would be continually and immediately near. And there are several very distant places to which we would travel, to expand our awe at creation and human history as we seek to continuously encounter the One who is making it all make itself in the grand evolution of love.

Second, our dream is to have each other for many years. I would have nearby daily the woman who has already loved me so faithfully, tolerantly, emotionally, and physically for two and a half decades. There would be a guest room and a place to visit friends, our three children and their treasured people too, preferably with a fireplace and windows through which to share the natural miracles. But a comfortable bedroom would be essential in which to be reminded vividly and often of the *incarnate love of God* in carnal human mutually pleasuring expression.

Third, there would also be a computer, a quick one, with an excellent word processor and connection to the Internet. Morning after morning I awake with thoughts, ideas, images, and concepts that become dreams of expression. The *Spirit of God* is there within me, and my introversion savors it, yearning to find ways to manifest it to others, anybody who would take it seriously. I believe Jesus would have wanted a computer too had He lived in our age, though He apparently never wrote anything that was saved in His own day. For my wife, her books, tapes, and meditation setting would be easily accessible and well used to daily facilitate the flow of her soul.

Nurturing our capacity to allow awe in our lives, to continually quiet our resistance to its power, is a chief project of the spiritual life. Having an awesome long-term lover in your heart, house, and bed certainly helps keep alive the ability to be awed and respond with affection, care of people, and worship of the Divine. Sexual loving is there if we can find and feed it to facilitate our constant thirst for meaning, purpose, and our inclusion in the awesome process of evolutionary love.

Notes

1. Howard Thurman, *Search for a Common Ground: An Inquiry into the Basis of Man's Experience of Community* (Richmond, Ind.: Friends United Press, 1986).

2. The author's definition. Wisdom is named in the Catechism but is not defined.

3. Pope Benedict XVI, *Deus Caritas Est*, encyclical, December 25, 2005, Part I, 2 (www.vatican.va/holy_father/benedict_xvi/encyclicals/documents/hf_ben-xvi_enc_20051225_deus-caritas-est_en.html).

4. Fortitude is also a cardinal virtue.

5. Tim Rice and Elton John, *Aida* (New York: Hyperion Theatricals, 1998). The musical was based on an opera by Giuseppi Verdi (1871).

CHAPTER FOUR

~

Death, Resurrection, and the Ending of Love

To love and win is the best thing;
To love and lose is the next best.

—William Makepeace Thackeray

In this life, love ends. Always. As sure as romance and intimate engagement stirs the soul, it will also come to a close. Whether it dies too soon or drags on beyond its spiritual liveliness, sooner or later the loving stops, and we are left with the project of what to make of love's whirlwind and breezes that have carried us, jostled us, abandoned us, and in the process uniquely shaped our lives.

So far in this book we have extolled the benefits of intimate loving. But the beauty of eros must not obscure the fact that love beginnings are followed by painful endings. Very few even last into maturity. The ending of a love relationship that sears the soul is an inextricable aspect of the loving mystery. Unless they die together, even lovers who commit to marriage early in life and remain faithful until death eventually face the end of their "we" and its emotional residue. Dashed or deadened romance almost universally finds a way to etch its pain into our love life theme and stand there forever as a spiritual cornerstone.

The particular grief that follows the loss of romance must have a reason anticipated by the Creator that we can continue to ponder. St. James' suggestion that pure religion includes caring for widows (James 1:27) is at least an invitation that care of people when the love of their lives has died ought to be held in high regard. Permanent love separations stand alongside death as powerful endings that feel profoundly tragic, deepen our view of life, and prod the growing of our wisdom. But first they darken our souls in a way that nothing else

47

does. What meaning can be garnered from breakups: the natural grief *feelings* of love's end, its parallel *faith event* in Catholic tradition, and the *future* that the transition seeks to sculpt into wisdom?

The Feelings

Among the inpatient population of any mental health unit walks at least one young person who attempted suicide resulting from the souring of a once-beautiful romance. The end of a love relationship can hurt that much. Although to outsiders it seems silly ("There are other fish in the sea"!), when such a beautiful animal turns on us to wound so deeply, it feels to many of us that it is not worth going on. It seems we'll never be happy again. As Skeeter Davis pondered in a 1960s song, Why do the sun and ocean go on even after a great love is lost?

Hurt may be the most basic feeling of breakup. It can often be neglected through ingrained habits of protecting it with masks of anger or contrived cheeriness. But lovers who allow themselves to fully experience the natural flow of their emotions after they part are likely to acknowledge that the word *hurt* best describes the most basic emotional tone of the grief.

But hurt is not alone in the response to love's failure. The jumble of emotions that invade the heart confuses us all with its complexity. Mashing together anger, fears, pervasive sadness, loneliness, and a yearning for the warmth of the past, the feeling hodgepodge of grief can be so powerful that it is life transforming. As it plows into our everyday life, overturning previous established ways of looking at ourselves and at the world, it is preparing beneath our awareness, potentials for new growth on the other side.

Virtually all ways of describing the bodily sensations we call feelings can be used in the impossible task of conveying to another person the experience of ending a love. C. S. Lewis's *A Grief Observed* stands as one of the best-written attempts to describe losing his wife to death. Here is my own brief description of the feelings that overwhelm many people who say good-bye to a lover in divorce, fed-up defeat, or being "dumped."

You feel like a failure, questioning your worth as a person. You feel like a fool for having been so vulnerable and for not being vulnerable soon enough. You feel ashamed of what you said and for not saying what you wish you'd said. You feel guilty for hurting your lover and for not taking better care of yourself when you got deeply hurt by him or her. You feel angry for how your partner trashed your love, clung to insensitive habits, and never understood your soul. You feel stupid for having been dominated for periods of time by the emotional intensity or physical intimidation of your partner. You feel foolish and embarrassed by the public scrutiny that you think sees you as a personal failure. You want to go under the porch and lick your wounds and simultaneously are driven to show the world that you're healed and again in charge of your life. You want no romantic engagement whatsoever and yet feel the profound emptiness of the bed in which you sleep alone. You feel a relief that there is again a modicum of peace in your days and glimpse moments of euphoria that descend unexpectedly on you in the freedom of being yourself. Then the bitter feelings of having had your guts torn out flare again.

These depictions of breakup's emotional hurricane are common patterns of how the unique devastation attacks the soul of the jilted or escaping lover. Efforts at assuaging the critical nature of grief feelings by being nice through it all mostly fail. Like straining to smile while being physically barbequed, the charade is just too much. Good grievers let the stark and natural feelings emerge, acknowledge them authentically to themselves, share them in whatever trusted personal context is available, and allow themselves to await any new directions or learned wisdom that eventually emerge. Doing so requires a measure of faith in the loving mystery, a quiet conviction that the Creator has designed some hope into this ambiguous aspect of an unpredictable world.

The Faith

What is called the paschal mystery has formed the core of Catholic practice from the very first days of Christianity. Typically defined as the death and resurrection of Jesus, its celebration in all Catholic parishes from Holy Thursday to Easter Sunday sensuously invites participants to join themselves to that self-donating love event as a contributing part of the world's redemption. One could say that the paschal mystery moderated the natural human fear of death by solidly confirming a fledgling first-century belief that there is a glorious life after dying.

The crucifix, displaying the dying body of Jesus on the cross, continues to visually teach that the Good Friday death of Jesus is an essential part of the paschal mystery. During the Middle Age reformation, newly forming iterations of Christianity changed the crucifix into a "reformation cross" without the body of Jesus in its obviously dreadful condition. The intent was to emphasize the glory of the resurrection rather than the "sacrifice" of Jesus the crucifix portrays. Both symbols feed Christian souls. The crucifix hangs today in many Catholic homes, churches, and hospital rooms, keeping alive the notion that dying inevitably precedes any significant rising to new life.

After forty-five years, the cross that was starkly attached to my mother's coffin still adorns a wall in my home. An ordinary crucifix made entirely of some inexpensive shiny metal, its uniqueness lies in its personal meaning. But its particular art also uniquely conveys honor of my parents' lives as intimate lovers. This crucifix includes two bold background circles that symbolize rings. My sisters and I chose it during mom's funeral arrangements when we were in our early twenties because it honors the marriage between our parents and their persistent Catholic practice, along with the portrayal of the dark side of the paschal mystery. In essence, it combines intimate love and Catholic tradition in one beautiful sacramental.

The original paschal mystery initiated a solemn practice of seeing death as a transition rather than an ending. Pre-Christian Hebrew belief had considered *sheol*, the place of residing after death, as a rather dreary place.[1] The notion of a happy afterlife was being formed among some thinkers only about the time that Jesus was born. It was boldly confirmed to early Christian believers by his resurrection. The notion of heaven as happiness with God was replacing sheol as a dark ending. Belief in a new beginning that follows the process of dying, the most tragically fearful aspect of this life, became a core element of Christian teaching.

The ending of a romantic love relationship can be seen as the personal parallel to the paschal mystery in the unfolding of a human lifetime. As a bold spiritual milestone, love breakup prods the learning of virtually every human being that there can be a beautiful future that follows. A love relationship that confirms one's essential goodness is possible even after devastating final separation. Loving, as the core of Christian practice and the crowning glory of human living, survives the ending of any particular love relationship.

The Future

The notion that a wedding is a permanent commitment to remain in partnership with a specific person until death of one or the other is a wonderful ideal that reflects a major feature of the mystery of intimate loving. The essential dream of lovers is to remain faithful to one another in the gloriously demanding endeavor of keeping their delightful love flowing for the rest of their lives. Even infatuated teenagers sometimes slip into fantasies of wafting forever in their vague impressions of a future together. This ideal of endless love is likely to remain a feature of intimate relationships for centuries to come, injecting hope into us humans in a uniquely spiritual way.

Breakup, however, will inevitably stand equally as stubborn as one of love's primary characteristics. To engage the loving mystery will continue to mean repeatedly facing the combination of seeking permanence on the one hand and traversing love failures on the other. Efforts by teachers, church leaders, and libertines alike to eradicate one side of the mystery or the other are likely only to mislead people into gnarly spiritual conundrums laden with guilt, confusion, resentment, and unnecessary wandering in their human endeavor of combining sex with love as a component of life fulfillment and spiritual maturity.

What can love pain teach? It can, for example, carve into our spiritual makeup some unspoken convictions:

- Nurturing an intimate "we" requires more attentiveness and imagination than we'd thought. In our next romantic adventure, if there is one, we may make more intentional effort at observing the relationship itself and pondering how to feed it.
- Emotionality and soul-flow sharing are as important as sexual mutuality. Women especially find loving inextricably attached to their emotions and cannot respond much sexually without heartfelt interaction that includes their feelings.
- Sexual mutuality is as important as emotionality and soul-flow sharing. Men especially have their love tied to genital sex and won't feel loved for long without it.
- Looking at oneself and the progress of one's own acquisition of virtues makes the intricacies of active loving possible. The psychoanalytic concept of projection makes it too easy to blame an intimate lover for one's own faults and need for growth. Only when both lovers are looking at themselves will intimate maturity progress beyond a certain/uncertain point.
- One side of a partnership cannot make a love relationship work. Mutual involvement is an essential element in the loving soup. If either stops investing for a significant period of time, the relationship is definitely in decline.
- Flexibility regarding one's own values needs balance with the solidity of honoring them. You don't have to give up "you" to love me, and neither do I. Relationships aren't impossible when partners hold different deeper values. But they are more difficult.
- Wonderful but deeply damaged people (e.g., from combat, sexual abuse, physical abuse, emotional abuse, mental illnesses, addiction, or other destructive family-of-origin dynamics) will probably need significant healing before engaging the depths of intimate loving relationships can be successful. Trying anything else than finding recovery when one of you is alcoholic, for example, is probably folly until that recovery finds quality.
- Romance heals, but its healing powers are limited. Many of our self-doubts, self-criticisms, and pockets of life reticence are healed by the adoring eyes of a genuine lover. But love can't heal addiction, character disorders, mental illness, and the wreckage of combat and abuse. It can only contribute to the complex processes of recovery.
- A compassionate heart is more important in love than physically appealing endowment. Hanging on to adolescent notions that big boobs

and penises result in greater ecstasy only misleads from paths to intimate maturity.

- Good sex is not love.
- Good sex both expresses and enhances intimate love.
- Soul flow can be learned. The best of us, whoever they are, continually learn how to share our inner dialogue in ways that feed one another personally without shock and damage to the relationship.
- Developed capacity for soul flow requires motivation, persistence, and the tolerance of learning from experience.
- There is no perfect lover.
- There are many exquisite lovers willing to grow together with a partner.
- Marriage counseling can help a struggling love.
- Marriage counseling may not heal a deeply damaged relationship.
- Marriage counselors vary considerably in expertise and professional wisdom.

Catholic canon law regarding marriage was fashioned before there evolved a readiness among humanity to see intimate loving from a spiritual perspective. Its heavy-handed condemnations and illusions of certainty that made contributions to the permanence of marital fidelity in centuries past could now benefit from a practice of constant revision that honors sexual loving as one of creation's greatest mysteries. Divorced people need some organizational structure that is pastoral, along with ministry to their hurting spirits.

In regulating the intimate loving aspect of life, secular law contents itself for the most part with curtailing domestic violence and making fair decisions about material rights when a love life has failed. Church law, however, may have overextended its attempt to influence marital success by unrealistically insisting that people take communal restrictions as consequences for not staying together in poisoned relationships. A more pastoral perspective will likely be implemented in future iterations of Church law when maturing lovers are included in the widespread consultation needed to fashion regulation that honors the Church's pastoral identity and its spiritual mission.

Note

1. John L. Makenzie, S.J., *Dictionary of the Bible* (Milwaukee, Wis.: Bruce Publishing, 1965), 800 ff.

CHAPTER FIVE

~

Lust or Lusty Love—
The Moral and the Spiritual

It is a continual demonstration of the truth that we are composite creatures,
rational animals, akin on one side to angels and on the other to Tom-cats.

—C. S. Lewis

The Roman god Janus could symbolize the sexual mystery as both beautiful
and dangerous. Janus was represented by a head with two faces, looking in opposite directions. He was worshipped at "beginnings" such as plantings, weddings, births, and pivotal events in a person's life. In Roman mythology he
represented transitions—between the primitive and the civilized, between the
country and the city, between peace and war, and between childhood and
adulthood in coming-of-age.

The intense pleasure of human sexuality carries the powerful capacity both
to enrich life through the expression and fostering of mutual love and to hack
away at it through many forms of loveless assault and obsessive preoccupation.
Moral thinking around sexual behavior has so long overshadowed intimacy's
spiritual nature that the latter is only now beginning to be seen. Only in the
twentieth century did sexuality's comely face of spirituality begin to be increasingly appreciated opposite its stern face of morality.

From a spiritual point of view, the work of moral reasoning at its best seeks
to give direction to human decisions by identifying those that are destructive.
Moral theology, as it is called in Catholic tradition, is any major religion's "wisdom about bad" or understanding of "what should not be." Considered functionally, it studies and teaches what kinds of human behavior displease the Deity because they hurt people. Moral views have dominated religious thinking

about sex for centuries because of morality's power to use condemning, judging, forbidding, ostracizing, and punishing to protect some people from others—and from themselves.

Spiritual theology, on the other hand, seeks to define and describe what is beautiful in human living, "what should be," what is virtuous, and what contributes to human happiness and unity. Spirituality can be defined functionally as the entire *array of beliefs, practices, and values that people use to cope with and enjoy the profound, uncontrollable mysteries of life*. It includes sexual loving as one of its components that can enrich the lives of most people.

Catholic moral tradition can contribute to a spirituality of intimate loving by reminding us of how difficult it has been to find meaningful perspectives on sexual behavior. Morally condemned behaviors, because of their partially observable nature, continue to offer some wisdom about intimate spirituality. Looking back at moralists' teaching on how the human spirit languishes and sabotages itself (i.e., sin) can be useful in exploring ways in which the loving mystery fails to thrive.

One group of moral concepts worth exploring, for example, became well defined by preachers during the Dark Ages and now can be seen as a collection of styles of spiritual failure. Seven of those were eventually gathered together in a cluster of vices called the seven deadly sins. They become styles of love-life failure when seen through lovers' eyes.

Specifically named *lust, pride, wrath, greed, sloth, gluttony,* and *envy,* the seven deadly sins had their roots in Old Testament law as it gradually developed over many centuries and in New Testament preaching as Christian leaders observed patterns of living that inhibited conversion. St. Paul noticed that certain human characteristics hardened people against the power of the Holy Spirit coming on them. In fact, his list of the fruits of the Spirit in Galatians 5:22–23 was preached largely in contrast to his condemnation of personal evils he saw preventing deep and positive life changes, named a few verses earlier in Galatians 5:19–21.

Through the Dark Ages and the Middle Ages, preachers focused on these patterns as they observed them in their extremes, in people whose lives had degenerated into ugly evil. They were called "deadly" because they were seen as ways of living that kill the human spirit. They were also called the "Seven *Capital* Sins" from the same Latin root as "decapitate" because people seemed to "lose their heads" to these dangerous proclivities that could cause them eternal damnation.

The moral theology term "sin" is useful to a spiritual perspective only as a warning about the destructiveness of specific behaviors when the evil inherent in them is veiled through various forms of self-deception or inexperience. The seven deadly sins can still offer insight into failures of intimate love, as human tendencies to forms of excessive *self-indulgence* that inhibit *mutual indulgence* of romance. While a good measure of self-indulgence is necessary in order to enjoy passionate mutuality, the intricacies of loving relationships can't stand it in excess. Too much "me" defeats the "we."

Indeed, as we will see in the next two chapters, all these seven are distorted preoccupations with good things. Like the wild overgrowth that constitutes cancer in body tissue, these seven preoccupations strangle healthily growing love. They can unpredictably do so in every phase of a relationship. They cloud assessment of potential lovers in romantic beginnings. They steal energy from loving relationships in their developing stages. And they can erode even decades of marriage, with the potential to eventually defeat intimacy entirely.

Looking at these classic brands of evil relative to intimate loving can also enhance their visibility as spiritually deadening in general, making them more useful for personal guidance in our age. The first one, lust, deserves its own chapter since it features evils directly related to sex itself. The other six follow in chapter 6 as ways of inhibiting the flourishing of intimate love. But seeing it from a spiritual rather than a moral point of view may help it find its place when joined with genuine love among all the other grand human behaviors that buoy the spirit and feed the soul.

Sex as Spiritual

The emergence of full-blown sexual arousal introduces one of the most powerful spiritual forces that shape adolescent lives. It confronts all of us humans, some more powerfully than others, with the life mystery that is the most immediate of all. It boldly presents itself over and over within our own bodies. As a basic corporal function, it erupts in ways we cannot ignore, creating a spiritual arena all its own. A mere curiosity in childhood, it becomes powerfully transforming in adolescence. Seizing our attention with intense pleasure, it frustrates our efforts to control it, prods our romantic courage, curtails our parental sharing, and alerts us to the sobering fact that now as almost adults we can actually generate offspring.

Emerging seemingly from nowhere in early adolescence, sexual arousal brings with it similarities and differences from all other bodily functions. Like our heart rate and our breathing, arousal materializes and finds its rhythm on its own, at whatever age our bodies become ready. Like urination and defecation, it intricately combines bodily sensations, intention, and decisive action, presenting us with frequent but unpredictable corporal urges that compel our will to unite with them to release bodily pressure. And like our cravings for food and drink, its pleasure cries out for satisfaction of its incessantly recurring appetite.

By the time passionate sex takes over lovers in its sweeping storm of carried-away pleasure seeking and pleasure giving, both partners have previously faced the exquisite mystery of sexual arousal alone. Somewhere in the secretive seclusion of budding, self-explorative adolescence, both lovers, if endowed with normal levels of hormones, have encountered the nearly irresistible pleasure of their own penis or clitoris. Most of us, especially men but a majority of women as well according to Kinsey[1] and many other researchers, have at some time or another cooperated with those bodily urges to orgasmic release. This mixture of one's own action collaborating with unmanageable sexual arousal has mystified most of us long before we manage to employ sex in relationships for the fulfillment of intimate loving passion. The term *commit*, from Latin "put together," fits this collusion between one's will and a power beyond arousal.

C. S. Lewis once made a distinction that is key to seeing sexual love as spiritual. He distinguished sex itself, which he called "Venus," from sexual *love*, which he called "Eros." In his classic book *The Four Loves*, he wrote that sexual desire is focused on getting "it," sexual pleasure. Eros or sexual love, on the other hand, wants the beloved. Venus makes a heterosexual man want any woman, while eros will be satisfied by only one particular woman without whom he will not be happy.[2] Although the exceptional thinker Lewis might argue with the oversimplicity of this statement, the difference between sex itself on the one hand and sexual loving on the other is the presence in the relationship of at least a sliver of genuine mutual love.

The virtue that traditionally assists a person to deal with the two-faced aspect of the sexual mystery is chastity. It was defined in the later catechisms as *the successful integration of sexuality within the person and thus the inner unity of man to his bodily and spiritual being*. Related to temperance, it sought to permeate the senses, impulses, and appetites with reason, and it was acknowledged to be achieved only by a long and difficult process of combining a gift from God with consistent personal effort.[3] For people pursuing a life of ever-maturing intimate love, chastity could be defined simply as *continually seeking to bring sex and love together and keep them entwined*. Indeed, it is a lifelong task.

Even assessing the degree to which a specific relationship edifies one partner's soul is no small project. The question "Is this the love of my life or merely my desire for the pleasure of bodily warmth, sexual satisfaction, and the high of 'being in love with *someone*'?" enters the minds of many of us as we begin to engage the sexual loving mystery. Mostly a matter of the heart, answering that question well requires honest use of one's mind as well. Sometimes consulting with a "big brother/big sister" type of friend, mentor, or counselor can help. But in the end, nobody can provide absolute clarity. One is often left with questions such as the following: Do we both genuinely care for each other as persons? Are we truly in love? Are we both fooling ourselves because we so badly want it to be love? Is one partner fooling the other to obtain mere sexual pleasure or material benefit? Is one of us fooling our self about our own inner knowing the truth that this is not really love but mere sexual desire?

When Sex Is Spiritually Harmful

The ancient Latin meaning of the word *lust* was quite positive. It meant simply a *very strong sexual desire*. Its later use in some languages (German and Dutch) retains the positive connotation of *pleasure* or *delight*. Even in English, where it has taken on a mostly sordid nuance, it can still be used as a compliment in such hyperbolic phrases as "He was really lusting after me last night!" In that sense, lust refers to times when the intense desire for loving pleasure overrides the patience necessary for quiet emotional sharing and relational gracefulness, catalyzing glorious passionate romps. Unpredictably, the intensity of ardor overcomes the need for intimate sharing, an exquisite experience occasionally, to both men and women, though men may be more prone to seek it frequently. Such "lusty love" often provides a couple with some of its grandest memories, from early romance to the nursing home.

The sexual mystery has always presented a powerful paradox to humanity because the glory of lusty love stands so remarkably close to damaging sexual experience in the forms of clueless experimentation and destructive abuse. Sex constitutes some of the best and the worst of life. At its best in passionate loving, it crowns the glory of romance, while at its worst in violent or furtive abuse, it may be the greatest enemy of intimate love.

There are three paths to the damage. They could be called *seduction*, *induction*, and *reduction*. All from Latin origins, they refer to being (1) lured or "led away" from loving support by indulging the attraction to pleasure, (2) being "led into" loveless sex with no promise of intimate relationship, and (3) being "led back" to a place of less-than-human treatment for the sake of somebody else's gratification.

The Seductions

In the contemporary dark comedy *To Die For* (Columbia Pictures, 1995), Nicole Kidman's character, a married woman, boldly seduces an inexperienced high school boy into a highly sexual relationship for the explicit purpose of persuading him to kill her husband. Offering him sex in a wide variety of venues with reckless abandon and charming allure, she seduces him into actually loving her and then convinces him that the only way they can consistently be together will be if her husband is dead. Predictably, after he completes the murder, she abandons him to the imprisonment he questionably deserves. He had been "led away" intentionally from the earnest support of his friends into the bare, manipulative sex that he thought was love.

Seduction is not always so dramatic and openly sinister, of course. In fact, it is not always destructive. In the midst of a loving relationship, leading one another into a pleasuring event makes up some of the most delicious fun of intimate loving. But outside such a relationship, seduction can be devastating. As a form of Venus, or sex without love, it could be defined as *either misusing the motivating power of sexual pleasure, or feigning love, for the purpose of obtaining either sexual gratification or material benefit.* It is by definition loveless.

Not so clear, however, is the partially conscious using of sex or feigned affection in order to benefit in small ways from the warmth of closeness, the spending of money, or the promise of later enthusiastic fun together. What makes intimate loving a continual mystery is that its intricacies can never be completely analyzed. Love is of the heart and cannot always be recognized by someone outside the relationship itself or even immediately by those engaged in it. As a classy and middle-aged female physician once quipped on a woman's TV show, "Men will do almost anything for that [orgasmic sex] and we women can sometimes benefit from that." Sorting out that kind of loving indulgence from what is loveless advantage-taking is part of maturing as an intimate lover.

Other, less harmful forms of seduction are not spiritually recommended at all. Leading another away from the loving context of parents and friends into the intensity of sexual pleasure when you believe you love her or him may be understandable and even effective. But that kind of attempting to manipulate the unpredictability of love has its hazards, materially and spiritually. The woman who seeks to get pregnant to solidify a relationship and the man who impresses a girl with opulence are reaching a bit far into the disingenuous land of manipulation. The intimate engagement that may result will need to heal that subtle deception later before the love can ever mature.

Sexual Reduction

The term "reduction" is chosen here for its reference to "leading back" (Latin *re* meaning "back" and *duco* meaning "to lead") a person into a place of less-than-human treatment. Defined as *treating another as an "it" either for purposes of sexual gratification or for material profit,* such as in prostitution, pedophilia, rape, and incest, it is the most damaging of all, the substance of what the word "lust" now commonly means. There is no question of love in these cases, and the damage is severe, perhaps permanent. There is no redeeming view of sexual reduction. It has been described as "soul murder" in that its personal damage mars the core of an individual so seriously that hope of successfully reclaiming a life of intimate loving, even with excellent therapy, is questionable.

Intimate loving does carry a healing potential, however, and that theme has not been lost on songwriting and Hollywood, probably because most lovers need that healing to some degree. The Billy Joel song "An Innocent Man" (1983) is sung by a fellow who pledges to assist his once-abused lover to overcome her woundedness through his faithful and loving presence in the relationship. The much-viewed film *Pretty Woman* (Touchstone Pictures, 1990) carries the same theme. A prostitute played by Julia Roberts falls in love with a wealthy patron of hers, played by Richard Gere, and "love will out." The healing power of genuine romance is vividly portrayed, an antidote to previous sexual wounding of both partners that is implied though never really seen. Both *A Beautiful Mind* and *As Good as It Gets* carry the healing theme as far as seeing it helping the seriously mentally ill overcome major disabilities.

Harmful Induction

When an adolescent "sex club" was broken up in a posh large-city suburb in the 1990s, it was discovered that for months a group of barely teenagers had frequently gathered at one kid's home after school and engaged in various genital sexual activities. When some of the youngsters were interviewed afterward, one of the girls was quoted as saying, "It wasn't rally that great. Actually I don't like sex that much. I think it's mostly for boys anyway."

That event, carried briefly on national news, illustrates parents' fears that have fueled centuries of attempts to protect daughters with secular law and religious teaching. Insensitive, loveless sex, even sometimes in youthful experimental groping rather than hardened rape and incest, can ruin a person's chances at loving bliss all her life. She was "led into" sex, with no indication or real promise of a loving relationship.

One could distinguish such luring through sordid curiosity or peer pressure, from intentional seduction, by the notion that there was little if any promise of anything for this young lady except being accepted and feeling like she was part of an "in" crowd. One could not necessarily accuse the boys of seduction since they may have been as foolishly experimental as the girls. Yet the damage to her future love life may be considerable. It may be years now, after some effective therapy and relationship with a genuine lover, before she experiences the joy of sexual love. The confused impressions she carries about the carnal loving arena may result in her never experiencing it at all.

Induction into loveless sex could be defined as *being led into carnal pleasuring without any implied promise of love or material benefit*. The leader-in is often oneself, not necessarily another person or group of influential peers. One can induce oneself into such pervasive habits of autoeroticism that one slows or even inhibits the emotional-level relating that allows the gradual formation of relationships of genuine intimacy. That being said, however, the chances of serious damage from solitary sex seem to be very small.

At fifteen, I was stunned walking home from going to confession one Saturday afternoon. I'd told the monsignor about my recent escapades of sexually pleasuring myself, not even knowing the word "masturbation." He'd made it clear that such behavior was mortally sinful, and I knew that meant I would go to hell if I hadn't confessed it and heard the absolution. Way behind many of my Catholic school peers in coming to sexual manhood, my head whirled in a bewildered haze to know I'd come so close to damnation. It was the most serious moment of my life so far.

How sexual pleasure took on such a solemnly negative cast is the story of other, more scholarly and historical books. But indeed it had done so in the common practice of Catholic teachers and leaders. They once taught that all sexual pleasure outside marriage was seriously sinful. There was no sexual correlate to petty thievery or little white lies. Illicit pleasure was always as bad as you could get, alongside murder. The catechism defined lust as "inordinate" enjoyment of sex or disordered desire for it. It then defined "disordered" as sexual pleasure that didn't bring spouses together or that couldn't result in conception.[4] If it wasn't making a baby or bringing you closer to your wife, it was condemned and could send you to hell forever. Augustine even saw sexual intercourse in marriage as venially sinful if it wasn't intended to procreate.[5]

It is easy to believe that public officials of past centuries, including ecclesiastical leaders, were doing their best with what was known at the time about the sexual mystery. Newton knew nothing about quantum mechanics, Freud missed the oppression of women, and early biblical translators didn't use inclusive language. Even Einstein didn't think up a computer. Similarly, religious leaders of earlier centuries could not comprehend what is now known about women's anatomy, physiology, psychology, and spirituality. Their understandable failure to recognize the spiritual beauty of sexual love was certainly one component of their forbidding all unmarried sex, much like the U.S. government prohibition of all alcohol in the 1920s. Who can tell for sure even today which sexual partners actually love each other, even if one of them is a prostitute, gay, or on a one-night stand?

The employing of mere logic in attempts to discern a priori what aspects of sexual sorting and relational groping toward loving intimacy are seriously harmful has spawned such enormous preoccupation with sex in moral thinking that the very term "morality" now commonly implies errant sexual behavior rather than a broad range of destructive moral acts. Today if someone is deemed immoral by society, the reference is generally not to theft, murder, deceit, or embezzling millions.

Still, ecclesiastical leaders' historical attempts to overcontrol the sexual mystery have come to appear as folly by spiritually maturing Catholics. Clergy sex scandals have not helped. What any church leader says about sexual morality is now commonly ignored. That separation of sexual loving from authentic religious practice is now giving way to discerning and teaching how sex can be employed in the intricacies of intimate love.

Healing Sexual Misconceptions

As mutual partnering becomes the expected relationship style, how can we distinguish intimate love from destructive loveless sex in order to foster the one and continue to fiercely combat the other? A much more realistic theology of the transformative potential of the sexual mystery has long been needed. Perhaps theologically educated maturing lovers can now develop that thinking through (1) offering more *realistic perspectives* on the relative importance of intimacy to spiritual maturity, (2) incorporating *women's experience* into society's treatment of sexual issues, and (3) readdressing specific *gnarly moral issues* that have eroded Catholics' trust in its long-celibate leadership.

Realistic Perspective

Thinking about sexuality as spiritual experience must include honoring it as mystery rather than as a set of behaviors that can be controlled by one's will and regulated by decree. The entire concept of control has little use in spiritual practice. As we do not completely control our concentration during prayer, our intentions while singing hymns, and our reverie during meditation, so actual control in the arena of sexual sorting is elusive and ought not to be a measure of excellence. The exciting, necessary, and dangerous territory of engaging the sexual mystery, from early adolescence to aging, remains forever a worthy arena in which to develop our human spirit. Only experience teaches in that arena, and that teaching is never complete. One becomes a great lover by actually loving and learning from the efforts, through humor at the awkwardness, resilience through the hurts, and bighearted forgiveness for one another's insensitive mistakes.

When the medieval poet Dante Alighieri wrote about his visions of the afterlife in his famous political satire *The Inferno*, he placed the "lusters" just inside the edges of hell, not deep within. He found them in the air, being blown about eternally by howling winds, wrenched and jerked from one place to another, unable even to influence their own direction, pace, or destination. He didn't see them as deeply evil and to be disdained but rather as unfortunately foolish and to be pitied. Unaware of the significance of their sexual decisions while living, they had never experienced the profound joy that loving sex could have brought them in life. As they had let themselves be ruled by their own corporal passions, they were now forever at the mercy of external forces yanking their bodies about on the edges of hell.

Jesus himself made much less of sexual sin than the religious leaders of his time and many of those of our day as well. There is no officially recorded harangue from his mouth about the horrors of masturbation (never mentioned in the entire Bible), fornication, and prostitution. Several passages indicate that he was definitely against the destructiveness they can breed. But like Dante, he was clearly more concerned and angry about other human evils than the groping awkwardness of sexual development and the blurry lines inherent in romantic sorting that is honestly seeking loving expression.

To continually honor the mystery that sexuality will probably always present to the human soul, reference to a *continuum of sexual activity* may serve as a framework.

If one could survey all the sexual activity in Seattle on a given night, for example, perhaps 10,000–50,000 people engaging in some form of it would be spread across a continuum. At one pole would be insensitive sex, in such forms as incest, pedophilia, and loveless prostitution. Some of this behavior could be called lust but some more appropriately obsessive preoccupation, wrathful acting out, and lurid abuse of children. The destruction to the future potential for intimate loving of the victims would anger and sadden most any observer.

Clustering near the other pole would be the various degrees of sexual loving, from the emotionally intimate to the generously compliant and from the quiet leisurely to the wildly passionate. There lies lusty love in all its quieter, warmer, wilder, and passionate forms, the delightful and challenging endeavor of intimate loving that provides the subject of most of this book.

Between those poles, however, would stand a vast area that fits neither side. Made up of a huge variety of sexual experience that is neither solid loving nor insensitive sexual intrusion, it could be called "love-seeking." It engages the natural bodily gifts of creation that are designed to promote intimate relating, in endless forms of explorative, relationship building, flirty, awkwardness. Swimming in that pool of love-seeking is what disturbs the moral theologian and the parent. Dangerous and unavoidably real, engaging it remains generally necessary to establish one's identity, learn one's values, and incorporate skills, attitudes, and communication patterns of love the hard way—through experience.

Women's Experience

In the twentieth century alone, major discoveries about the anatomy, psychology, and spirituality of women have transformed the possibility of intimate partnering. That body of new understanding needs to be considered in any useful concept of a "natural law" and its correlate "Divine Law" that was originally formed by the reflections of celibate men. Several unfolding discoveries during the twentieth century serve as examples: the clitoris and "Grafenberg spot" in anatomy, oxytocin in physiology, and women's contributions to psychology and the understanding of human relationships.

Widespread recognition of the variety of ways in which women achieve orgasm, often requiring manual stimulation of the clitoris, took a step forward with Albert Kinsey's research in the 1950s[6] and that of Masters and Johnson in the 1960s.[7] But according to some women gynecologists, the physical aspects of anatomical understanding of women has even now, sixty years later, only begun.[8] Incorporating into spiritual teaching, the ways in which many women deal with their lesser frequency of sexual arousal in relation to their partners' seemingly incessant sexual wants and needs will require considerable careful interdisciplinary consultative discussion.

The concept of natural law that expected all intercourse to result in orgasm with the penis in the vagina has been disclosed as blindly unrealistic. It was designed by celibate men, mostly through logic, without even the advantage of autopsies on dead women, let alone the articulated experience of live ones regarding their love lives. The ways women experience sexuality remained, until the twentieth century, a scary mystery that precluded inclusion into sexual thinking. Sinister words like *cunnilingus* and *mutual masturbation* may take on more positive connotations when their potential to contribute to the personal fulfillment of women is taken seriously by moral thinkers.

Similarly, the discovery of the Grafenberg spot[9] may prove to be a factor in women's spiritual integration of sex and love. Thought by some to be an anatomical feature of high sexual gratification located deep in the vagina, it has added further speculation of women's pleasuring potential that was only suspected by individual women before they began to talk openly to one another in the latter half of the twentieth century.

In physiology, the hormone oxytocin is being studied for its role in complex physiological processes related to bonding, trust, and sexual arousal as well as childbirth, lactation, and moderating pain and anxiety.[10] Discovery of the way oxytocin is created more plentifully through caressing the skin of women than of men shows promise of physiologically confirming what individual females have known for ages—that caressing and cuddling are sometimes more satisfying for them than orgasm.

The implications of these physical discoveries for the potential of intimate satisfaction in partnering mutuality can be augmented by what society learned through women in the twentieth century about psychology and relationships. Examples would be the deep satisfaction that feeds us from the soul flow of emotional exchange, vastly differing levels of endowed hormonal stimulation, fortitude-based assertiveness, and the psychological nature of intimacy itself.

Rethinking Gnarly Moral Issues
Three specific love-seeking issues that unsettle parents and leaders regarding their potential damage to eventual loving bliss need special comment: autoeroticism (solitary masturbation), sex before life commitment (included in fornication), and artificial birth regulation (birth control). The intent of the opinions here is not to solve these gnarly issues of *moral* theology but to provide a

spiritual perspective on them from the view of mature lovers looking back. How seriously do unfortunate decisions made in the course of facing the sexual mystery actually inhibit intimate loving and the spiritual life in general? How can a more realistic view of the power of sexual arousal contribute to the life project of eventually bringing sex and love together and keeping them there as long as life allows?

The traditional Catholic position on autoeroticism confounded millions of people over decades during the twentieth century and eroded their trust of religious leadership during adolescence. Now solitary masturbation is seldom spoken about in religious education circles or retreat conferences, probably because many spiritual leaders have not clarified their own thinking on the subject, cannot find integrity in energetically teaching absolute condemnation, or are unwilling to grasp the courage to teach what they actually believe. Public teaching of a spiritual view of autoeroticism would involve intimate sharing of the teachers' own experiences that could put a leader in peril of his or her ministry or teaching position and esteem in the community.

Solemn darkness around developmental autoeroticism is now unmasked as almost humorous. Never mentioned in the Bible and almost universal among people in the unpartnered years before marriage,[11] no deleterious effects of explorative masturbation can be documented. Studies of priests disclose that a very small percentage of them believe that masturbation is always seriously wrong, and a large percentage engage in it themselves as their repeatedly acknowledged failures of committed celibacy.[12]

It is probably true that obsessive preoccupation with solitary sex distracts from the intricate work of emotional maturing for the sake of eventual intimate relating. But occasional events of autoeroticism or regular use of it as release of sexual pressure seem to be no more destructive than a few glasses of wine a few time a week. Obsessive sex and obsessive drinking are highly spiritually damaging. Yet that offers no justification for condemning carte blanche either developmental autoeroticism or drinking alcohol. There are much more dangerous forms and phases of love-seeking than solitary sex.

Describing developmental autoeroticism from a spiritual point of view would explore the inner *feelings* that masturbation enkindles. Vague impressions of loneliness and shreds of shame in the relaxing afterglow seem to be natural. They bring hints in the reflective experimenter that sex is made for sharing, not for self-indulgence. Even early Latin philosophers such as Petronius in the first century knew that lust as sex without love brings no joy but rather eventually becomes tedious. He wrote, for example, *Foeda est in coitu et brevis voluptas, et taedet veneris statim peracte* (Delight of lust is gross and brief, and one quickly wearies of its desire).[13] Finding solitary orgasm both intensely pleasurable and subtly lonely points the way toward anticipating a future time in one's life when sexual pleasure will be employed in the most loving coalescence between people that creation has designed.

Shared sex outside a committed relationship stands as a more current dilemma in Catholic culture and one that carries more serious potential consequences in deeply hurt feelings, the spread of venereal disease, relationship discouragement, and unwanted pregnancy. Like the term "lust," use of the word "fornication" continues to throw down a right–wrong gauntlet among people who actively practice Christianity. The question "Is sex before marriage always a sin or not?" immediately tends to divide Christian believers into distinct camps. Those who have incorporated a rigidly moralistic meaning to the word "fornication" can wax quickly superior to those who see love as the key to morality and personally know many couples who have fashioned wonderfully loving lives after engaging in sex before they were married.

The word "fornication" itself, not mentioned in the Ten Commandments, was recorded to have been used only twice by Jesus[14] and five times in the entire Old Testament. It has its roots in referring to prostitution, in ancient Latin meaning "a vaulted chamber." Its original meaning was likely "sex devoid of love" in its exploitive and oppressive forms rather than merely sexual pleasuring before solemn commitment. When a huge majority of practicing Catholics who have become successful long-term intimate loving couples have openly acknowledged engaging the sexual mystery together before official commitment to one another, it will be more difficult to categorically condemn that practice as deeply sinful with much conviction.

At the same time, a loving relationship is generally not well served by early sexual abandon. When sex gets ahead of love, disillusioned partners can find to their dismay that "good sex" doesn't necessarily lead to loving of the heart. Both men and women can easily deceive themselves in the blur of carnal pleasuring that sex is love.[15] The experience of women who are more likely to insist on meaning and beauty in sexual relationship have only begun to be heard. We ought to make no assumptions about what further, open, and extensive consultation will reveal.

Besides the physical consequences of sex without love commitment, there are personal perils as well. Disillusionment after being deceived and deceiving oneself in a relationship gone bad is common. People of high libido experience periods of sexual abundance as a love they've craved forever, and it may not be that. Others who naturally yearn for the warmth and closeness of intimate sharing can easily believe that the emotional component of relationship will naturally follow satisfying sex. Both paths lead to later disappointment.

Intimate love is of the heart, whose voice can easily be lost in the fascination with immediate pleasuring agreement. The compelling heartfelt, person-specific, mutual treasuring of body and soul of loving romance remains too elusive to be ensured by mere sexual compatibility.

The effect of the development during the twentieth century of methods that can prevent conception must also be considered in seeing sexual loving as spiritual. Increasingly easy birth control methods freed women, to a greater degree, to explore sexual expressions as a component of their love seeking and enriching their own lives and families after marriage. If the purpose of ecclesiastical policy is to support human spiritual lives, then the experience of successful intimate lovers must now lead the way in teachings about matters of intimate love. Garry Wills wrote compellingly in *The Papal Sin* of how Pope Paul VI included a few married couples in consultation regarding artificial birth regulation in 1965, beginning just such use of intimate lovers' experience.

Wills further details, however, that as the time neared for an official report of that commission, the pontiff ignored the substance of the sixty-five consultants in publishing the encyclical *Humanae Vitae*, which thus became what Wills calls the most disastrous papal document of the twentieth century.[16] Well-known Catholic priest and publisher Richard Ginder has reported the vote of those consultants in favor of including some means of artificial birth regulation as permissible, at sixty-one to four.[17]

That story is a striking example of ecclesiastical leadership allowing logic based on faulty knowledge to overshadow spiritual experience. Stubborn hope compels us to believe that at a future time, when love is consistently and authentically honored as the essential reality of spiritual experience, it will take its equal place with procreation in intimate and medical decisions about such issues as birth regulation, love seeking, and all forms of sexual pleasuring that are in the service of intimate mutuality.

Notes

1. Alfred Kinsey, *Sexual Behavior in the Human Female* (Philadelphia: Saunders, 1953), chap. 13, 510–43. Compare also Gina Kolata et al., *Sex in America* (New York: Warner Books, 1995).

2. C. S. Lewis, 134 ff.

3. *Catechism of the Catholic Church: With Modifications from the Editio Typica* (New York: Doubleday, 1995), no. 2337–50, 619–23.

4. *Catechism of the Catholic Church*, no. 2351–52.

5. Augustine of Hippo, *The Good of Marriage*, chap. 6; Roy J. Deferrari, ed., *The Fathers of the Church: A New Translation* (New York: Fathers of the Church, 1955), 17.

6. Kinsey, *Sexual Behavior in the Human Female*, 520 ff.

7. Virginia E. Johnson and William H. Masters, *Human Sexual Response* (Philadelphia: Lippincott Williams & Wilkins, 1966).

8. Compare Helen O'Connell, M.D., at www.abc.net.au/quantum/scripts98/9825/clitoris.html.

9. Although not firmly established in medical understanding, the content of the original article of Ernest Grafenberg, M.D., has received considerable attention. Published in the *International Journal of Sexology* in 1950, it claims discovery of a place of sexual supersensitivity deep in the vagina, now colloquially named after him as the "G-spot."

10. Nigel Barber, *The Science of Romance: Secrets of the Sexual Brain* (Amherst, N.Y.: Prometheus Books, 2002), 38.

11. Kinsey, *Sexual Behavior in the Human Female*, 520 ff.

12. A. W. Richard Sipe, *Celibacy in Crisis: A Secret World Revisited* (New York: Brunner-Routledge, 2003), chap. 4: "The Masturbations," 57–79.

13. Andronicas Petronius, *The Oxford Dictionary of Quotations*, 3rd ed. (New York: Oxford University Press, 1979), 373.

14. Matthew 5:32 (equivalent to Mt 19:9), Matthew 15:19 (equivalent to Mk 7:21), and John 8:41.

15. Matthew Kelly, *The Seven Levels of Intimacy: The Art of Loving and the Joy of Being Loved* (New York: Simon & Shuster, 2005), 7–33.

16. Garry Wills, *The Papal Sin: Structures of Deceit* (New York: Doubleday, 2000), chaps. 5 and 6.

17. Richard Ginder, *Binding with Briars. Sex and Sin in the Catholic Church* (Englewood Cliffs, N.J.: Prentice Hall, 1975), 114.

~

CHAPTER SIX

Six Other Styles of Intimate Failure

We make a ladder of our vices if we trample those same vices underfoot.

—St. Augustine

One of my dogs is a great metaphor for the mystery of eros. High-strung and appropriately named "Buster," he engages people indiscriminately by energetically nosing around them with ebullient enthusiasm. Tail literally wagging his body, front feet dancing, mouth panting and drooling, half open in a dog smile, he aches to be touched. He seeks above all not to be ignored. Similarly, eros as heartfelt, loving attraction is more than fetching. He's infectious, relentless, and shamelessly fickle.

Like Buster, however, if eros is ignored for long because of preoccupation or the reticence born of earlier wounding, he recedes into a corner to sleep or to await a chance to once again be noticed, encouraged, and stimulated into fun. A dog tied alone in a yard day after day with nobody to touch or frolic with him becomes either forlorn or hostile. Similarly, eros ignored for too long because of human preoccupations that distract from his natural joy limps for years and even for a lifetime.

Seven such preoccupations powerful enough to deeply discourage eros have a history in Catholic tradition as the seven deadly sins. The six remaining after lust include *greed, envy, pride, wrath, sloth,* and *gluttony.*

Greed Ignoring Eros

Greed could be defined as *the absorption of a person by money, things, "stuff," material worth, and the work it takes to obtain and maintain them*. It was nakedly illustrated in the repeated phrase of the song "Material Girl" (*Like a Virgin* album, Sire, 1985) sung by Madonna in the 1980s as she boldly boasted to be a material girl in a material world. No room there for the spiritual life—at all.

Greed mostly ignores the spiritual component of life and vigorously absorbs oneself in the material. Greed doesn't always deter sexual stimulation and activity and sometimes even seems to enhance it. But eros as sexual *loving* can't stand much greed.

Dante Alighieri, in his *Inferno*, described two kinds of people preoccupied with "stuff": the "hoarders" and the "wasters." Finding themselves on one level of Dante's hell, they had lived earthly lives of overfocus on money. One group had been absorbed in "getting and keeping," while the other was engrossed in "spending, using, and consuming." On his journey through hell, Dante finds them as two mobs on the same muddy plain, engaged in incessant violent conflict. They are encumbered by huge weights that they endlessly ram against each other in the mire, only to withdraw and clash again through eternity, all the time burdened and fatigued by the boulder-like tonnage and the bitterness between them.[1] Clearly there is no space for eros here, nor presumably was there in their lives on earth.

Since we humans are not angels without bodies, intimate loving needs a physical place. Privacy for soul-flow sharing, a bed, and some walls for leisure and passion eventually become essential. The backseat of a car is exciting for only so long. A man needs such a space for an enchanting cheerful woman he believes is enthusiastic about him and at least compassionate with his sexual rhythms. A woman is likely to seek a place of comfort, sensuously arranged, with visual appeal, music, aromas, the suggestion of abundance, and a man interested in all of her—body, heart, mind, and soul.

I was once frequently surprised by stories of couples' "best times" together in the history of their relationship. How often those peak months or years occurred when they had very little materially but were gradually fashioning a place for their romance. They were in college or entry-level jobs, newly in love, living on one or two small paychecks, and delighting in finding an apartment of their own, furniture they could afford, and appliances that fit both their budget and their style.

But the lure of bigger and better "stuff" is seductive. Naturally seeking to improve our material situation through more space, greater comfort, and easier days can progressively fuel a growing drive to affluence. No problem—until the tail begins to wag the dog. Then eros goes begging while one partner or both becomes absorbed in incessantly "moving ahead" materially. As an anonymous pundit once quipped, "Everything I've ever owned has eventually ended up owning me."

Perhaps men and women become trapped differently by material preoccupation, from allowing it to color the decision of who to marry to seeing it crowd out erotic passion in the middle and later years. "Marrying for money" is more spiritually dangerous than its humorous references in social conversations implies. Whether men are more prone to "getting more money" and women to freely spending it or women are more practical and men more "toy loving" is not important. What is most elusive is finding moderation in material concerns that keeps a major focus on eros as continuously attempting to energize the here-and-now delightful engagement between the lovers. Psychiatrist writer and radio show host David Viscount was not far off when he once wrote, in effect, that what everyone wants most is to be happy at home. Only those who do not have this want anything more.[2]

Greed, sometimes called "avarice," is the antithesis of charity, and all are vulnerable to it—rich and poor alike. The wealthy who share generously of their abundance may avoid the pitfalls of greed. At the same time, those who have little can become so fiercely protective of it that their erotic life wanes. The seriously greedy spend their lives getting more and/or spending what they have on themselves.

More recently, greed has been related to "workaholism," the excessive attachment to the excitement of doing more and more to get more and more, leaving progressively less time and energy for family fun and erotic indulgence. Traditionally, avarice was known as a sin of aging. Perhaps that is because eros had been left behind in aging discouragement, with the old one seeing little left to embrace other than money and things and their illusion of security and power.

The concept of "collusion" can be useful in appreciating how greed multiplies in power when two people become entangled together in the illusion that material ownership can deeply feed the soul. Workaholism differently punishes both the work addict and the family. Collusive greed refers to *both* partners being entangled in the acquisition/consumerism "rat race," submerging eros in their lives until the emptiness is recognized, if it ever is.

In the Gospels, Jesus is seen as warning against the spiritual danger of greed in such parables as the man building barns to store his excess grain rather than sharing it with the poor (Lk 12:13–21), wealthy Dives suffering after death for ignoring the poor during life (Lk 16:19–31), and comparing the difficulty for the rich to enter the kingdom with fitting a camel through a narrow local traveling passage called "the eye of a needle" (Matt 19:23). He had probably learned well from Hebrew Scriptures such as Ecclesiastes 1:2, 2:21–23, which decries the preoccupation with "stuff" that eventually causes discouragement when its emptiness becomes obvious.

Most people in the Western world are rich by global standards. How long will we be preoccupied with our own material well-being from consistent, integrated efforts to assist the world's development? When it comes time to acknowledge that the planet may not support its entire population at our level of affluence, will we compromise our own bottom line and level of convenient comfort for the sake of all people having a basic level of "enough"? Will we not find room for the undeveloped world in our policy decision making and daily consumption until we are forced to do so by economic decline? Will we someday begin to enable collaboration and community rather than perpetuating resentment, discouragement, and the rage that breeds terrorism in those who cannot feed their children? Will we allow our intimate loving sensitivity to extend beyond our own convenience?

Gluttony: Sometimes Addiction

The common drinking song, long sung by reveling drinkers with reckless abandon on campuses and in taverns, proclaims, *There is a tavern in the town, and there my true love sits him down, and drinks his wine as happy as can be, and never ever thinks of me.* If you have ever heard those words sung in a languid blues style, however, the pain is much more palpable, especially in the following verse:

> Fare thee well, for I must leave thee,
> Do not let the parting grieve thee,
> And remember that the best of friends must part, must part.
> Adieu, adieu, kind friends adieu, adieu, adieu,
> I can no longer stay with you, stay with you,
> I'll hang my harp on a weeping willow tree,
> And may the world go well with thee.
>
> —Anonymous

The phenomenon of addiction has been recognized for centuries, probably since cave persons found fermented grapes. Only in the twentieth century, however, did alcoholism begin to be understood well enough for recovery to become a realistic hope. It still causes more love-life pain than virtually anything else. The self-deception that characterizes this illness precludes consistent intimacy. Indeed there is question of whether a person "under the influence" or whose everyday life is still in the throes of alcohol addiction is even capable of committing to love "until death do us part."

Excessive ingestion of even good things causes problems. A pinch of salt adds flavor to life. A mouthful of it could be deadly. In Catholic tradition, excessive seeking of pleasure from food and drink was called gluttony. It featured patterns of immediate self-indulgent ingestion that grew into soul-defeating preoccupation. Gluttony as excessive eating was sometimes distinguished from drunkenness as excessive drinking of alcohol. Both gradually sucked up energy from relationships and eventually defeated them.

Alcohol is harmless in itself. A bottle of it on a shelf will cause no problem to anyone. But drinking it is another matter. Nine out of ten people can drink a bottle of whiskey in the course of a week or so and suffer no ill consequences. But that tenth person—it affects her differently whenever she imbibes. She would likely finish it before the sun goes down, and it might not be enough even for today. Her behavior would likely change in ways that concern the people who know her, even if they hadn't long ago become accustomed to her frequent metamorphoses.

Some of what in classic Catholic moral tradition was seen as gluttony and drunkenness is better understood today as addiction, the complex causes of which remain in question. Getting drunk once can be somewhat harmful because it erodes prudent judgment for a while and precipitates destructive decisions and behavior. Chronic drunkenness, however, is likely due to the illness of alcoholism or its kin, drug addiction—diseases that can be treated and from which recovery is possible. Unfortunately, a key feature of the illness is that the consequences of drinking cleverly, stubbornly, and comprehensively hide from the drinker.

Despite all the public education and celebrity attention to drinking problems and recovery over the past eighty years, alcoholism continues to have a reputation as a sin, a fault, a moral weakness, or a personal failing. The attitude that "drunks should just quit doing that to themselves and to the ones who try to love them" continues to prevail.

One of the greatest achievements of humanity during the past century was the long and painful discovery of a relatively successful way for people at the mercy of alcohol addiction to live with that condition in a normal, quality life. Alcoholics Anonymous[3] remains mostly a mystery to all of us, even its members. But the way it includes a spiritual perspective on recovery casts enormous light on a genuine illness that used to be taken for self-neglect, insensitivity to family, wanton selfishness, and life-wasting perversion.

Much of the pain resultant from alcoholism is born by those who genuinely love the victim of it—the drinker. Attend a single meeting of a healthy Al-Anon[4] group, and you will not forget at least one story told there. It is difficult to overemphasize the fortitude, knowledge, understanding, and self-control required to recover from the damage done to an alcoholic, generally not even noticed because of overfocus on the drinker. Psychological and religious efforts alone typically fail to deal with the painful habits that grow unnoticed in those who love an alcoholic. These ways of coping preclude intimacy as surely as the drinking itself.

The story of Naaman the Syrian (2 Kgs 5) presents a model of the addict's lover's plight in seeking help for her own issues rather than obsessing about the stuckness of her partner. Naaman, a king's army commander from a distant land, had come to the prophet Elisha because of his reputation as a healer. When Naaman arrived in Israel, the prophet told him to wash in the Jordan River. Naaman's response was that the advice was too simplistic. He could wash in any of a number of rivers in his homeland. He had to find the humility to seek the help where and how it was recommended, at which point he was healed.

Similarly, the lover of an alcoholic typically resists Al-Anon as an overly simplistic solution—until she agrees to earnestly try it.

The lover of an obese person faces a similar challenge. How do you raise the issue of being overweight to one whose body constitutes a major component of your intimate loving? When you love intimately, your body is, strictly speaking, not totally your own anymore. It is shared. Never again will your body be only your responsibility, nor will it ever be the responsibility of anyone else. Partnering means that we share these bodies now, including the right to know, to a reasonable extent, where these bodies are and how we are taking care of them. We are deeply invested in one another's bodies as well as the persons they house. The combination of sexual attraction to your lover along with deep concern for his or her health is intricate indeed to address in intimate confrontation.

Along with substance addiction, the term "gluttony" commonly calls up images of overeating, getting carried away with the appetite for food. Obesity as a spiritual topic is even more sensitive than alcoholism since a glance around yourself almost anywhere in the United States will confirm that two-thirds of U.S. citizens are overweight, half of those qualify as obese, and three million as morbidly so.[5] As a health problem, obesity is not as insidiously harmful as alcoholism, but it does tend to shorten life, slow the enjoyment of bodily activity, truncate romance, and lower self-esteem.

There are many reasons for being overweight, and eating too much is only one cause. But we are a nation with an abundance of foods along with the affluence and freedom to partake in any of them we choose. Overindulgence in eating is a constant temptation. As a people, we are far fatter than most other nations. Diet books vie with cookbooks for enormous shelf space in libraries, both public and private.

Fasting has diminished as a spiritual practice, though in some circles it is making a comeback. Abstinence from meat is almost gone from society's means of spiritual nurture. The worst thing about Catholic leadership making a *law* out of meatless Fridays was that it obscured the value of fasting as a *spiritual practice*. Then when the law was abolished, very few Catholics continued a healthy custom that could contribute greatly to the strength of spirit we need to face every-day food decisions as well as endure the challenging crisis times that try human souls at some points in every life.

In a partnering spirituality, it is clear that gluttony and addiction affect both the partner and the relationship. When one partner becomes lost in self-indulgence, where is the room for shared pleasure? Just as habitual masturbation robs a partner of some of the dynamism of sharing the vulnerability of mutual sexual need, so do overdrinking and overeating often rob a partner of the joy of shared healthy love exchange. It is painful to see the self-destruction of somebody you like, let alone one you dearly love.

When both partners are addicted or obese, the problem multiplies. The powerful mechanism of denial hides one's own ingestion problem, and a partner similarly afflicted solidifies that denial. One viewing of the Oscar-winning love story movie *Days of Wine and Roses* (Warner Brothers, 1962) easily brings tears to anyone who has been hurt by the addiction of a spouse. As two lovers seek sobriety, they repeatedly sabotage one another's efforts. The pain and pathos mount with very little redemption.

Eating, drinking, and sexual loving have traditionally been called "the passions" because of their similarities as natural hungers. The shared joy they foster when engaged in together, perennially celebrates life. At the same time, eating, drinking, and sexual loving naturally provide constant reminders of the interdependence among people. None of us grows or prepares all that we eat and drink. And the way lovers deeply rely on one another for affection, companionship, and pleasure is a constant reminder of how all humans rely on one another globally for virtually everything we need.

Envy: Drunk on Comparison

I once bought an airline ticket from Seattle to Chicago for $168, the cheapest price I'd ever seen. I grabbed the deal. A few weeks later, however, I noticed on the Internet that the fare had been reduced to $138. I didn't know whether to feel good at having gotten my best fare ever or bad because lots of people got prices even cheaper. The former is gratefulness. The latter is jealousy.

Envy and jealousy are close kin. Both compare one's own situation unfavorably to that of another. Traditionally the difference is that jealousy wants what the other has, while envy doesn't really care to have it but just feels nasty over the other's delight. The Grimm's fairy tale that illustrates envy features a dog that chases a cow from the hay. The dog cannot eat the hay himself, but in his envy he can't stand seeing the cow so happy savoring it.

A little jealousy in romance feels good and probably enriches the relationship. Seeing your lover being charmed by an attractive guy enkindles a shade of jealousy with a hint of inward glee that she is "yours and not his." A later private quip to her that you felt like "beating his balls blue" may prompt a giggle from delight that you noticed and cared.

But serious jealousy, generally born of fear, can cause the kind of overcontrol that kills partnering and romance. Demanding to know the destination of every errand, your whereabouts every moment, your intentions in every venture, and your motives in every relationship—these are deadly to the spontaneous trust and joyful sharing that are an absolutely essential food of long-term partnering. They are signals of serious difficulties in the relationships that probably need outside help if the romance is to survive.

The opening of the first martial arts class I attended with my ten-year-old son found us standing silently in careful lines with about thirty other neophytes of various sizes, ages, shapes, and genders. All eyes were focused and ears alert for introduction into the healthy philosophy of a widely respected sense. As we all faced him in the personal openness of disciplined stance, one of the first things he said was, "Compare yourself to no-one."

He didn't elaborate much, but what I understood his further sentences to mean was something like, "Focus on your own performance. That is what matters. Partner and compete with your own potential, not that of anyone else. Use and develop what you have been given. Ignore the impulse to feel superior to some and inferior to others. Learn to focus without comparisons."

The *sense* was urging us to avoid developing any habits of either false pride or envy and bringing such previously established attitudes into our engaging this new arena of karate. He was reinforcing John Dryden's concept of envy as a "tyrant of the mind."[6] Probably without knowing it, he was also preparing the youths to contend with the impulse to jealousy and envy in their later excursions into romantic love.

We in the United States have become so accustomed to functioning from envy that we do not even notice how pervasive a force it is in our financial decision making. It is the water we swim in and thus do not detect. Why, for example, does a fad of purchasing sport-utility vehicles take hold and propel an automobile market for decades when it makes no economic sense in a world of shrinking fossil fuels? Why do so many young women become despondent about their physical appearance in an age when women are arguably becoming more and more beautiful every decade? Why do sneakers at $80 to $200 per pair become so popular without much recognizable difference from those in the $30 to $40 range? Aren't fads in general fueled by envy of what somebody else has, whether I need it or not?

Comparison—of our own bodily endowment, possessions, and life situation—to what others seem to have is a spiritually destructive habit. Moses wrote two of the Ten Commandments warning of the dangers of envy—or "coveting" as he put it. The ninth commandment emphasized envy of somebody else's lover, and the tenth warned about looking comparatively at someone else's "stuff." Obviously, even in days of early communal development, the problems from looking too often and too closely at the situation of another person's apparent happiness was seen as highly dangerous to the community as a whole.

Are some weddings motivated by envy? Does the opulence of that day distract from the sacredness of the formal commitment at its core? Are some love seekers attracted to the comparative physical attractiveness of a potential partner for his or her public appeal rather than the heart-piercing reality of romantic love? All lovers would do well to ask ourselves these questions in the sacred inwardness of our own personal reflection before sealing a marital bond.

The antidote to envy and jealousy is a combination of two habits: simple gratefulness for your own endowment and graceful appreciation of beauty and good fortune wherever you find it in others. Awareness of your envious feelings and openly acknowledging them to yourself and to your lover are prerequisite to both. Intimate loving helps heal jealousy by confirming our own deep goodness as human beings, enkindling gratefulness, and providing a regular arena in which to share it.

Graceful validation of beauty wherever you encounter it and willingness to communicate that appreciation are ingredients of magnanimity—bigness of person and maturity of spirit. It may not always be prudent to express genuine delight at another's physical or personal beauty or obvious good fortune, but capacity to do so when you choose definitely keeps envy at bay.

While we Americans tend to see ourselves as mostly envied by others, we also can sometimes feel the bite of envying countries who achieve superior organizational arrangements, such as cheaper health care, more effective schools, and more functional social service structures, despite lesser resources. And envy can keep us preoccupied with the illusion of "staying ahead" rather than learning how to promote structures that allow sharing worldwide.

Pride: "Me" versus "We"

In Catholic tradition, pride was the primal sin—exaggerating your own importance, magnificence, and worth so much that you didn't need God. Pride made you "cocky," like the man too sure of his lover's "yes" one night. On the list of the seven deadly sins, pride was the root cause of other sins and capable of destroying a soul. "Hubris," in Hebrew, was an excessive fascination with oneself to the diminishment of God and anybody else.

Such self-absorption was well illustrated by the Greek myth of Narcissus, who became so attracted to his own image as he glimpsed it reflected in still water that he couldn't fall in love with another person and couldn't really care about anybody else, even the lovely Echo, who tried so hard to love him. Endowed with magnificent beauty of appearance, Narcissus was nonetheless damned to isolation by his own self-preoccupation.

What junior high would-be lover doesn't know disgust at a girl so preoccupied with herself that nobody else gets on her emotional "radar screen" or a guy so self-absorbed that he oozes disdain? Intimate partnering requires considerable investment in the "we" of the relationship. Intimate loving of a treasured person, however, can easily reveal that conceit is often a veil for self-doubt or even self-loathing.

Some women theologians have argued that pride is not the root sin of females.[7] They contend that "triviality, distractability, and diffuseness" or hiding their essential strengths and gifts would more appropriately qualify as the primary way women have historically failed themselves, their own goodness, their potential relationships, their accomplishments, their daughters, and, in the end, the fulfillment of their own lives. Indeed, when St. Bernard wrote that any spirituality based on anything but humility is folly,[8] he was referring to humility as *accuracy of self appraisal*, neither putting oneself up in hubris nor putting oneself down in hiding. There is a bit of Alcoholics Anonymous oral wisdom intended to help recovering people dodge a return to deadly pride. It states, "Nobody on this planet is any more important than you are, *nor any less*."

The natural human experience of feeling good about oneself and one's accomplishments is wonderfully unique. That glorious joyful awe at the athletic, academic, or artistic success of your son; the public poise of your granddaughter; the face of your wife; or the solid self-appreciation you experience at a job, a relationship, or a life well lived, is some of the fruit of the Spirit of God in the forms of deep joy and profound gratefulness.

But pride as excessive self-importance eventually destroys partnering. Who is too good to clean toilets or vacuum carpets? Who wouldn't work for minimal wage when times are tough? When one erotic lover considers him- or herself to be more important than the other, the partnering virtually dissolves. Relationship may continue, but the partnering quality will not survive one member's gradual realization that the insensitivity of the overly narcissistic other will not heal. Loving partners don't estimate the worth of themselves relative to the other. Partners are, in a real sense, equal. If one partner becomes too "big," too dominating, and thus too controlling, the gloriously elusive mixture of power and vulnerability that makes love partnering possible wanes. Eros is dying. You may have something at that point, but it is not partnership, and it is no form of mutual love.

Pride at its worst interferes with any close relationship with Transcendence as well as with human relationships and global care. When Ernest Kurtz, a Harvard University historian, researched the Alcoholics Anonymous movement in the 1970s to discover why it works for some and not for others, he titled the resulting book *Not God: A History of Alcoholics Anonymous*.[9] When the first recovering alcoholics were attempting to capture the principles that seemed to be helping them remain in the fragile new lifestyle they called recovery, they aimed the very first step at the pride that had prevented any helping partnership to succeed for decades in any of their lives.[10]

Most all of us secretly believe, at least at times, that we would do a better job being God than God does. That thinking goes something like this: "Why do children die, millions suffer incessantly under poverty, and earthquakes destroy entire cities? A God as compassionate as I am wouldn't let that happen." That is pride. Humanity has never successfully answered the question of "why is there huge pain if God is good?" classically called the "problem of evil." But to presume that we can see a better way to create and maintain a universe is the folly of pride. In the ancient story of Job, the protagonist got put in his place when he reached the edges of that abyss. "Have you ever given orders to the morning, or shown the dawn its place?" (Jb 38:12). "Have you journeyed to the springs of the sea, or walked in the recesses of the deep?" (Jb 38:16). In several chapters, Yahweh is described as asking Job, in effect, "Where were you when I created the whale? Can you do that?" (Jb 38–41).

The heartfelt expression of worship is one of life's best antidotes to pride. Not just "going to church" but actual soulful utterance of awe at the "Beyond-me, Beyond-us" of the Divine puts us in our rightful place as both marvelous and limited. Some traditional Catholic practices have helped generations of active members grow humility and nurture it:

- Genuflecting on entrance to the worship space, if reverently intentional, invites a second or two of authentic reverence, an acknowledgment of the greatness of the Divine and our proper place beneath Her.
- Using our thumb to make a little cross on our forehead, lips, and heart as an outward sign of our taking a place of humility to listen carefully to the gospel message opens us in mind and heart and informs our speaking of the wisdom it contains.
- Offering our entire selves and all we have to God at the offertory of the mass, uniting our gift with the sacrifice Jesus made by his death on the cross, reminds us that our entire worth is something we have charge of only for a time.

A church I once attended, St. Charles in Tacoma, Washington, has one word of foot-high letters etched boldly in mosaic at its entrance so that all people entering the front door pass directly over that word. The pastor once asked the question to start his Sunday homily: "How many of you can name the single

Latin word on the floor at the entrance to this church?" A few of the several hundred present raised their hands and knew that word was "Humilitas." What better term to adorn the entrance to a place of Catholic worship?

On a global level, are Americans really entitled to a huge percentage of the resources of this planet while fathers in some places chronically can't feed their children? Isn't that feeling of "entitlement" an issue of the worst kind of pride? Can ecclesiastical leaders truly lead without the humility it takes to admit when we were wrong, about Galileo, the Holocaust, evolution, cover-ups of pedophile atrocities, and artificial means of birth control? Gary Wills has called this inability of the Catholic leadership to admit mistakes the "papal sin."[11] Eugene Kennedy has suggested that the "unhealed wound" of sexuality in the Catholic Church will be addressed only by the humility of its leaders.[12]

Focusing on our own self-regard is our first spiritual project. In that process it is the deepest humility to come to richly appreciate our own dignity, worth, and value and a major mistake to exaggerate it.

Wrath: Anger Chained and Unchained

A key component of partnering progress during the twentieth century was the assertiveness movement of the 1960s and 1970s. Many people, particularly women, were taught that their anger was the fuel of their self-care and the fire finding their voices after centuries of silence. Then in the 1990s, the focus turned to "anger management" for people who had been unable to keep the ferocity of their anger within the normal limits of behavior that are acceptable to society. Too much and too little of the human indicator of personal pain—the emotion of anger—continues to present a significant issue for developing lives. It eventually becomes so for every love relationship worth keeping.

If there is one area of historical religious contention that rivals sexual morality in fervor, it is the place of anger in spirituality. Jesus clearly favored "turning the other cheek" and "going the extra mile" when accosted (Mt 5:39–41). Yet he railed at the leadership of the religious leaders of his day (Mt 3:6–8), sternly reprimanded Peter for his easy avoidance of conflict (Mt 16:23), and flogged business leaders for using money to defile sacred space (Mt 21:12). He clearly validated the selective use of anger, primarily in expression of spiritual outrage.

There is a powerful inclination in all of us that seeks control in order to get our way as much as possible. That is natural. We can't get rid of it completely. Hidden fear is often at the base of it—fear of being left out, left alone, missing something, or being hurt (again). Not getting our way in an important matter naturally generates anger inside us.

How we deal with that anger in our verbal expressions and behavior is a perennial spiritual problem. Religious teaching has traditionally emphasized overcontrol of it, prisons protect societies from undercontrol of it, while the assertiveness movement encouraged freeing it for use in self-care and effective personal relationships.

In Catholic tradition, *wrath* was listed as one of the seven deadly sins, no doubt because it was seen at its destructive worst in incidents of retaliation, rage, tantrums, "losing your temper," torture, and killing other human beings. Now anger is best seen as a continuum, from annoyance on one end to violent rage on the other, with such common terms as being "miffed," "ticked," irritated," "torqued," "aggravated," "pissed," and "enraged" all in between. Learning how to acknowledge and use anger artfully in society and in close relationships is a major project of spiritual maturity.

In the emotionally charged arena of intimate loving, the tendency to use whatever power we have to get our way as much as possible can grow just on the edges of our awareness. We catch ourselves abusing anger only when there is energetic resistance from the partner—in other words, in a fight. Whether in the form of physical coercion or emotional manipulation, overuse of power eventually repulses any partner. The best scenario, then, is a confrontation that hopes to disclose the oppression to the oppressor.

Expressed anger is a "pause button" in romance, a temporary turnoff. When one partner is clearly acting angry, there is a wall to erotic enjoyment. It may be temporary and hopeful of "making up." Both partners may learn indispensable things about one another from the fight, and one may find the other "beautiful when you're angry," but for the moment, the pleasures of soul flow and "shared skin" will definitely be interrupted.

Domestic violence, or hitting the one you love or claim to love, signals excessive anger more clearly than anything else in intimate relationships. Four million women suffer severe assaults each year by husbands or boyfriends, and one in four women will be victims of domestic violence in their lifetime.[13] Wrath in close relationships has not been eradicated.

Anger management is available today for any perpetrators who may discover their own misuse of anger in hostile verbal berating or violent behavior. Excellent shelter and counseling is also available for victims. No person ought to be too proud to get that help. Most victims wait too long, and some die every year in the hope-against-hope of waiting too long.

Physical violence, tortuous as it is, belies the emotional and verbal violence that almost always precedes, provokes, and accompanies it. Educating on physical violence makes a contribution, but it is still like glancing at the surface of a pond, not seeing all that teems beneath. Referring only to anger misses the hurt, fear, and loneliness that hostility veils. When "anger" found its way onto the list of "capital sins" in traditional Christian morality, it was before Freud had come along with the "unconscious." The intense anger that eventually fuels a good "quit" to romance inevitably has a history that includes loneliness, discouragement, misunderstanding, fear, and especially that most neglected of all feelings, hurt.

The mutual vulnerability of a sexual pleasuring relationship is one of life's best places to learn mercy. In romantic partnering, somebody you deeply love needs your loving in the way she needs it, not the way you want to give it, all but begging you to understand that. The levels of anger and hurt that are born by misunderstanding need some maturity to work through. Like the merciless debtor of Matthew 18:21–35, the perpetrator of domestic violence is incapable of doing that. He (85 percent of domestic violence victims are women[14]) remains clueless about the vulnerability sharing that is the bedrock of intimacy. He reflexively fuels anger instead and emerges as an insensitive assailant. Only professional help will facilitate positive change once that happens. Prison alone is not likely to succeed.

Anger itself is not a sin. It is a beautiful expression of the hurt self, like the physical pain that signals bodily damage needing attention and care. But when anger is allowed to stew into wrath—hostility, resentment, cynicism, and violence—it is enormously destructive to human well-being. Excessive, seething anger is the cause of divorces and wars. Anger in perspective, combined with the acknowledgment of vulnerability and need, will one day guide religious and national leaders to vigorously do all they can to nurture loving partnerships of all kinds and prevent military conflicts altogether.

Sloth: "Who's the Givin' For?"

The *New Yorker* magazine once sported a cartoon with a clearly overweight businessman complaining about his frustrating day to a physically trimmer colleague over martinis at a bar. The heavier man is whining to the other, "It was awful when the power went out today. There I was stuck for six hours on the escalator."

Was he too clueless to know how to walk down or just too lazy to do it?

One doesn't hear much about laziness anymore. Accusing the poor of being lazy would seem like obnoxious blaming of them for their own misfortune. Suggesting it of the rich and privileged is to imply that some guilt is in order for those who enjoy material comfort. And, of course, guilt of any kind is out of vogue. But sloth as *reluctance to work* was traditionally named as one of the seven deadly sins, able to defeat entire lives. It referred to laziness in both the physical and the spiritual aspects of one's being.

Partnering lovers easily feel annoyance at laziness in one another that hinders the flourishing of partnership in at least three ways: (1) it inhibits the *physical work* that needs to be done, (2) it hinders investment in the free flow of *emotional availability* that is essential, and (3) it slows the *sexual response* energy required for committed mutual pleasuring.

Physical Work

The childhood morality most all of us learned in relating with our siblings, classmates, and playtime chums requires significant involvement in shared projects by everyone who benefits. The pristine communal experience of the kindergarten classroom taught laziness as a justice issue. Slackers simply aren't being fair.

So when lovers embark on attempting to share virtually everything, the impression easily emerges that one's partner is no longer "pulling his weight." After the honeymoon period, there is so much to do—making a living, feathering a "nest," maintaining vehicles, preparing food, and keeping track of shared funds, to name a few. Which partner will keep a job? Both? Then who will keep the house, vacuum, launder, wash windows, clean carpets, paint walls, and replace appliances? Both? Who keeps track of bills, taxes, loans, investments, and donations? Who maintains the yard and relationships with relatives, in-laws, and neighbors? Children complicate the operation at least twofold—each. Indeed, we all want to slack sometimes. And we all need to sometimes. There is a wide path of work and responsibility on which partners trust one another to tread about evenly. But like horses pulling in traces, complications arise when one "lets George do it" a bit too much.

Families and cultures differ strongly on the specifics of how the communal sharing of responsibilities and work is negotiated. Swiss streets, for example, are immaculate, while Mexican *calles* always look neglected. But the Swiss don't seem to have much fun, while the Hispanics appear to enjoy life constantly with siestas and fiestas. Suppose a Hispanic marries a Swiss? Will the one eventually seem insouciantly lazy while the other waxes strident and emotionally joyless? Won't both need to adjust? How will they do that? Even on a physical work level, sloth can be a barrier to flourishing romance.

Emotional Availability

Sloth infects the spiritual realm by feeding reluctance to master the art of emotional sharing—something we all need to do in order to partner deeply and persistently. Intimate partners stay in touch with one another's feelings, an ongoing process that requires a level of listening investment not so important outside of romantic relating. Without too much stereotyping, John Gray's books and talks taught that men listen more nonverbally and need to invest the energy it takes to listen often, at length and without a "fix-it" attitude, to a partner who is about ten times more verbal.[15] Women are accustomed to more words in communication and will likely need to work harder at teasing words and feelings out of their men without denigrating them. In the midst of this expenditure of relational focus and energy, the question, "Is it worth it?" eventually emerges. The slothful are more likely to answer, "No, I'm out of here."

Sexual Response Energy

Even mediocre sex requires a fair amount of movement of one skin across the other. When the mutual energy isn't enough, the culprit may be fatigue or compromised health, but it also may be downright laziness. And the latter can masquerade as the other two. We humans do get tired and sick and thus may be unable at times to respond to a partner's invitation or feel reluctant to embark on passionate engagement we won't be able to finish. But declining to invest what is necessary under the guise of "a headache" or being "too tired" can become habitual, a lazy attitude of one in a pattern of being just too lethargic to strike the match that would set the kindling aflame.

Laziness in romance is not always easy to see. A man, for example, who fails to slow his hands to a leisurely, loving, twenty-minute back tickle may actually be too lazy to do so, as he is thinking far ahead to the three minutes of intense preorgasmic ecstasy. A woman may be simply too lazy to "give him what he always wants" or to generate the bodily enthusiasm that would nonverbally convince him it is love rather than burdensome obligation that motivates her. Only loving sexual generosity will motivate these investments of energy over the long term. Laziness impedes that investment.

Mental health professions have given new meaning to at least two old concepts related to sloth—depression and dependence. The concept of depression now better describes some of what was once seen as sloth and points to effective treatment that helps it. What is depressed, or "pressed down," in depression is the human spirit. Depression can be helped by medication and therapy. About 17 percent of the U.S. population will experience it in its serious proportions during their lifetime, and almost 10 percent of all American adults now rely on some antidepressant medication assistance.[16] Depression is not laziness.

The other term, "dependence," is derived from two Latin words that mean "something hanging down" or "hanging on," which can contain elements of laziness. The natural phenomenon of the "parasite" life form that lives off the health of a larger organism is the vivid epitome of dependence. Romantic partnering is founded on *inter*dependence between lovers, each relying on the involvement of the other for pleasure, companionship, and the health of the relationship itself. Partners learn how to avoid too much dependence of one *on* the other and too much independence of one *from* the other. The slothful person has grown too much dependence.

All seven of these failure styles involve excess in various forms. Catholic tradition grew wisdom of four fundamental characteristics that spiritually confront the seven deadly lifestyles in the form of the four cardinal virtues, the subject of the next chapter.

Notes

1. Dante Alighieri, *The Divine Comedy: Hell; Purgatory*, trans. Charles Elliot Norton (Boston: Houghton Mifflin, 1941), 19 ff.

2. David Viscott, *How to Live with Another Person* (New York: Simon & Schuster, Pocket, 1983), 45.

3. *Alcoholics Anonymous*, 4th ed. (New York: Alcoholics Anonymous World Services, 2001), 50.

4. *Paths to Recovery: Al-Anon's Steps, Traditions and Concepts* (New York: Al-Anon Family Group Headquarters, 1997).

5. The National Institutes of Health regularly update statistics at http://win.niddk.nih.gov/statistics/index.htm#preval.

6. *The Works of John Dryden*, Song of Jelousie from *Love Triumphant* (Hertfordshire: Wordsworth Editions, 1995), 382.

7. Valerie Saiving, "The Human Situation: A Feminist View," *Journal of Religion*, April 20, 1960.

8. G. R. Evans et al., eds., *Bernard of Clairvaux: Collected Works* (New York: Paulist Press, 1987), 99 ff.

9. Ernest Kurtz, *Not God: A History of Alcoholics Anonymous* (Center City, Minn.: Hazelden Educational Materials, 1979).

10. *Twelve Steps and Twelve Traditions* (New York: Alcoholics Anonymous World Services, 1952), 21–25.

11. Garry Wills, *The Papal Sin: Structures of Deceit* (New York: Doubleday, 2000).

12. Eugene C. Kennedy, *The Unhealed Wound: The Church, the Priesthood, and the Question of Sexuality* (New York: St. Martin's Griffin, 2001).

13. Sara Glazer, "Violence against Women," *Congressional Quarterly* 3, no. 8 (February 1993), 171.

14. Glazer, "Violence against Women," 171.

15. John Gray, *Mars and Venus Together: Relationship Skills for Lasting Love* (San Francisco: HarperCollins, 1994), chaps. 5 and 6, 94–159.

16. Rebecca Lundquist, *WebMD: Better Information, Better Health*, available at www.emedicine.com/rc/rc/i7/depression.htm.

CHAPTER SEVEN

~

Four Cardinal Virtues
of Love's Foundation

Each man should so conduct himself that fortitude appear in labours and dangers: temperance in foregoing pleasures: prudence in the choice between good and evil: justice in giving every man his own.

—Cicero, repeating Plato and Aristotle

To love romantically one must at some point get "carried away." One sheds the reticence of the solitary for the promised delight of being near. Boyhood falls away like a snakeskin that served it well in an earlier day but no longer fits the adventuresome eagerness of youth. Budding womanhood replaces the fears of rejection, misunderstanding, and being thought a fool, prodded on by vague yearnings for a new kind of warmth and fun. We risk the serious newfound dangers for the sake of love.

Yet as in every aspect of the spiritual life, if we do not use our heads, we lose our souls. Engaging the mystery of romance requires walking that edge between abandoning ourselves to impulsive excess on the one hand and passively missing the radical, life-defining call of the Spirit on the other. Partnering with siblings and friends, complex as these relationships can be, pales in difficulty beside sexual love in which our thirsts for intimate soulfulness and intense pleasure jostle us into scrambling for perspective in the midst of ecstatic joy.

The Catholic tradition that grew as spiritual remedies for tendencies to the excesses illustrated by the seven deadly sins came to be called the cardinal virtues.[1] The term "cardinal" is derived from the Latin *cardo*, meaning "hinge," a most useful invention that allowed doors and gates to smoothly open and close. The four cardinal virtues, named *prudence*, *justice*, *temperance*, and *fortitude*, came to be seen as pivotal, the basis of all virtues that help people relate to one another. Since we are essentially relational beings, some measure of these virtues is indispensable to spiritual health. When seen through lovers' eyes, they become four basic traits essential to any quality relationship.

Originally, these four qualities were adopted from Greek philosophers by early Christian writers and were extensively developed theologically by Thomas Aquinas in the thirteenth century. Unlike the theological virtues, which are "infused," the cardinal virtues are acquired by a combination of endowment and practice, much as athletic or musical excellence emerges from endowed giftedness that is formed and honed by disciplined repetition and competitive experience.

While a certain kernel of each of these personal qualities is essential even to early romance, they tend to grow in the fertile context of lovers learning both to employ and to temper their self-interest for the sake of loving mutuality. They are qualities of the love that gives relationships a chance by keeping our natural inclinations to *self-indulgence* from completely sabotaging the *mutual indulgence* of the loving spirit.

Prudence versus Prudery

My fifty-year-old male colleague Lincoln tells the story of a day he stopped to rest while jogging. Looking ahead on the trail, he noted a female form biking toward him, and his gaze became fixed on her bouncing boobs. As she drew close enough to speak, he still had not noticed her face when he heard a voice he recognized quip, "Hey Linc, I'm up here!" He knew he quickly flushed with a mixture of *embarrassment* at his mindless gawking and *relief* at her good-natured attitude about it.

That woman knows that most males, from the time they are about twelve years old, frequently search their immediate area for the most attractive female faces and forms coming toward them and bottoms going away. This is not a sin, a fault, a disgusting habit, a virtue, or a vice. It is simply a fact. It is our state of evolution that the initial stage of mating prods a natural tendency to make connection through our eyes to women we consider attractive. In response to a young lady's letter lamenting about boys' preoccupation with girls' bodies in her junior high school, Ann Landers once put it this way: "All people everywhere look more at women than at men."

Traditional morality named several concepts, dating from the biblical wisdom literature (written down during the seventh to third centuries B.C.), to combat the dangerous excitement generated in men by women's physical attractiveness (Prv 6:24, 7:10, 9:13, 11:22, 14:1). One such concept, *prudence*, is generally defined as the virtue that helps us figure out what is most excellent for us in any situation and choose the best means for achieving it.[2] As applied to the sexual loving arena, it means *employing the mind in uncommonly common sense when responding to the natural urges of sexuality.* In other words, it refers to using your thinking, along with your sensuality and your heart, in the project of finding and growing from intimate love.

Sexual prudence is a balancing act. On one side of prudence lies prudery—a fearful attitude of overprotective avoidance in response to the relentless sexual urges. In Catholic tradition, *custodi oculorum,* or "custody of the eyes," was a spiritual discipline intended to keep appropriate distance from the visual attractiveness of erotic beauty to moderate or even avoid the hassles of engaging the sexual mystery. The proverbial "Catholic girl" term referred to women so overly self-protective regarding sexuality that they truncated the passionate loving aspect of their own lives.

On the end of the intimate loving spectrum opposite to prudery lies impulsive foolishness. Ignoring or remaining clueless about consequences for oneself or other people of insensitive sexual behavior can be criminal. The biblical wisdom literature is full of references to "the fool" (e.g., Prv 10 and 14). At its worst on that end of the spectrum lies destructive impulsivity in rape, incest, and pedophilia.

Neither prudery nor insensitive lust offers the blissful satisfaction of intimate loving. Prudence keeps us between them, even during inexperienced youthful love seeking.

The seeds of prudence as a lifelong virtue are initially shaped in childhood by imitating adults and developing a natural inclination to self-management. We want to figure out "what works" in daily living and peer relating. So when children are sexualized or otherwise abused, the foundations of prudence have little soil in which to germinate. Substituted for the giggling intimacy, adoring glances, functional savvy, basic teaching, and self-protecting lore we crave from parenting ones, we settle for survival. Too busy with devising our hypervigilance and strategizing for survival, many of the abused gain little of that intuitive relational know-how for intimacy called prudence.

In the best of families, whatever fledgling prudence is garnered from childhood is invariably challenged and reshaped in adolescence by the intensity of sexual stimulation and the natural human search for affectionate companionship.

As an inward and terminally reflective teenaged boy in the mostly placid 1950s, I watched rather than engaged girls, including my sisters, as they all faced the question of "modesty"—how much to stimulate boys with exposure of bare skin and curvy form. Some seemed to decide mostly in the direction of prudery, minimizing attractiveness with overprotective attitudes and drab visual self-presentations that kept them a bit safer but stimulated less fun. Others more often decided in the direction of the lustily provocative, attracting more male interest while increasing the risk of being misunderstood, insulted, and even attacked. I gathered that prudence likely grows through trial and error between these two poles, eventually fashioning that uncanny public image that in those days would be called tastefully attractive, wholesomely fetching, or freshly winsome. Moods seemed to prod individual girls to move closer to either end of the spectrum at any given time.

Men do not come to sexual prudence naturally either but only through experience. Many boys eventually find that brash impulsiveness is attractive to girls only fleetingly. On the other hand, it can take reticent, prudish "good boys" like me years to find the hearts of girls who are interested in fun, warmth, and feeling loved. The sexually teeming, chaotic, junior high atmosphere challenges both boys and girls to find and fashion prudent approaches that avoid meanness, monitor charming antics, and hazard frequent glances at the mood of the loved one. Some of us learn faster than others, but virtually all of us get hurt, most of us deeply, a few times in the process.

However one comes to find the mature place of prudence between insensitive lust on one side and prudery on the other, it is essential to do so, especially for anyone who proposes to be a fulfilled lover. When my wife and I recently revamped our shared home office together, my interest was the practical organization of hundreds of books for ease of retrieving them when needed. Her approach was the visually aesthetic—what looks good—in the clusters of large, small, hardcover, paperback, and so on. The two methods obviously don't always coalesce. We prided ourselves after twelve hours on one day, refraining from frustrated conflict while finding an arrangement that was both pragmatic and aesthetic. Motivated by interest in closeness through the day and in bed at night and fortified by some learned prudence in negotiating with one another over the years, we made countless decisions that worked. I don't believe we could have done it twenty years ago. The demands of prudence would have been too high for two strong-willed people earlier in our lives.

The most difficult function of prudence for many of us is in distinguishing between various forms of seduction on the one hand and budding intimacy on the other. For many men, sex pulls us in with excitement and the promise of unfettered pleasure. But the entanglement of intimate relating can quickly turn confusing. For many women, the reverse is true. The pleasing feeling of having an attractive guy want to be with you, including the promise of fun experiences and warm connectedness, holds the hazard of his sexual expectations that can feel a bit rushed. The question is "Is this powerful attraction to a single individual, mere sexual preoccupation, or the pleasant feeling of being found attractive, or is it indeed the love I've been looking for?" The ambiguity about whether I actually love her is matched by the nagging question of whether she really loves me. In the vast area of love seeking that flows between insensitive lust on one side and sexual loving on the other, prudence can serve as adviser even while it is growing within you. "Does he (or she) love me?" is indeed the classic "lover's question" ("A Lover's Question," Otis Redding, Atlantic, 1969), which demands some measure of prudence to answer and simultaneously promotes the growth of prudence in the one who is seriously asking that question.

Mature prudence is as essential in ecclesiastical leadership as it is in one's love life. Prudery in a spiritual leader, especially in an oversexualized society, truncates the growth of prudence in followers. If the pastor is perceived as condemning engagement of the sexual loving mystery, seems clueless about its compellingly attractive power, or is cool or awkward when talking about sex and intimacy, our initial impression will be "This guy doesn't know much about real life as I experience it." Advice on prudence in romance will need to come from someplace else.

Overt seduction or sexual coercion in a spiritual leader, however, inflicts even worse consequences. As has been seen boldly in Christian organizations during the past decade, sexualizing ministry relationships, even a tiny bit, destroys the pastoral relationship, sours religious practice, and can inhibit the victim's pursuit of sexual loving enjoyment for years or for a lifetime. Ministry training that includes a time of careful supervised self-exploration is essential to anyone embracing spiritual leadership of any kind.

On a global scale, prudence is a primary characteristic of leaders entrusted with making pivotal administrative decisions regarding relationships among communities and nations. When a mature perspective on the global improvement of human living conditions is omitted as a criterion for making international decisions, prudence and wisdom are failing, and we can legitimately fear for the entire planet.

The Justice Base of Sexual Love

The powerful ring to using the word "justice" implies that everyone knows what it is. Emphatic accusations of injustice command attention. But in reality, true justice is elusive. We all believe in the accuracy of our individual senses of fairness, but twelve people on a trial jury typically haggle vigorously before finding even a majority opinion about what is just in a given situation. Because of this subjective quality of actual justice, the word can easily be wielded unjustly, particularly by anyone in power.

Whoever created the old saying, "justice depends on whose ox is being gored," had noticed that one's prejudged view of a situation can determine what "fair" looks like to him that day. The word "justice" can even be used as a euphemism for "vengeance" by anyone who feels wronged. "We will bring the (infidels), (terrorists), to justice," for example. Wars and entire systems of law have been devised to bring some order to people's differing views of what is just.

In Christian tradition, justice is a virtue. It is not a generality that exists in some objective place, but it resides *inside* us and grows there as we mature—or not. Defined simply as *giving everyone their due*, [3] it is considered by Catholic tradition to be a "cardinal virtue" on which other virtues depend. Those who live making their decisions completely incognizant of justice as a behavioral criterion are called names—jerks, sinners, sociopaths, anarchists, or tyrants, for example—by people earnestly attempting to organize freedom in communal life.

In ancient Hebrew culture, there is no single word for "justice," but its meaning in contained in the concepts of "judgment" and "righteousness," to which humans only strive to attain. Only Yahweh was considered to be just. The rest of us merely seek to attain justice as a personal quality that is eminently worthy of being continually sought. The natural context of intimate loving relationships presents us with an almost endless arena in which to do so, gaining three types of justice benefit in the process: 1) a basic sense of fairness learned from the necessary, nitty-gritty decisions of everyday shared lives; 2) a solidifying sense of justice from vigilance regarding actual oppression that may arise between the two lovers; and 3) a global sense of justice garnered from observing that justice is a necessary platform on which their love must be built and applying that observation to world relationships.

Everyday Fairness

Whatever new lovers have learned about justice in their childhood—from supervised play with toddler peers and from rule-laden preadolescence—gets challenged later in the arena of romantic love. In the unique new vulnerability created by intimate emotionality and mutually shared pleasuring, what feels unfair can bite. And what bites often teaches. Misuse of the power we give one another in the shared vulnerability of emotional intimacy and carnal pleasuring "bites to the bone." Many of us don't learn what it is trying to teach, even through our first three or four romantic adventures. When we see the visible hurt on the face of a partner we've betrayed even slightly, we're being prodded to grasp a lesson of intimate justice.

The flow of decisions about who will attend to every aspect of shared lives becomes a school of love that won't feel loving if it feels unfair. The inherent questions regarding "who is responsible for what" emerge immediately in romance, and they continue to form a justice-learning milieu all days of a couple's lives.

Early in the relationship, such questions may be about who will initiate contacts, provide transportation, decide about entertainment, host liaisons, bestow gifts, and remember anniversaries. Later these give way to who will make a living, do the dishes, keep track of bills, vacuum floors, schedule child care, and initiate making love. The unpleasant feeling of seeing the one you love feeling mistreated by you or even sad about what was decided motivates lovers to find fairness on a daily basis. In the best of relationships that habit becomes a solid sense of overall fairness, the virtue of justice.

Intimate justice is seldom a direct focus in loving decisions. Most lovers quickly learn that excessive emphasis on fairness reduces the spontaneity of eros and spoils the fun. Fairness is rather an unspoken expectation that needs debate only when violated. It is the floor on which love stands and grows.

Is it fair, for example, that he initiates gentle touching more often than she? Or is it irrelevant as long as she responds warmly and initiates affection often enough for him to feel himself cherished? Is it fair that he works more outside the home than she? It is as long as a mutual, albeit informal, decision concludes that such an arrangement is optimal for the "we," the finances, and the human growth of both partners. Is it fair that her mother visits them longer and more often than his? Is it fair that one of them had a half million dollars in the bank when they met, while the other was deep in debt? On this level of inequality, what needs to be learned may be simply tolerance and the realization that loving is about far more than being equal in every *jot and tittle*. Graciousness in the face of the many small events of unfairness soothes both lovers and widens their souls. Grace begins with and then transcends justice.

Vigilance about Oppression

Any intimate relationship is an organism, a system organized to function beyond the capacities of either of its components alone. Like a hanging mobile, any part is affected by significant activity in any other part. St. Paul referred to this phenomenon regarding the early church by comparing it to the human body (1 Cor 12:12–27). A person living day to day in the "we" of intimacy is highly influenced by whatever of importance happens to the other partner.

As the daily sense of fairness forms in romantic partners, they tend to develop a more vivid sense of human oppression. Any serious reflection on the ways in which significant unfairness impedes the love translates into recognition and disdain for actual oppression of others. A lovingly married woman naturally develops empathy for other women living in relationships that are not basically fair and antipathy for aspects of cultures that oppress feminine freedom, rights, opportunities, and expression.

Oppressed would-be partners eventually respond to the unfairness with inward discouragement, outward rage, or "going elsewhere" for sustaining affection, if the latter is even possible. The potentials for 1) *depression*, 2) *hostility* and 3) *"cheating,"* all efforts at coping with or reestablishing relational justice, then begin to erode the intimacy. The chances of continued richness are already suc-cumbing to stubborn injustice.

The extent of depression in our society, including its inability to use annoy-ance, hurt, and disappointment to fuel action in addressing concerns, to some degree witnesses the failure of relational justice. Feeling betrayed and not know-ing what to do about it leaves many lovers hopeless and resigned to the failure of a love that once sustained them.

The second option, hostility, is now often seen as the cycle of abuse that may even end in death. Without a sense of justice, there are no limits to contain what grows into rage. Whether by stinging words, forced sex, or physical blows, what was once affectionate quickly turns to chaotic woe. The movie *The War of the Roses* (20th Century Fox, 1989) boldly illustrates with dark humor how in-cessant retaliation between husband and wife eventually slaughters a great love. In that story, wrath literally kills the partners as they stubbornly go to their deaths together still vengefully fighting one another for dominance.

Going elsewhere for affection—cheating, infidelity, or abandonment—as the third option may be the most common of all. Guilt about the injustice one in-flicts is largely rationalized away in our society where the unspoken entitlement is to get one's own way. Rather than continue to engage the mystery in this re-lationship, some look for it in greener pastures where satisfaction may be easier.

Facing the potential for violence, depression, and a decision to sever their re-lationship, lovers can be scared into seeing how justice is the bare-bones plat-form on which love is built. Without it, there simply can be no love. Intimate loving discloses a view of justice that can't easily be gained elsewhere.

Global Justice

Philosopher John Stuart Mill, among others, suggested that romantic relation-ships can help a person learn about the reality of justice in global aspects of life:

> The moral regeneration of mankind will only really commence when the most fundamental of social relations [marriage] is placed under the rule of equal justice, and when human beings learn to cultivate their strongest sympathy with an equal in rights and cultivation.[4]

In romance, without justice, there is no trust; without trust, no vulnerability; and without vulnerability, no mutuality. Without mutuality, there is no inti-macy, and without intimacy, there is no lasting satisfaction. Without satisfac-tion, there is either apathy or resentment. With apathy comes nothing worth-while. With resentment eventually comes violence, which on deeper levels is called oppression, domination, and terrorism. By the same dynamics, genocide has been rationalized and practiced several times on our planet in the past hundred years. And thousands remain committed to a terrorist way of seeking justice through violence when they feel powerless by any other means.

The prophet Malachia (Mal 1:14 to 2:8–10) warns people to "lay it to heart," or take very seriously, the way we "show partiality in decisions." The Gospel of Matthew (Mt 23:1–12) contains an actual tirade of Jesus on the horrifying injustice practiced by the religious leaders of his time. While God alone is truly just, we clearly have an obligation to seek justice wherever we can as a basis for other virtues needed to fashion and nurture human relationships of every kind.

The Fortitude of Partners

A classic film portrayal of partnering fortitude is *High Noon* (Fred Zinnemann, 1952), which starred Gary Cooper and Grace Kelly and is one of the most famous western movies ever made. The entire story takes place between 10:30 A.M. and just after noon on their wedding day. Immediately after the brief ceremony, Cooper's character, Will Caine, receives a telegram notifying him that a ruthless convict he apprehended years ago has been released from prison and is headed for the town with three cronies, intending to kill him.

Will's quandary: "Stay and fight, ending the longstanding conflict one way or the other, or leave with his bride to the hoped-for safety of hardware store management in a distant city." The position of Amy (Grace Kelly), his Quaker bride: "End the violent life now, don't be a fool and throw your life away for a town that doesn't appreciate you anyway." The haunting song woven throughout the movie captures his dilemma as if sung to his lover. In paraphrase it pleads, Don't forsake me darling. Not on our wedding day. I'm not afraid to die facing this killer, but what would I do if you'd leave me?

Will initially believes he can muster the entire town to help him face the bad guys but finds nobody fit to fight who is willing to do so. He is able to garner no support from anyone, including his deputy, his lifelong aging hero, the judge, his friends, the town leaders, the local pastor, and the entire church congregation. His bride does forsake him, and he determines, hurt and disappointed, to stand alone. He does prevail, of course, with the dramatic assistance of Amy, who returns to fight with and kill for him despite her pacifist religious convictions.

Seeing that story in my boyhood probably helped shape my own stubborn commitment to "good" and an eventual search for lasting love. It clearly has parallels to the Jesus story—widespread respect collapsing into abandonment in a short time, solid personal resolve to persist for the good of unappreciative others, and eventual resurrection though love. As a boy I remember asking my father at bedtime how Jesus was able to carry the cross that, on my childhood crucifix, was so much bigger than Jesus himself. My dad, uneducated but deeply good, simply replied, "He was a very strong man." I'm sure he never had an idea how much that brief event strengthened my life at times when I have needed fortitude.

Whence fortitude? It is defined in Catholic tradition as the developed capacity to find firmness in difficulty and reliability in pursuing good.[5] It is not totally natural to humans and is found in us in various measures. How do humans garner and muster this beautiful mixture of stubbornness, integrity, courage, functional savvy, personal strength, and capacity to find meaning in a worthwhile cause? God knows we will need it several times in our lives. Where does it come from, other than from naked faith and praying for it from the sincerity of our hearts and the depths of our souls?

Some fortitude comes from letting yourself "give a damn," to care about someone enough to stand anywhere with them and for them. A teenaged boy's fortitude naturally grows a bit when he allies himself with a girl who is physically weaker and may need protection. It then grows exponentially on the day he becomes a father. Fortitude seems to burst forth from loving deeply what and who is given us to love.

Some fortitude comes from finding clarity on just what is worth standing for and what can be let go. Traditionally, fortitude is a virtue of budding spiritual adulthood when one realizes that many Christians have been persecuted and have died for their faith throughout history and that one day you too might have to stand publicly for your soulful beliefs.

Some fortitude comes from stories about the courage and resilience of magnificent spiritual heroes like Christian martyrs, Jesus, Will Caine, Martin Luther King Jr., and my dad.

And some fortitude may come from having successfully endured with strength and grieved with integrity what hurt us deeply and we simply could not control. How one faces the necessary and desperately unwanted major losses of life—death of a mom at seventeen, death of an infant daughter at thirty, a casual good-bye by a treasured "love of my life" wife at thirty-five—probably helps hew fortitude into the soul as well.

There will be times when we'll need fortitude—like when we lose a job our family desperately needs; when we're thrust into combat for a cause we don't understand; when seeing yourself as part of the remnant that will stand and work for the communal justice that considers all people actual siblings, at least as deserving of enough food and shelter as I am; and when fighting for life against cancer while straining to know when to abandon the fight and quietly surrender to a waiting Dad/Mom God.

But we also may need it at lesser times, like when our daughter colors her hair green just before Easter and we need to stand beside her in church, as we face team parents after our son misses the seemingly easy goal that could have qualified his team for the state meet, when we need to make a decision for ourselves in opposition to our spouse regarding her drinking, and when we've got to decide how long to insist our teenager attends church without further alienating him from the Catholic traditions we hold so dear.

Great religious and political leaders have exhibited the fortitude necessary to stand for the higher values of the good of all humankind against whatever odds emerged. Honoring such values inside oneself is not enough. One day, some fortitude will be called for to make difficult decisions and prompt actions that imperil one's own well-being in the service of fostering the goal of inclusive global community we all need and seek.

Some fortitude undoubtedly comes from praying for fortitude today and for a partner that will stand with you at "high noon," one with whom you will willingly stand when he or she desperately needs you.

Temperance: *In Medio Stat Virtus*
(Virtue Stands in the Middle)

A most exquisite aspect of romantic love's mystery is the way in which its richness requires both excess and balance. A love beyond prudery is not ashamed of carried-away passion. And a passionate love soon finds need for return to balance to enable stability and personal depth. Passionate loving feeds on getting carried away while quickly returning to patterns of eating, sleeping, and working that make practical life possible. Any illusion that one has control of life is lost in genuine erotic love. But at the same time, any erotic relationship that lasts must find flexibility for incorporating a fair amount of excess in the service of frequent joyful celebration of the goodness of humanity, pleasuring experiences, and the glory of one another.

This cycling between excitement and stability, fun and common sense, passion and planning, celebration and reflection, could be called "moderation" or, in traditional Catholic terms, *temperance.*

In the early part of the twentieth century, the word "temperance" adopted a specific meaning that nearly ruined the word. Ever since the great drinking prohibition attempt was called the "temperance movement," in the minds of many people that term now refers to a strident attitude toward alcohol, not only abstaining from it altogether but also working in some energetic ways to reduce and even prevent its consumption by others.

But traditionally, the Christian term "temperance" carried a broader meaning. Temperance was defined as the ability to moderate our natural attraction to pleasure and balance our use of created resources.[6] One could say it is the ability to avoid excesses that tend to defeat spiritual wellness or a developed capacity to moderate the human appetites for food, drink, and sex in the service of fashioning viable relationships and making quality spiritual decisions. In short, it meant seeking a base of moderation from which mild excesses could be used in celebration for the sake of spiritual nurturance.

In Catholic tradition, a few drinks or a little overeating could be seen as enriching life in partying celebration, while drunkenness robbed a person of reason, and gluttony deteriorated health and contributed to spiritual malaise. Temperance was the ability to find balance in situations where "moderate excess" would contribute to fun, while "excessive excess" leaned toward disaster.

Almost nothing was known until the twentieth century about addiction and the disease of alcoholism. It is very clear now that what was once gluttony and drunkenness can better be seen as addictions that frequently need specifically focused help to give recovery and a decent life a chance. Addiction slowly slays partnering. Excess in all things is the hallmark of the addictive personality, and a great deal is known now about how to help people with it, physically, emotionally, and spiritually. The remarkable treatment modalities and growing awareness of recovery dynamics, developed only in the last two thirds of the twentieth century, dramatically exemplify return to temperance after being lost in excess.

The fundamental value of temperance can also be seen clearly in the effect of excessive excess on love relationships. One definition of intimacy would be the *capacity of a couple to consistently and openly share their inner dialogue with one another.* Excesses that become habitual defeat the freshness of that emotional connecting. A drunk thinks he or she is more scintillating when drinking than when sober but quickly bores and offends a lover who is not also "under the influence." The drunk literally doesn't know that it is no fun even to talk very long with an inebriate, much less sleep with one. Couples with a recovering partner often find when one of them sobers up that they actually have not known one another very deeply and don't even like one another very much. Addiction had "superficialized" the relationship from the beginning.

A cosmic metaphor illustrates what love needs in order to survive. The universe as we know it contains temperatures that range from heat at thousands of degrees Fahrenheit to cold that is hundreds of degrees below zero (absolute zero at –476°F). Humans, however, can exist without insulators (clothes and shelter) only in the extremely narrow range of about 50°F to 120°F. We need sleep at least every twenty-four hours and can eat relatively few very complex substances, needing them at least every several days. Without the simple compound called water every three days, we begin to die. Prolonged excess beyond these stringent limits quickly cancels life within us.

So too it is with intimate partnering. Romance needs eye contact, caresses, soulful conversation, conveyed warmth, and sexual expression in some uniquely discovered combination and frequency that feeds both partners. The "we" of romance especially needs mutual exchange of emotion virtually every day even to survive for long. Habitual excesses of food, mood-altering substances, money, and even sex or religion hinder and eventually preclude this consistent soul connectedness on which partnerships subsist.

Even great thinkers have struggled to describe how balance between the glorious joy of mild excess can coexist with the horrible destructiveness of abandoned limits. St. Augustine was speaking about worldly goods, including sexual intercourse in marriage, when he wrote, "Many, indeed, more easily abstain from them so as not to use them at all, rather than control themselves so as to use them well."[7] Not many in our age seem capable of "total abstinence" from dancing with eros over a lifetime. But "perfect moderation" with eros seems impossible for all. Temperance is a virtue that grows only with experience. And even the fumbling sexual experimentation of adolescence makes its contribution to that learning of moderation and balance in the service of romantic love.

Notes

1. *Catechism of the Catholic Church: With Modifications from the Editio Typica*, First Image Books ed. (New York: Doubleday, 1995), no. 1805–9, 495–97.

2. *Catechism of the Catholic Church*, 496.

3. *Catechism of the Catholic Church*, 496.

4. John Stuart Mill, *The Subjection of Women*, ed. Susan Moller Oskin (Indianapolis: Hackett, 1988), chap. 4, 103.

5. *Catechism of the Catholic Church*, 496–97.

6. *Catechism of the Catholic Church*, 497.

7. St. Augustine, *On the Good of Marriage*, xxi, in *Fathers of the Church: A New Translation*, vol. 27, trans. Ruth Wentworth Brown et al. (New York: Fathers of the Church, 1955), 41.

PART II

EROS AND COMMUNITY

Christianity has always featured agape love as its primary motivational energy. When Mother Theresa stopped to care for that first dying person on a street in Calcutta, she was not motivated by eros. It was agape that catalyzed her splendidly endowed human empathy and generosity into a lifetime of active caring that inspired and transformed the lives and deaths of thousands worldwide.

The kind of love that motivates us to actively care for each other regardless of previous familiarity endures as the central ideal of Christianity. Inspired by gospel stories like the Good Samaritan, told by Jesus in answer to the question "Who is your neighbor?," it compels people with naturally gifted sensitivity and bigheartedness to pursue lives of ministry and charity to do what they can to enrich the daily living of all people.

Love in any of its forms burns to express itself outside itself. As the Hindu poet has written, "Can any lock keep love confined within, when the loving heart's tiny tears escape and confess it? The unloving belong only to themselves, but the loving belong to others to their very bones."[1]

Creation however, has primarily featured eros. Long before Pentecost, erotic energy compelled people to transcend mere animal reproductive sex in a magnificent process of evolving love. The poetic and scientifically based writings of French paleontologist Pierre Teilhard de Chardin during the middle of the twentieth century painted inspiring pictures of the ways in which love has been evolving over the billions of years of continuing creation. The forefront of that process is communal unity and the various forms of energy that drive it.

In his classic book *The Four Loves*, C. S. Lewis distinguished four forms of human loving that are clearly distinct from one another. All of them can be seen as contributing in their unique ways to the evolution of communal connectedness. Family caring (*filia*) is the love one experiences for offspring, siblings, and others in the direct line of reproduction. It differs from the selfless generosity of agape, which is the gift of genuine altruistic care for all people that does away with the notion of "stranger." Both friendship (*amicitia*) and sexual love (*eros*) unite us in pairs, the latter adding carnal pleasuring to the former.[2]

When agape abruptly began to flourish in the Middle East after Jesus' death, eros was overshadowed and eventually seen by Christian leaders as peripheral, even something of a distraction to the "real" love of agape. As we have seen in this book so far, however, a consistent, intimate confluence between two people at the level of their bodies and essential cores (eros) tends to sensitize them to the pains and joys of the rest of humanity (agape). Inversely, lovers need a dose of agape (selfless love) in order to meet the challenges of intimate (erotic) loving for it to endure and achieve its maturing tasks. In other words, eros and agape ide-ally collaborate like dancing siblings, never uniting but consistently working in partnership together toward the common goal of a magnificent form of world community we cannot yet even imagine.

In Catholic culture, however, and to some degree in wider Christianity and other world religions, those dancers have become estranged. Dark Age fearful-ness, cultural dominance of the physically stronger men over the childbearing women, and a thousand years of celibate spiritual leaders, among many other factors, have split the two enough that religion and sex continue to spat and even feud all over the world. As women have found their voices, dominance is receding as relationship solution. Spiritual perspectives on sexual love that are taking its place foster greater partnering among people. The structures promot-ing agape may now be able to learn from eros. What insight can be gained about Catholic traditions fostering communal excellence, sacramental practice, social spirituality, Catholic social teaching, and spiritual leadership by looking closely at the ways in which eros unites and matures individual souls?

Notes

1. Tiru Valluvar, *Tirukkural*, 8:71–72, Satguru Sivaya Subramuniyaswami, trans. (Hi-malayan Academy Publications, www.himalayanacademy.com.)

2. C. S. Lewis, *The Four Loves* (New York: Harcourt Brace Jovanovich, 1960).

~

CHAPTER EIGHT

Sacramental Enhancement:
Can Agape Learn from Eros?

There can be no knowledge without emotion. We may be aware of a truth,
yet until we have felt its force, it is not ours. To the cognition of the brain
must be added the experience of the soul.

—Arnold Bennett

Tom Williams is an eighty-year-old Jesuit priest who continues to pastor a
Catholic church in the Pacific Northwest. Before every mass in his blue-collar
parish, he prays the Lord's Prayer with all the ministers for that celebration
gathered in a hands-holding circle. He begins with a short spontaneous prayer
that always includes "that what we do here will be useful to these people in
relating with their God." Sometimes he uses the word "helpful" instead of
"useful." In his low-key servant way, he ministers from his version of a growing
perspective—"functional spirituality." Religion is intended to be functional,
always, in the judgment of a prudent person, serving the spiritual experience
of people. True ministers of any sort strive to make religious practice useful, concretely assisting people's spiritual lives.

The seven sacraments that form the core of traditional Catholic practice are
arguably the most effective array of religious words and symbols that have grown
through human history. Essentially, they honor and sanctify key life events and
communal development in order to feed human beings spiritually through the life
cycle. Soulful participation in these sacraments continues to bring spiritual benefits to both individuals and communities for hundreds of millions of people worldwide. These seven can also be seen, however, as enhancing the sanctity of intimate love and as being far more richly understood when seen through lovers' eyes.

Maturing lovers learn to pay attention to the moment, to "what works" in keeping their love warm and active, and to the importance of celebrating events that are significant to either or both of them. A simple kiss both celebrates and enhances affection. A vigorous hug appreciates a success as small as second place in the D-league bowling tournament. Conflict resolution, intimate reconciliation, shared work, and all the rest of what makes up an intimate week allow the love to continue. Several times a day, "here and now" words and actions fit the moment and feed the love.

The seven sacraments have lived for centuries because they capitalize on real and meaningful life events, important endeavors, and human needs for frequent support and encouragement in facing life's difficulties and inevitable heartaches. Focusing on *belonging, communing, reconciling, confirming, leading, marrying,* and *dying,* the sacraments parallel the needs and challenges of maturing intimate love.

In Catholic history, human imperfections have often allowed these seven exquisite religious practices to become ritualized, overregulated, and obscured by patterned obligation. Our humanity repeatedly tempts us to protect ourselves from the awe of communally intimate engagement with the living God. Perhaps we can gain from eros some insight into how to fend off this reducing of sacramental excellence to policy, procedure, and the seductive neatness of empty ritual. How might the sacraments look through reflection on their parallel with intimate loving relationships? In an age in which partnering is emerging as a primary model of human alliances and spiritual richness, what can eros teach agape?

Belonging

When lovers connect body, mind, and soul, they almost magically create space in which they both "belong." Pre-romance life is mostly solitary in terms of relating from the soul. In that mostly insular existence, punctuated with intermittent connection with parents, siblings, groups of pals, and budding friends, we only intermittently feel a deep belonging. Then, with the spark of erotic engagement, lovers find the belonging situation reversed. They suddenly begin living in a world in which a pervasive "belonging" quality permeates their days, interspersed with interludes of loneliness and missing one another.

In a real and palpable sense, lovers carry their belonging with them. Loneliness mostly eradicated, lovers have found a life place in which somebody else wants them to be, enjoys them, looks for them, anticipates reuniting with them, and yearns for the sight of their face. A song John Denver made popular and I sang at my own wedding conveyed the message that whenever you're there beside me, we will be at home ("Follow Me," 1970).

Among the many sources of the feeling that one temporarily belongs are a parent's home, a friend's presence, your grown children's welcome, a sister's kitchen, contributing membership on a team, a favorite club or society, and a genuinely needed support group. On a list all its own, however, sits the belonging of romance, a powerful source built into the sexual configuration of created humanity. The potential of bodily pleasuring catalyzes a unique brand of soulful belonging that can enrich understanding of baptism as a sacrament of initiation and suggest hints at the process by which all of humanity is gradually including itself into a world community.

In most Christian denominations, baptism is considered to be a fundamental sacrament. In the 1960s, the fathers of Vatican II identified baptism along with the Eucharist as the central core of the sacramental array.[1] They didn't so bless Holy Orders, which might have contributed to the fat threads of both clericalism and anticlericalism that wind through the historical and current church. Matrimony wasn't seen as central, nor was confirmation. Baptism is the initiating core that seeks to unite people in one eventual world community in which everyone belongs. Baptism challenges all members to contribute their God-given gifts to this goal and to the values that promote it while their spirits benefit richly from the communal love it is gradually fostering.[2]

The concept of belonging is partially observable in the interpersonal dynamics of the formation of any small group. In the study of group dynamics, the concept of "inclusion" refers to a naturally occurring interpersonal project that begins in the first session as each member actually joins that group—or not. Impartial observers note that the group actually forms itself as each person present, one by one, speaks to the group as a whole. As they speak something about themselves with what feels to the group like congruent emotion, they form a little community that the others gradually join. Those who do not include themselves in this simple way remain peripheral and are not likely to contribute deeply to the group life and its work until they do.

Baptism sanctifies this natural phenomenon, builds on it, and enhances it. Emerging from an ancient practice of washing away past regrets, this simple water ritual is primarily about belonging, and by that belonging, it births a fresh new spiritual life expunging previous regrets. Baptism is initiating a person into membership with a community, enkindling the feeling of being accepted there without question, and receiving expressed communal hopes that the group will eventually benefit from the new member's giftedness. It is also a commitment by the community members to the well-being of the new person. They all symbolically hope for an eventual personal commitment of that person at the age he or she is able, to the good of the community. But first, baptism is about belonging and feeling that you belong. You have to "get in" a communal relationship before you can "get with" its functioning, reap its benefits, and contribute to its flourishing and its mission.

The human heart is key to true belonging. When the heartfelt alliance between lovers wanes, so does the feeling of wanting to be in one another's space. In romantic relationships, one partner's realization that "the heart is not in it" for either oneself or one's other is a signal of relational hunger that needs to be fed by encounter.

Similarly, biblical writer Luke (Acts 2:14a, 36–41) describes in enthusiastic terms how the early Christian community initiated into itself thousands at a time in its early days through the preaching of leaders that "cut to the heart." Clearly, belonging is more than being on somebody's registration list, deserving a certain label, or claiming to believe. It must involve the heart and its flow with other souls. It was this issue of need for heartfelt belonging that motivated the pre-Protestant Anabaptist movement to insist that one must be able to speak for oneself to authentically join Christ in Christian community. You had to be adult to accept baptism. But whether baptized as infant or adult, eventually the initiation must touch your core.

Baptism is fundamentally against the loneliness of humankind. Loneliness can be most painful, and when persistent, it can even be lethal in the forms of self-neglect, isolative thinking, and suicidal despair. When habitually withdrawn, minds distort realistic appraisal of issues, exaggerate urgency, minimize basic responsibilities, and otherwise maladapt to the hurt of too much being alone. Country singers like Waylon Jennings often bemoan the loneliness of humanity in songs such as "Mommas Don't Let Your Babies Grow Up to Be Cowboys" (*Greatest Hits*, 1979). Much earlier, at least one of the composers of the biblical Book of Genesis recognized four thousand years ago that "it is not good for man to be alone" (Gn 2:18).

A clergy colleague and friend of mine learned this anew from a Jewish therapist he was consulting. My friend had been seeing the psychiatrist for several weeks, pouring out his woe of recent and past failures in career, marriage, and life in general. He was discouraged, alone, and continually questioning his own worth as a person. After thoroughly listening for weeks, at one point this Jewish therapist sat back in his chair and simply said, "It sounds like your baptism never took."

Baptism, intimate loving, and the growing Christian community all fundamentally combat loneliness. Together they promote growing self-appreciation and self-treasuring that only arise from personal connectedness, soul flow, loving validation, and the repeated experience of being loved. Lovers know that one needs to respond to the incessant thirst for belonging and foster it, follow it, enjoy it, and go where it leads, not mechanically but personally. One aspect of quality spiritual leadership is the gifted ability to foster the feelings of belonging in communal gatherings, facilitate expressions about self from the members, identify ministry gifts, and validate them for use by the community for which the Creator gave them.

Jesus was against loneliness too, though he no doubt suffered more than his share of it. He spoke to people's souls, and they naturally responded and in following him began to belong to the community generated around him.

The Catholic Church's four constitutions (on the Sacred Liturgy, the Church, Divine Revelation, and the Church in the Modern World)[3] written and promulgated for the first time in the 1960s at Vatican II, are also against loneliness. They declare that the Church's mission is global unity.[4] The people who are initiated into Christianity are to do more than belong. They are to be a surging, burgeoning fellowship of energetic, gifted, loving, and generous worshippers who enjoy one another and work to include the entire global population into one collaborative community, not through membership rolls and implied obligations but through feeling the loving acceptance of widespread inclusive energy and then ministering from the personal solidity such belonging generates.

According to the documents of Vatican II, global unity will not necessarily happen under a form of ecclesial governance that is monarchical or dictatorial. Although in some sense hierarchical[5] as an organism related to the Divine, the Church is referred to as a mystery, and the type of polity is not specified. Several collaborative ecclesiastical models are suggested that imply less attempting to control (the People of God, a Sheepfold, the Body of Christ, and a Building of God[6]). The project inherent in baptism is the gradual mission to lend a true and loving belonging quality to literally everyone's life. The Vatican II constitutions employed a centuries-old concept, "the priesthood of all believers,"[7] to capture the notion of shared responsibility of all humans to participate in this global communal care mission. It is not the leadership's mission. It is ours. But it does require leadership that comprehends and feels belonging in their own lives beyond organizational membership and regulatory neatness.

Communing

Communing, or *relating with a group of people from the core of one's being*, has been the staple spiritual practice of Christians from the beginning. The awesome mystery of celebrative group cohesion, so attractive to people of most cultures that experienced it in that first century, has been generally accepted as a defining characteristic of the early Christian movement. Excellent leaders and thinkers have strained throughout the centuries to keep thriving agape alive and protect it from becoming ritualized, institutionalized, and sapped of the spirit of its authentic élan.

Romantic lovers similarly struggle to keep alive their intimate loving beyond the initial, irresistible, high-emotion experience of falling in love. As powerful human mysteries, both of these love forms—eros and agape—feed the soul without ever being comprehended. But can something be learned by agape from the up-close, personal arena of romance? How are these two forms of human love both distinct and parallel? Could the *public loving* inherent in grateful worship be enhanced by exploring elements of the *private loving* of eros? Besides the obvious and fundamental differences, there are at least seven significant similarities that can lend deeper understanding to both eros and agape. They are described in the following sections.

Loving Declaration

A romantic relationship transforms from initial excitement to deeper potential at the moment when one person risks authentically declaring love for the other. Eros limps when neither one hazards the gamble. Love stories invariably include a major focus on the moment of love declaration as a key to the relationship's flourishing. When the love that seems enormously problematic at times and its glorious success appears to be beyond the reach of both lovers is actually expressed clearly in words, the relationship takes on new energy and begins to expand into a life together.

Similarly, heartfelt addressing of the Deity, soulfully expressing love, gratefulness, allegiance, or the willingness to follow any call is a traditional hallmark of religious spirituality. Genuine prayer that engages from the heart, the core of one's being, alters the person who is praying, sometimes dramatically. The Eucharistic presence of God in the traditional forms of bread and wine invites such dramatic personal pledges that actually change lives. So declaring one's love obviously doesn't preclude "backsliding" in religion or divorce in romance. But there is a parallel spiritual benefit to soulfully manifesting one's love, to God or one's human lover, even once.

Heartfelt Authenticity

Declaration is one thing, sustained authentic relationship is quite another. While evangelistic ministry emphasizes the *first* dramatic conversion avowal, Catholic tradition has featured *frequent* soulful manifestations of loving the God who loves us unconditionally. It is not the wedding that matters as much as the ongoing love expressions in maturing a love relationship. Many are the couples who, inwardly fearful of the irresistible intimate milieu, lose the magic of the moment, the spontaneous passionate romp, or the élan vital to romance through disingenuous "faking orgasm for the sake of relationship" or "faking relationship for the sake of sexual satisfaction."

Maintaining authentic soul flow after initial spirited romantic connection has its parallel in the Eucharistic participant struggling to intentionally invest in the celebration. As Inspector Clouseau quips in the movie *The Pink Panther* (Columbia Pictures, 2006), "A woman is like an artichoke. It takes some work to find her heart." Similarly, catechists and the Catechism define prayer as "lifting our *minds and hearts* to God," not mere words or beautiful public phrases.

None of us, however, means every phrase we sing or say in a worship service, nor can we concentrate on every word or gesture of our lover at home. We are far enough advanced in the evolutionary process to consistently mean what we say but not constantly and not perfectly. Where is your mind 50 to 80 percent of the time during a church service? Electronic media, despite its awesome advantages, seems to make maintaining genuine attention at worship even more difficult. We're now conditioned to sumptuous multimedia presentations that combine color, angle, movement, background music, and innumerable vivid and rapidly changing images to literally seize our attention, manipulating time and space to carry a point. Worship leaders can't match that.

But we gather in church for heartfelt worship in addition to any recreation or entertainment we seek elsewhere. It is in the sustained effort to find frequent soulful connection in fostering both eros and agape that matures us. How many times during a one-hour worship service do we need to call our minds back from wandering and inject our hearts into meaning what we are saying? Repeatedly generating attention and sentiment is the hallmark of feeding both a love life and an authentic worship experience.

Sustaining Repetition

Counting on your partner to respond positively to your needs and hopes provides a measure of stability to intimate relationships. Never removing the mystery, comfortable patterns offer some assurance of an oasis in the midst of a world full of unpredictable realities. Even in the midst of disagreements, we trust that we can risk honesty because the strength of the bond between us will eventually return to its sustaining patterns.

In the relaxed and lingering caresses that convey erotic love so beautifully, however, overpatterned repetition is immediately noticed as lacking love. If genuine affection is not generated in the actual intention of the caressing partner, the one being caressed will not feel the love for long. Compulsion and obsession—excessive repetition of thought and action, respectively—steal the mystery and deaden the loving efforts. While regularly expected loving encounters can provide delightful anticipation, sexual loving engagement generally can't stand much ritualizing. Returning to the well again and again quenches the body's thirst. But in both romance and religion, the spirit needs feeding that is both familiar and always new.

Since the deadening effect of compulsive behavior can be noticed more immediately in bed than in church services, it may hold benefit for agape to learn from eros the limitations of patterning. The awesome mysteries of communal love flee and hide against senseless repetition and hyperregulation. Both liturgical leaders and participants can learn to combine in-the-moment genuineness with established ritual to fend off meaningless repetition.

Word and Action Coalescence

In romance, it often happens that one partner naturally emphasizes words of simple sharing and affectionate endearment (often the feminine) while the other favors active and passionate expression (often the masculine). But "talk is cheap" without action, and passion is brutal without affection. As romantic relationships need both action and words regularly for the love to be expressed and nurtured, so communal worshippers need to artfully combine them in liturgical expression.

Both Eucharistic celebration and romantic engagement combine words, actions, and material symbols in intricate ways that exude transforming spiritual power. Water, oil, gesture, music, food, drink, and the bodies of people in love mingle as vehicles with which to stand in the mysterious awe of love in any form. Only constant attention to the wonder of this happening allows us to creatively contribute to its orchestration and, at the very least, refrain from impeding it.

Shared Celebration

Celebration holds a prominent place among the many faces of sexual sharing. Periodically, lovers naturally feel compelled to do something fun together, with at least an impression of excess, a feeling of being "carried away" from burdensome realities of work, children, health issues—any serious negative perspectives. Motivated by mutual appreciation of "something magnificent"—a success, an accomplishment, a bit of good fortune, or just an exceptionally beautiful day or the essential beauty of one another—lovers celebrate. Sharing the richness of life multiplies joy.

One of the most magnificent aspects of early Christianity must have been the communal celebrative sharing every week. Crossing all cultural, gender, familial, and social class lines, it included everyone who believed in joyous active appreciation of the love of God fired by the powerful Spirit that was beautifully uncontrollable. Eucharistic celebrations need to portray and celebrate themes that fit the congregation, capture what is currently of concern, memorialize past greatness, and honor deceased people of note, always working to touch the heart.

Grateful Expression

The joy of romantic loving is made up largely of shared pleasures of all sorts—eating together, party conviviality, the cuddling warmth of bodies, gleeful appreciation of one another's life victories, daily humorous stories, indulging each other's preferences, and all the sights and sounds of one another's souls and bodily presence. Gratefulness a person may feel for all that is not so much an obligation as a natural outpouring resultant from awe at recognizing its goodness.

In early Christian practice, the worship gatherings were intrinsically Eucharistic. Derived from the Greek *eu*, meaning "well," combined with *kharizesthai*, "to offer graciously," the word *Eucharist* means simply "grateful." Early Eucharistic celebrations were times of expressed gratefulness—spontaneous thanking for the abundant flow of palpable agape and for all that was good in life. Sharing the presence of Jesus in bodily form as present in the consecrated bread and wine has been the primary way of Christians giving thanks together since the first century A.D. The Creator must be as pleased at us using our personal gifts in carnal love as at an entire community gratefully praising as one.

Anger Positioning

Expression of anger in some forms can be quite destructive to both eros and agape. Mean nastiness immediately ruins loving, both in church and in bed. Yet anger is a reality that sometimes contributes energy to the wildness of passion in romance and the authenticity of fortitude that is sometimes necessary to protect sacred space and overcome obstacles to a religious mission.

Both agape and eros prompt us to find expressions of our dissatisfaction that are productive without ruining the moment of truth in loving, either intimately or communally. In some Eucharistic atmospheres, one wonders how the "wild man" of John the Baptist would fare as a congregant. Where is the place for realistic masculinity and assertive femininity in the pervasive inane "hypergoodness" of overly domesticated Christianity?

Partnering Leadership

When one healthily mature lover feels a patronizing attitude coming from the other, trouble is already brewing. Researcher John Gottman at the University of Washington has learned to see in years of videotaping married people's conversations facial or verbal indications of *disgust* expressed by one partner at the other as clear signs that the relationship won't last.[8] "Power over" one another in romance simply doesn't fit the relationship and ought to be disclosed quickly as phony, pretentious, or dangerously close to violence.

Likewise, "power over" becomes quickly distasteful in leadership of Eucharistic celebration. Called to be invested in the spiritual benefit of all present rather than convenience, neatness, or regulatory correctness, priests are solemn and sacred ritual leaders "from among us" as well as "from above" in hierarchical structure. The communal Spirit of God cannot be killed by human leadership, but it can be held back, deterred, and sidetracked into material concerns for periods of time that truly burden gathered Christians who are simply seeking to enjoy one another in heartfelt thanksgiving celebration.

This problem regarding the quality of liturgy presentation came up in medieval times. Theologians debated whether the Eucharistic sacrament could be valid if the celebrant was a jerk, living in sin, drunk, or inept. They created the language of "ex opere operato" (from the work of the worker) and "ex opere operantis" (the work of the work working) to deal with it. They concluded that the sacrament's validity depends only on the intention of the celebrant, not on his integrity or spiritual health.

However theologically true that may be, the decision may have let celebrants relax too much. If their soul condition didn't matter, they didn't need to try very hard at connecting with the congregation, at soulfulness, at actually meaning what they say. They could sink into ritualized mediocrity and count on grace to overcome their own shortcomings. That attitude raises questions about spiritual laziness and the hope-sin of presumption.

Eventually, perhaps some celebrants weren't really celebrating. They were complying, following procedural rubrics, getting through it, doing it "right." Rather than authentically celebrating, they could be well intentioned but mindlessly faking it.

Lovers could tell them that they couldn't fake it for long. Celebration soon pales if it isn't real. Sexual activity quickly becomes dull and even tedious when loveless and mechanical. It is still something, but it isn't much. It contributes little if anything to the growth of the romance. Maybe it is even helping to kill it. Vatican II Jesuit theologian Karl Rahner is said to have once quipped that grace is evident "wherever people refuse to surrender to the mediocrity of compliance."

Worship celebrants need to be gifted in order to regularly overcome that "mediocrity of compliance." If they are truly called to liturgical leadership, they likely have some semblance of charism for authentically celebrating with gathered communities and praying from the heart while they do so. They may not be gifted for administration, organizing, accounting, preaching, recruiting, sacramental forgiving, or inspiring to contribute financially. But if they are to truly serve the spirituality of individuals and the community, they must be gifted to lead worship with true reverence.

Marrying

Father Ray, a now-deceased Iowa priest friend of mine, began many of his wedding sermons like this: "Humanly speaking, a man and a woman simply can't live together for very long. It's too easy for any two people to hurt one another

deeply and repeatedly. . . . So it's a good thing we're not just humanly speaking."
Paul Stookey's "Wedding Song" (*One Night Stand* album, 1973) still captures
this notion at many nuptials, proclaiming softly that "this troubadour" will be
among these two lovers whenever they call from their hearts, to help the "we"
of their love survive and grow through the difficult times. Father Ray would
continue his sermon by illustrating how the Spirit of God is necessary and available to any couple who would be "calling from your hearts" for help when they
need it. "Not the calling of your words, or your minds or your wishes," he would
say, "but the calling of your hearts."

As a human endeavor, a wedding is essentially a mutual, socially witnessed
commitment between two people to engage the loving mystery exclusively with
one another for the rest of their lives—"until death do us part." Clearly, the
official commitment event does not ensure a lasting love. But it does tend to
crystallize the relationship as an enormous life change for anyone. In the 2006
romantic comedy *Failure to Launch* (Paramount Pictures, 2006), the thirty-five-
year-old still-living-with-his-parents playboy is thrust into the commitment
confrontation by the words of his most entangling lover: "Do you want to have
fun all your life, or do you want to be with me?"

Weddings took place long before Jesus as a natural attempt to maximize the
possibility of relationships enduring. Bonding for life is a leap of faith in any
case. But if, in the "presence of God" and all the people important to me and to
you, we vow publicly that we invest in this relationship for the rest of our lives,
then we have the best likelihood that we can muster at living into maturing romantic love. Sometimes the actual commitment has been made long before the
wedding, at the proposal, the engagement, or the intimate conversations of
planning a life together. Sometimes it is not made at all, even at the wedding,
as one or both lovers blithely plan and merrily perform an opulent ceremony in
which the bride and groom never touch their own souls.

But in traditional Catholicism (and still in some Protestant traditions), marriage is also a sacrament—a mixture of word, ritual, and symbol that unites a
couple together with the love of God in a bond made sacred. Something profound is added to human relationship when two lovers acknowledge that the
Divine is ever present in their love. The relationship is not made up only of "we
two" but is a greater "we" that includes a powerful positive energy beyond our
control, operant and available to sustain, inspire, support, guide, and energize us
through "good times and bad," in "sickness and in health."

The medieval reformers of Christianity largely abandoned matrimony as a
sacrament, mostly because their scrutiny found no scriptural basis for it, and
they had become highly suspicious of "tradition" because of Catholics' use of the
concept as more coercive than spiritually enriching in their time. But there was
cogency and grace in the Christian traditions that retained matrimony as a
sacrament. It emphasizes that romantic loving is indeed a source of "sanctifying

grace," the indwelling presence of the resurrected Jesus, or, in other words, an actual source of regular experiences of the living God. It asserts that indeed we can rest assured that Divine grace is acting and available as we traverse the labyrinthine paths on which eros leads.

The evangelist John was perhaps the most poetic and theological writer of his time when in his later years he wrote in his first letter, "God is love, and he who abides in love, abides in God and God in him" (1 Jn 4:11–16). John penned these words about the primacy of love—over law, thinking, wisdom, and everything else—in his old age, presumably after decades of reflection. With married lovers, God abides constantly but especially "at the calling of our hearts."

The most dramatic contemporary question alive about this sacrament asks, "Is marriage made up of a man and a woman, or can homosexuals actually marry?" Several U.S. Christian denominations have been struggling in tortured ways with the issue of whether homosexual unions should be "blessed" by ecclesiastical organizations in sanctified weddings. Is God in that love between gays and lesbians or not?

These questions obviously have no clear answers on which, at this point in history, all can agree. But from a spiritual rather than moral perspective, the questions themselves can thrust us into deeper exploration of the meaning of marriage as sacrament for anybody. The piercing issue that puts at stake the life integrity of people on both sides of the debate may lead us to ask key questions: Is marriage primarily about love or about law? Is love from the heart the primary criterion for marriage, or is it political correctness? What is the role of churches and governments in deciding who actually loves and thus who can marry?

Such questions are both disturbing and unavoidable. If one understands the biblical letter of John with interpersonal sensitivity, then how can one exclude any true love from the phrase "abiding in love"? Whose responsibility would it be to determine when two people are actually "abiding in love"? If "God is love," then is there some actual love that is not God? Was the use of the Greek term *agape* for "love" meant to exclude eros as actual love that indicates presence of the Divine? Can "abiding in love" be determined with certainty in any heterosexual couple? Who then can appraise the presence or absence of love in a gay couple without even knowing them intimately? Does the physical configuration of how love is carnally expressed override authenticity of the love as criterion for socially celebrated lifelong commitment? Can gay and lesbian people in justice be excluded carte blanche from the sacrament of sexual love sharing, let alone from church membership or leadership?

Clearly, not all that looks like love really is. Some of it is manipulative exploitation, some lust, some genuine love seeking, some legal or political convenience, some staying together for the sake of material rights, and some the wounded relational debris from another person's lust long ago in rape or childhood abuse. Could the external structures of a spirit-filled communal body go a bit further determining who is "abiding in love" though we will never do so with certainty? Are there perhaps Christians who never find their way into leadership but are gifted in assisting lovers in this imprecise discernment? Could such people be involved in the pre-wedding preparation phase of romance? How can communal worshippers support, assist, nurture, and enhance romance in young lovers of any sexual orientation without invading their privacy? Who is taking these questions seriously? Where is the leadership to facilitate the widespread involvement of maturing intimate lovers to do so?

Functionally, the sacrament of matrimony is a grace-enhanced, natural gift to humanity intended to assist us in the most difficult endeavor of finding, fashioning, and feeding romantic partnerships that continue to grow and prosper throughout the life cycle despite beleaguering odds and formidable obstacles. A wedding guarantees nothing, just as a father can guarantee no success of his son's life directions, accomplishments, and richness of enduring relationships. But weddings as beginnings of matrimony, well planned and sincerely celebrated, do help. The troubadour truly is available at the calling of our hearts.

Reconciling

I once confessed masturbation to over two hundred priests at one time—and two bishops. At the age of twenty-six, I'd been asked to speak at a clergy conference on "What We Expect of One Another" in the late 1960s. It was a diocesan clergy conference at a time when young priests were contending both subtly and openly with established ones who'd not yet been imbued with the new theology of Vatican II. When I shared a story of seeking a confessor in the middle of the night so as not to say mass the next morning in mortal sin, the archbishop was overheard whispering to his auxiliary, "There's such a thing as being too honest!"

The age-old spiritual issue of guilt could be called the "mother of all spiritual issues." It could be defined as *a feeling of sickness inside for failing to live up to your developed expectations of how you treat God, people, and yourself.* The Catholic traditional term for whatever causes that feeling is *sin.* All major religions have developed ways of defining what is worth feeling guilty about and how to assuage that sick feeling. There are huge differences in what individuals and religions believe are the worst human actions and what it takes to heal the damage from those acts. But the efforts of faith groups to address the guilt phenomenon are universal. Sufi poet Jaleluddin Rumi asserts that there are eight doors to paradise. All of them are sometimes shut, but one of them, the door of repentance, is always open. "Carry your baggage there at once," he advises.

Protestant theologian Paul Tillich once wrote a small book, *Love, Power and Justice*, on what he called "the power of re-uniting love."[9] He referred to how lovers part and return to one another repeatedly and the power that dynamic has on their growing relationship. He was referring not only to the daily parting and reuniting of all lovers but also to how we hurt one another, sometimes even intentionally, in rationalized retaliation to each other's wounding words and actions. He believed, along with many marriage counselors, that we can continue intimate relating only if we learn to use effective and repeated reconciliation.

As a twenty-something seminarian learning about the sacrament of reconciliation, then called "confession," I remember a popular song frequently blaring from the radio sung by Petula Clark entreating her lover by the title "Don't Sleep in the Subway Darling" (Warner Brothers, 1967). "Forget your foolish pride" was only a cliché, but it was sung with earnestness; it fit our learning about repentance.

Like that lyricist, all successful lovers know something about the dynamics of forgiveness. They find that guilt ruins the love, that painful conflict can often be resolved, and that the ability to "forget your foolish pride" is essential to the process. They either learn about forgiveness through repeatedly encountering one another's humanness or eventually part, defeated by resentments and self-pitying victimization.

Experienced lovers find out that cheap words about "always forgiving one another before the sun goes down" are more poetically beautiful than practically useful. The vulnerability inherent in the intimate arena, from naked needs for daily affection and frequent physical pleasuring, inevitably becomes a breeding ground for hurt. That hurt grows into pools of resentment and guilt, partially hidden below the surface of everyday getting along. Some of these never heal and build themselves into insurmountable barriers ending in divorce of two who initially loved sumptuously. If they do heal, it is only with particular care, generosity, graciousness, and an effective process that takes place beyond a superficial "trick of the mind" to "forgive others as you would like to be forgiven." Reconciliation is as complex and difficult as it is absolutely necessary.

The classic process of personal forgiveness formed itself in Catholic tradition over centuries in order to pastorally address the spiritual need of guilt. Failure to do so led to remorse, resentment, hostility, or discouragement, all of which tend to impede the growth of human wellness. The spiritual value of the well-known steps—*contrition, confession, absolution,* and *penance*—make good sense and are highly effective when performed with sensitivity and integrity. They can be found in therapy sessions, friendship repair, and thousands of patient–chaplain conversations in hospitals, hospices, and penal institutions every day.

But as a sacrament administered by celibate clergy, reconciliation has fallen into general disuse in the United States over the past thirty years. Perhaps that is because its revisions without consultative input from the faithful have lagged behind society's needs. Many of the "rich juices" of the classic forgiveness process have been lost from practice of this sacrament. Could the functional effectiveness of it be revitalized? How could eros teach agape about enriching this fundamental spiritual practice? Perhaps maturing romantic lovers could offer some suggestions of why use of this sacrament has declined and how it could be revived. If that consultation were to proceed, some of the initial suggestions might include the following:

- Genuine apologies do help: Hearing *heartfelt* words that your partner openly acknowledges sorrow for harmful words or actions, soothes the soul, and opens up possibilities for future fun. Without such open acknowledgment of regrets, the "we" continues to hunger for something missing in the making up. On a purely personal level, confession is spiritually valuable. The biblical practice of "confess your sins to one another" (Jas 5:16) in some private ritual form needs to be retained.
- Retain the "seen or unseen" option: For lovers, the darkness of the bedroom can sometimes feel safer as a context for apology and forgiveness than in the light under your partner's gaze. The sacramental option of "face-to-face or behind the screen?" is a useful one.
- Revive "general confession": Clearing the air of saved-up apologies, sometimes only in a marriage counselor's office, can free lovers for deeper incursion into the loving mystery. Such openness requires enormous courage because it renders us so completely vulnerable to one another. Blame from another person multiplies the pain of guilt when it is already painfully searing. If confessing invokes blame from the other, the pain can be unbearable and literally close off a partner in total defeat, essentially ending the relationship. Yet gathering some old, already forgiven regrets in a retreat, spiritual direction, counseling office, or marriage enrichment setting, as a genuine "cleaning house" effort, revitalizes most any wounded relationship. In the twelve years between 1979 and 1991, I personally listened to roughly a thousand "fifth steps" of newly recovering alcoholics and drug addicts at a treatment center in northern Wisconsin. The fifth of the famous Twelve Steps, originally distilled from the best of Christian tradition and the recovery experiences of early members of Alcoholics Anonymous (AA), has renewed the conviction in me and at least a million recovering people that summing up past regrets at key moments of your life is extremely healthy for the soul.

- Practice annual confession: Relate an annual confession practice to wedding anniversaries, penitential seasons, or a society's celebration of the New Year—Intimate loving needs little focus on failures. Adults in general need to apologize and move on. Shame is too painful to dwell on or repeat excessively. Likewise in religious practice, too much confession is burdensome. Once a year as a regular tradition would be enough for adults who emphasize joy over remorse. What time of year would be preferable? Celebrating a wedding anniversary is no time to bring up regrets of the past. However, an informal "cleaning house" conversation that emphasizes the future, leading up to the anniversary party, could be preparatory. There is no need to revise the liturgical year to better emphasize intimate loving as a spiritual arena. But more thought could be given to augmenting existing calendars by including references and practices that honor it.

- Empower gifted confessors: The interpersonal context of a confessional atmosphere is crucial to promoting an openness that is genuinely healing. The hurt eyes of a lover, the promise of the warmth of reconciliation, and the tolerant, forgiving stance of lovers to one another makes acknowledging failures possible. Catholic ordination once guaranteed a knowledgeable, trustable, objective, listening presence for promoting confessional confidence and openness. It is becoming more apparent, however, that many people are gifted for specific communal spiritual functions that don't fit the rigid structure of ordination for *all* functions. And many already ordained are not gifted for the interpersonal intimacy required for a confessional context. If revising the practice of this sacrament affects a wide influx of people wanting to use this sacrament, can there be training and an ordination of men and women gifted with sensitive, savvy, and mature wisdom only as confessors?

- Improve training for confessors: Lovers who don't actually listen to one another are doomed to intimate mediocrity at best. "Erotic obedience," listening to one another in a relaxed context, is essential to maturing intimacy. Most all of us have to learn to listen, though we all seem to believe we are "good listeners." Men in general need to adjust to women's communication styles, which include what seems like excessive wordiness. Women in general need to adopt their listening to men's style of communication, which tends to be more nonverbal. Both need to do this with gracefulness rather than judgment. A great deal is being regularly taught now in ministry training circles about how to listen personally and deeply without needing to advise or project one's own needs and issues onto the person for whom one is caring.[10] All confessors today, whoever they are, need to be both gifted and trained. They need to receive specialized training in compassionate listening and spiritual sensitivity. How can confessors facilitate an intimacy of self-disclosure if they practice it only meagerly themselves?

- Eradicate moralism in confessors: A love partner who acts morally superior through teaching, preaching, or advising from a patronizing place is quickly dismissed as obnoxious. Such unrequested instruction from confessors to already spiritually savvy penitents has contributed heavily to the decline in use of this sacrament. Confessors need enough life experience to habitually and authentically acknowledge weakness as human rather than implying, even subtly, that people need to be "better," seek perfection, improve everything, and constantly convert. Idealists and perfectionists may make it for a while in the pulpit but ought to stay out of the confessional until they have grown to accept more graciously their own limitations and thus the limitations of all humans.

- Personalize absolution: When lovers apologize to one another, they quickly yearn for a forgiving comment and gesture in return, even a minimal one. Similarly, absolution spoken clearly and personally is a key component of this sacrament. People will benefit from self-disclosure of regrets in many venues, but what makes this a sacrament is hearing ritually spoken assurance that God does forgive, here and now, this person for these actions. Confessors need to learn to make absolution a personal assertion, neither a ritualized formula nor an overly dramatized gushing. Absolution needs to be spoken with personal connectedness, assurance, and sensitivity.

- Honor uniqueness: After a serious apology, lovers benefit from a symbolic action that expresses and demonstrates an intention to do better on the issue involved. This is generally a gesture, a caress, a kiss, or words of a positive intentional future. Confessors need imagination in suggesting meaningful penances. Ritualizing the penance ruins the grace. Realistically symbolic actions that imply a gesture toward remedial action, without offering patronizing advice, often further the healing.

- Promote communal reconciliation: At times regrets do not require an apology, and "owning up" to a lover for some actions would only hurt him or her worse. As step nine of the Twelve Steps states, "Make amends for our wrongs unless doing so would cause more harm."[11] The growing Catholic ritual of "communal penance" rituals without direct confession is a positive development, fostering internal contrition and an experience of forgiveness when personal confession is not necessary.

While Pope John Paul II failed in many ways to implement the Spirit-inspired constitutions of Vatican II, his public apologies to world communities about historical Catholic Church institutional failures was a demonstration on how reconciliation can be effective on an international level. That practice can grow as politicians, diplomats, and national leaders continue to learn from reflecting on how forgiveness and reconciliation actually happen in our primary relationships.

Maturing

When you parent a teenager, you get a great chance to experience what it is like to be God—not in God's power but in God's vulnerability. Adolescents are a metaphor for all of us people in relationship to God. As parents of an adolescent, you deal daily with a person who is self-absorbed, dependent on you, moody, free, ungrateful, entitled, demanding, sullen, impolite, and occasionally endearing. You love her deeply and would die for her, but she is free to either ignore you, reject you with one flippant quip, or melt you with a smile. And you made her yourselves! You have faith that she is on the way to maturity and hope for the day that her adulthood can be confirmed by people who validate her as a woman and reflect their appreciation of her back to you. Doesn't that sound like God must feel relative to us humans?

When my daughter was twenty with a college year left, she took a trip with a friend from our home on the West Coast back to the Midwest, where she was born and lived until she was ten. As they drove from city to city, they stayed with and visited several relatives and some old friends of mine, from Texas to Louisiana to Wisconsin. She didn't know that I was calling some of them immediately after they left each city, garnering any comments from the hosts that would convey their impressions of my daughter as a woman. I was universally delighted in their views of her as personally engaging, capable, articulate, and delightfully fun. They confirmed for me her budding and already considerable maturity.

Traditionally, the sacrament of confirmation is a reception of the fullness of the Holy Spirit usable only by adults to empower them to function spiritually as mature Christians. It was recognized in the Acts of the Apostles as bringing on the radical personal changes of Christian conversion (e.g., Acts 8:18; 1 Tm 5:22; 2 Tm 1:6; Heb 6:1–3).

Functionally today, confirmation is the Spirit of God in the community of Christians affirming together a person's spiritual maturity. In current practice, a bishop confers confirmation, but it is basically a communal experience, as the term "confirm" or "made firm together" implies. As symbolized by the bishop's word and gesture, when a person is being confirmed, a community of validating and collaborating people is affirming your readiness to take your place as a spiritual adult among them. This sacrament says and symbolizes that you have enough developed capacity to use the Spirit within you and the resources of other Christians to care for your own spirit and be a part of the global mission of humanity in a difficult adult world.

In recent tradition, confirmation is generally conferred at some point in the teenage years, between the ages of eleven and eighteen, the most explosive era of hormonal sexual energy. How then did confirmation become so sexless? Maturing in adolescence is intimately connected with early romantic loving, making some sense out of sexual drives, the unpredictable and powerful realities of adult bodily living. Shouldn't confirmation preparation and celebration be more reflective of what is most intensely happening in the lives of those receiving it? Can it somehow reflect a young person's taking responsible charge of engaging the sexual mystery, as portrayed in Billy Joel's song "My Life" (*52nd St.* album, Columbia, 1978), in which he proclaims that whatever you do in the love-seeking individuation project of finding your own personal and sexual identity you "wake up with yourself."

In creative parishes, "sex education" is already being replaced by something like "romantic love education." People in adolescence are being introduced by maturing lovers with teaching savvy to the basics and some of the intricacies of intimate loving, the nitty-gritty sharing of bodies, minds, opinions, material "stuff," and emotions required of long-term romance. The men meet with the boys and the women with the girls as part of their learning of what it takes to be an adult love partner. Then the girls meet with some sensitive husbands and the boys with some understanding wives. In the future, perhaps all will learn as part of confirmation preparation, something more practical and realistic about making long-term romance enjoyable and fulfilling as well as possible.

A "Song of Songs" model of Catholic tradition would ask these persistent questions: How can confirmation be entwined with romantic education? How can the organized church minimize the disconnection that typically occurs between teenagers and Christian practice, due at least in part to their perception that leadership is ignoring what is most intensely going on within and among them? How is confirmation an opportunity to foster the integration of perspectives on bodily development, emotional maturing, and adult spiritual experience?

This transformative integration of sacramental confirmation may take a long time. But it may not if experienced romantic lovers are enlisted for their giftedness and professional success in relating to adolescents.

In actuality, the entire community confirms the maturity of a young person in many little ways by the impressions they share of him or her as a grown-up person. Once when I was seventeen, I met an older man I didn't know on the street in our small city. He stopped me and told be how much he had enjoyed my scoring fifteen points in the first half of our final basketball game, even though I fouled out early in the second half as we lost again—a simple interaction for which I didn't at the time have the presence of mind to thank him. But I never forgot his informal "confirmation" of my worth as a capable male human being. Sometimes girlfriends and the elders—uncles, coaches, neighbors, clergypersons, and teachers—confirm our worth as richly as any bishop. But the evolution of sacramental celebration is moving us to grander and more authentic communal ways of symbolizing and effecting the maturing Spirit of God through Christian adults as both lovers and servants.

Healing and Dying

When my mother died at age fifty-four, it nearly devastated my father. It took him over two years to be anything like himself again. Her death changed his life, and he never remarried. I believe he was frequently lonely during his last seventeen years. He hunted and fished with his brother and brother-in-law, visited his kids and grandchildren, played cards, and laughed a lot. But his partner was gone, and he seemed to attend more funerals. Longtime romantic lovers find out just how profound death can be. For dad, that loss signaled the end of a life-sustaining romance, a future of eating alone, and a very empty bed.

Every week, many pastors read during the worship service the names of parishioners who have died that week. Someday it will be me. Someday it will be you. Several people reading this won't be alive in a year. If we can say anything about how the Creator wanted the world to be, one clear certainty is that it's "built in" for everybody to die. As the old African-American spiritual song laments, we all "gotta walk that lonesome valley, we gotta walk it by ourselves.[12]" We can only guess, theorize, and theologize about why it is so. But it is so.

Dying is one of the oldest and most profound of all spiritual issues. Finding a cave mate dead must have been an awesome and awful event for primitive humans. Most of the oldest religious artifacts archaeologists have dug up were found with skeletons. Primitive religion must have emanated at least in part from coping with the tragic eventuality and apparent finality of death.

Biblical stories frequently refer to dying, along with love itself, as the most powerful of human experiences (e.g., Songs 8:6). Over the centuries, Christian tradition developed communal practices intended to help people deal with death, both those actually dying and those standing around losing a loved one and in the process learning how to someday face their own death. In the twentieth century, the hospice tradition began to teach more specifically how to take charge of our own dying, as sung by John Denver in "Around and Around" (*Poems Prayers and Promises* album, RCA, 1971) as he proclaims his hopes to still "be there when I die."

In the Hail Mary prayer, repeated one hundred and fifty times in the entirety of the Catholic rosary, people ask for Mary, the Mother of God, to "pray for us sinners now and at the hour of our death." We've noted in our souls over and over that there are only two times in all of life—the present hour and our time of dying. The distinction sobers us. All else pales in comparison. During the offertory of every mass, we participants are encouraged to give back to God all that we've ever had, emphasizing that we have it for only a limited time before it is naturally gone.

Primarily, however, the Christian spiritual practices addressing the process of dying are the sacraments—Eucharist and Anointing. Vatican II named "Viaticum," or the last reception of the Eucharist, as the sacrament of dying.[13] But in the twentieth-century tradition with which most Catholics have been acculturated, the sacrament of preparation for death was what is now called the "anointing of the sick" and was previously known as "extreme unction" or, colloquially, the "last rites." If you've ever participated in its being administered to someone you love who is actually in the dying process, it probably affected you deeply—especially if the priest possessed a gift for authentic ritual, pastoral sensitivity to the situation, and the time and inclination to pray it with heart and soul.

There is a slang term for priests who overritualize this sacrament. They are called "thumbers" in some circles because they quickly anoint the head, hands, and forehead with the oil on their thumbs, mumbling inaudible words, relating to nobody present, and disappearing quickly. Apparently fearing awkwardness, they create it. They are busy with other things, and they are not necessarily pastorally gifted. They dutifully serve, following procedures, staying within canon law, and showing up when they are called. At times in history, that was enough. Little was known about grieving. A sacramental presence was an experience of the benign Transcendent at an awful time of life. It served people well in that day.

Now, however, many people are more educated, spiritually sophisticated, and sensitive to the intended function of religious practice as well as its dogma and forms. In the early 1960s when my mother died, there were about three books written on grieving. Two of these were A Grief Observed by C. S. Lewis and Take the High Road by John Gunther. During that same decade, two women psychiatrists, Chicago's Elizabeth Kubler Ross and English hospice originator Sicily Saunders, started a wave of sensitive caring for the dying and writing about it. Now there are hundreds of books on dying and on grieving losses from infants and parents to uncles and pets.

In recent years, "end of life care" and "palliative care" have found a surge of societal energy. Both the Sacrament of the Sick and Viaticum have a place in that care. Widows or lovers whose partners have died could teach something about how to enrich these sacraments so they can take their rightful place in the continuum of interdisciplinary health care with dignity, reverence, respect, and integrity. Some suggestions they might make include the following:

- Sensitive, personalized rituals can be spiritually helpful, but overritualizing can bore, offend, and even disgust. When something important is happening, empty ritual is easily disclosed as an insensitive substitute for having nothing important to say.
- Grieving is a process, and we all need to learn more about it—continually.
- A small community of loving family and friends helps dying best, with calm presence and simple acknowledgment of the pain—if the uniqueness of the family allows such a scenario.
- Spare grievers all platitudes.
- We could do a better job of discerning who is gifted in the local community to assist the dying process of parishioners and the grieving bereavement after. Rather than leaving it to the clergy or currently active parishioners who may be minimally gifted and dutifully overinvolved already, we need to learn to recognize, empower, and legitimize all people pastorally gifted to help people grieve.

When you've lost somebody you loved—a romantic partner, a sibling, a child—and have learned from seriously reflecting on the experience, you may have become a bit more sensitive to the care that is needed at those times. You likely have learned something about "the hour of our death" for yourself as well. The ancient practice of the sacraments of Viaticum and Anointing are available as a profound vehicle for that care. Let us use them well and keep on learning.

Leading

The Scripture readings for the thirty-first Sunday of Ordinary Time (A) are aimed at spiritual leaders, a group of whom Jesus was highly critical in his day. The Old Testament reading from Malachi (Mal 1:14b–2:2b, 8–10), written almost three thousand years ago, is scathing in its criticism of the disingenuous ineptitude of many Levitical priests. The reading from Paul's letter to the Thessalonians (Thes 2:7b–9, 13) tenderly describes his style of leading with actual affection for his followers. Then the gospel reading (Mt 23:1–12) returns to the critical tone, as Jesus is quoted assailing some Jewish leaders for their pretentiousness, insensitivity to actual human struggles, and missing the deeper meanings of many spiritual practices.

Anyone called to risk the leadership of people who are facing the profound mysteries of human living ought to reflect on the phrase, "Fools rush in where angels fear to tread."

In Catholic and some Protestant denominations, ordination is considered a sacrament, the Christian tradition of empowering leaders for communal spirituality. Modeled after the Jewish Levitical priesthood, almost all ordained Roman Catholic leaders are unmarried men, exclusively authorized to preside in communal spiritual functions. They are educated and officially approved as ready to lead worship and administer religious rituals of initiation, reconciliation, marrying, healing, and dying. Then they are communally "ordained" and "officially designated" to be priests.

The paradigm of romantic partnering has had little influence on the preparation or designation of leaders, at least since mandatory celibacy was administratively made a condition of official liturgical leadership in the twelfth century. How would the endeavor of priesthood differ if the spirituality of intimate partnering were taken seriously as a part of the data of systematic theology? What if romance were consulted as one central arena of the spiritual life that is lived on a daily basis? If most people live day to day amidst the tides, breezes, and thunderstorms of eros, couldn't the spiritual leaders learn from using romance as one of the windows from which to view spiritual health? Aren't sermons disconnected and frequently boring, at least in part because of the failure to do so?

A partnership spirituality gains wisdom from intimate loving as it is experienced among people and sees parallels in how individuals can partner with the Divine and the Christian community. What is the Spirit of God showing humanity in the *erotic* form of love that could be of benefit to leaders of *agape* love in liturgical community? What can leaders learn from looking at what impedes eros that may also be impeding agape? Here are some suggested perspectives:

- Legal: Law is virtually useless in romance and other arenas of spiritual experience. Two valuable roles of law regarding love relationships are to set boundaries in combating sexual abuse and domestic violence and to assist in material division during divorce. But law offers no help in any form to nurture the partners' loving of one another or to overcome the inevitable barriers to love's maturing. Spiritual leaders immersed in law miss the power and importance of religious practices as well as other forms of nurturing the human spirit. Likewise regarding communal spirituality, law is mostly valuable in attempting to organize the structures of ecclesiastical life. But all of ecclesiastical regulation adds little worthwhile to the spiritual lives of Christians. Similarly, the oral AA tradition, "We make no spiritual laws or regulations—we only offer spiritual suggestions," is a better fit to helping people develop spiritually than requiring or forbidding specific actions that contribute mostly to managerial smoothness and organizational neatness rather than spiritual nurture, richness, and depth. Ecclesiastical leadership needs to divest itself of so much legal focus and concentrate on assisting the spiritual lives of actual people.

- Power: "Power over" is less than useless to would-be partners. Rather, it is enormously destructive. "Power for," "power with," and "empowering" may consolidate the mutuality of partnership. But "power over a partner" is an oxymoron. When one romantic partner uses power to influence the other, either directly through coercion or indirectly through manipulation, there needs to be a very good reason that the temporarily more vulnerable partner can acknowledge. Women may playfully seduce with sex and men with money, and sometimes it multiplies the fun. But cogent reasons rarely exist for heavy use of emotional coercion, physical force, or intentional deceit. Assessments for an alcohol problem or mental illness of a lover or confronting a financially disastrous decision may be a few exceptions. But universally, loving partners don't push each other around, physically, verbally, or emotionally.

  Power use is likewise generally destructive in spiritual leadership. Have we ever really forgotten the Inquisition, the witch hunts, the Crusades, the excommunications? How much good did they do for the spiritual well-being of either individuals or the communities involved? In their day they may have found some usefulness in the maintenance of authority, order, and the material resources of the organization. But among today's educated seekers and lovers, "power over" has little value in either romance or spiritual care, both of which thrive on attention to vulnerability and the assiduous *use* of power rather than *abuse* of it.

- Administrative: Management is only minimally useful to lovers. Who can "manage" a love relationship? A little organization and structure can facilitate romance by enhancing efficiency and ease of doing the material business involved, such as a filing cabinet and a shared calendar. But the élan of eros has a life of its own that responds to its primary foods of shared emotion, mutual pleasuring, empathy, listening, waiting, and intimate celebration. The human spirit in general is not assisted much by management technique. Overused and poorly defined words such as "obedience," "compliance," "uniformity," and "good Catholic" find most of their value during the formative first ten years of life. The roots of those words reveal interesting lost attitudes, however. "Obedience" has roots in words that mean "listening."[14] "Compliance" evolved from words that mean "being formed together." The term "uniformity" came from "forming as one." The fact that these words carry little current relevance to creativity, imagination, excellence, and intimacy ought to inform spiritual leaders of the limitations of their present use in ministry.

- Liturgical: Ritual has a small but significant place in romance. Patterning the occasions of sexual intercourse seems to enrich the relating of some couples more than others—and most for only a period of time. Spontaneity needs to intertwine with consistency. Likewise, the liturgists who designed the Roman ceremonies to include a portion of communal rituals that change daily and weekly and a permanent aspect that is rarely if ever altered were attempting to reverence this need in human spirit for impressions of both permanence and freshness, side by side. Modest ritual feeds, but excessive ritual bores and kills. Spiritual leaders seem to be tempted even more chronically than most of us by the human need to overritualize for order, convenience, and the illusion of control.

- Political: Politics has little relevance to the growth of romance in its perjorative sense of making decisions through means that ignore giftedness, competence, and excellence of function in favor of who the decision makers know, trust, like, or can exploit. Politics in ecclesiastical circles is inevitable because of our humanness. But the politicizing of major societal issues such as abortion, gay marriage, and pedophilia among clergy does little to edify and inspire.

- Pastoral: Charisms, or gifts, are vital to the intimate partnering life. Lovers unashamedly appreciate the physical endowments of the current "objects of their affection" and even of any *potential* romantic partners. They naturally recognize, validate, confirm, empower, implement, and use carnal endowment for mutual joy and functional effectiveness of the partnering. Having the various components of your body and personality noticed, extolled, employed in the love sharing, and complimented repeatedly over the course of years, even into aging, is powerfully confirming and building of self-confidence and worth.

  Likewise, a chief function of any pastor is the identification of the various gifts of the members of the congregation, validating them, calling them forth, employing them in communal spirituality events, and complimenting them again and again as they are seen to enhance the communal experience of God. That ability to thus orchestrate individual gifts for communal benefit is a unique and apparently rare gift itself and a talent not bestowed on all ordained leaders. To some degree it may be a learned skill as well. It is a matter of hope among faithful Catholics that a church structure based more on personal and spiritual giftedness than on order and regulation is in our future.[15]

Leading communities with a partnering model of spirituality would differ significantly from leading it with a preoccupation with neatness and order. It will require widespread spiritual maturity to fashion and enjoy such a church.

Notes

1. Austin Flannery, ed., *Vatican Council II: The Conciliar and Post Conciliar Documents* (Northport, N.Y.: Costello, 1975), 4, 55.

2. Flannery, *Vatican Council II* , 365.

3. Flannery, *Sacrosanctum Concilium*, 1963, 1; *Lumen Gentium*, 1964, 350; *Dei Verbum*, 1965; 750, *Gaudium et Spes*, 1965, 903.

4. Flannery, *Gaudium et Spes*, 903 ff.

5. Flannery, *Gaudium et Spes*, 369–96.

6. Flannery, *Gaudium et Spes*, 359 ff.

7. Flannery, *Gaudium et Spes*, 353.

8. John Gottman, *Why Marriages Succeed or Fail: What You Can Learn from Breakthrough Research to Make Your Marriage Last* (New York: Simon & Schuster, 1994), chap. 3: "The Four Horsemen of the Apocalypse: Warning Signs," 68–102.

9. Paul Tillich, *Love, Power and Justice* (New York: Oxford University Press, 1954).

10. See, for example, the website of the Association for Clinical Pastoral Education at www.acpe.edu.

11. *Twelve Steps and Twelve Traditions* (New York: Alcoholics Anonymous World Services, 1952), 83–87.

12. J. H. Crone, *The Spirituals and the Blues* (New York: Seabury Press, 1972).

13. Flannery, *Constitution on the Sacred Liturgy*, no. 39. Viaticum, 124.

14. See also chapter 9.

15. See also chapter 12.

CHAPTER NINE

~

The Evangelical Counsels for All

The Rule of the Friars Minor is this, namely, to observe the Holy Gospel of Our Lord Jesus Christ, by living in obedience without anything of our own, and in chastity.

—St. Francis of Assisi

From its beginnings, Christianity has been a communal movement. In every age, a few people have spurned secular values of "the world" in dedicating their lives entirely to the ideals of communal living. Indeed, before his public life, Jesus probably spent some time living in such a community of people dedicated to spiritual growth and compassionate ministry. That practice lives today in religious orders variously organized to promote spiritual excellence and human care in diverse forms.

Much of this organized effort, inspired by several New Testament references that suggest communally sharing everything until the second coming of Christ (e.g., Acts 4:32–35), has been shaped by promoting three pivotal characteristics among followers: *poverty*, *chastity*, and *obedience*. The three evolved somewhat differently from one another through the development of monastic traditions during the Dark Ages. By the early thirteenth century, they were consolidated into what came to be called the "Evangelical Counsels."[1]

The practical value of these "vowed virtues," as they are also called, was to free community members for spiritual development and ministry. They were intended to remove from the lives of people consecrated for ministry anything that would inhibit the excellent practice of charity. Minimizing preoccupations with money, sexual relationships, and major life decisions, the counsels guided lives toward more freedom to be spent in supportive relationships with one another and in the care of people, materially and spiritually.

Catholic teaching continues to suggest that following these counsels is a "better way" of life and encourages all people—clergy, religious, and laypeople—to live by them to enhance their spiritual lives.[2] When preachers have urged congregations to live these virtues in daily life, however, parishioners have often gone away confused and annoyed. How do they apply to love seekers and married people? One could legitimately ask inversely, How can intimate partners' sexual loving experience deepen and broaden the usefulness of the Evangelical Counsels for all people? How can they even be seen as related to the mission of fashioning a community of global proportions?

Erotic Obedience

Obedience as an adult virtue is out of vogue in societies of increasingly educated individuals. "Doing what you're told," except in some specific situations (e.g., in response to law enforcement and military command), is mostly a phrase of childhood. Being an "obedient child," thoughtlessly complying with another's wishes, doesn't give honor to one's own God-given adult mind. This is particularly true in the spiritual life. Embracing the responsibility of caring for one's own maturing spiritual life doesn't include conforming to the unexamined regulatory spiritual framework of somebody else.

Yet obedience has a long history as one of Christianity's central community-building virtues. Derived from the Latin words for "listening" (*audire*) and "to or toward" (*ob*), obedience essentially means "directional listening," making solid judgments about whom you will attend to for guidance and advice. The spiritual value of listening to the Spirit of God within one's heart was highly valued by early Christians. But Christian leaders soon noticed how difficult and confusing it can be to distinguish that inner voice from what a person inwardly wanted for oneself (e.g., Ananias and Sapphira, Acts 5:1–10). Making authentic decisions between the leading of God's Spirit and the well-rationalized ego needs of a given person who simply "wants his own way" continues as a perennial issue in the growing practice of spiritual direction.

The religious disconnect that occurs so frequently as Catholic children transition from idealistic childhood to the sexual torrents of early adolescence includes an ache for a maturing of their notion of obedience. At that time, to many young people approaching the whirlwinds of intimate relationships, elders they once followed eagerly and trusted for wisdom suddenly seem to known nothing about life at all. In order to honor the solid tradition of obedience as a spiritual practice, there is need for a mature spiritual understanding of that virtue that could be useful for sexual lovers, both youthful and maturing.

Essentially, obedience means taking seriously the heart and values of a trusted source of soul wisdom, traditionally a communal leader, for the development of your own spiritual excellence. In romantic love relationships, our current lover becomes one of those persons. A partner's view of us is always slanted somewhat by the pleasure-sharing intimate dynamics, making lovers completely unsuitable as spiritual directors, therapists, or pastors of one another. Yet a love partner functions as a witness to our life from an absolutely unique perspective that needs to be taken very seriously in making any significant spiritual decisions about ourselves. The unique perspective from a close-up lover can contribute exceptional feedback on just who we are and who we're coming to be. Even junior high girlfriends hold a power to influence the self-concept, identity, and future relationships of a boy, simply by the fresh, emotionally charged input they offer in response to what they see and hear from him in the fledgling self-disclosure of budding romance.

Mature obedience in intimate loving could be defined as *seriously considering, with both heart and mind, the core inner dialogue that someone you treasure carries on about you.* In other words, it means eliciting the content of your partner's perceptions of you as person and reflecting on it for your own benefit. His or her opinions, feelings, attitudes, and observations about you need not take precedence over your own self-appraisals, but they comprise some of the best data you have of coming to know and treasure your own person.

We are shaped as lovers largely by the clues we get from how our various partners see us and what they communicate about "how we are" as persons and as lovers. "Do I look fat in this" has come to humorously refer to the peril that feedback to a lover can contain. The brutal message of Elvis Presley's 1950s song "Hound Dog" has been felt by many of us in fledgling romance: "They said you was high class, but that was just a line. You ain't never caught a rabbit and you ain't no friend of mine."

The unique personality characteristics with which we emerge from our families of origin include complex "defenses" that work to keep our self-esteem positive while allowing our self-understanding to remain vague. When specific feedback slices through that defensive structure to describe us "in the moment," we get a variously welcomed opportunity to know ourselves a bit more accurately. A wife who uses words like "arrogant," "stubborn," "insensitive," and "stodgy" in a piqued fit of honesty may be unintentionally providing a spiritual opportunity to a husband big enough to take it seriously. Such authentic feedback is rarely provided by friends.

Much of the fruit of erotic listening is more subtle, however. One functional definition of intimacy would be *the sharing between persons, of their "internal dialogue"*—*that jumble of feelings, impressions, hopes, dreams, intuition, thinking, sensual experiences, and direct observations that makes up the human reverie.* When one person risks opening her inner dialogue to a person she loves, in a way that makes her vulnerable, the result is intimate connection. When that shared reverie is spoken about the present moment and the relationship itself, that closeness takes on its most intimate form.

The verbal soul flow of peaceful attentiveness that feeds the building of sexual passion and then sometimes follows orgasm in further sharing constitutes the essential food of ongoing sexual love. When you decide to take seriously the content of your lover's internal reverie about the relationship between you or about you specifically—your personality, decisions, habits, inclinations, "issues," faults, and virtues—you are engaging in the earthy virtue of "erotic obedience." That combination of humility, counsel, and reflective thought is a primary platform on which maturing love can be built.

What makes the erotic form of obedience unique is the character of the vulnerability brought by mutual reliance on one another for sensual pleasuring. To *keep on listening* to one another's souls over the years of a long-term relationship is a growth issue of major proportions. People change drastically over time, and if the soul flow between them is thin, lovers wake up one day out of touch with who they are to one another. Virtually everyone is challenged by continually developing this consistent listening aspect of romantic life. Paying attention to the impressions a lover has of you, without being totally imprisoned by that view to the exclusion of your own self-observations, cannot happen with an adolescent identity. It either grows with maturity or fails.

A mature understanding of obedience also includes spiritual sources other than your lover. The maturing person makes increasingly wiser decisions about to whom she listens carefully in order to gain self-insight and spiritual nurturance. People in religious leadership vary as much as any of us in the wisdom they have to offer about spiritual experience for the flourishing of our souls and the beauty of our lives. Those spiritual leaders who speak to your heart deserve careful listening. But specific leaders that seem overly interested in neatness of procedures or mere conformity to regulatory frameworks based on a concept of obedience as *compliance* may not know much at all about mature obedience as a spiritual way. Growth in the Evangelical Counsel of obedience for lovers benefits from careful discernment of the direction of your listening. One of those directions is always your cherished lover's heart.

Chastity: The Dance of Venus and Eros

In the sumptuous film *A Passage to India* (Columbia TriStar, 1984) set in 1928, Mrs. Moore muses, "Sometimes I think there's too much fuss made about marriage. Century after century of carnal embrace and we're still no closer to understanding one another." That may have been more true for centuries past than it is today. The twentieth century brought Freud, Kinsey, sexual liberation, feminism, marriage counseling, and vastly improved awareness of women's anatomy and physiology. We have much more knowledge with which to fashion understanding and wisdom regarding the sexual loving mystery.

The concept of chastity, for example, traditionally defined as "the virtue of purity in thought, word, and act," was taught more by infractions against it than as a positive virtue. A richer understanding of chastity can now be shaped by incorporating what has been learned about sexuality in the past hundred years and by uniting it with intimate love.

The Roman goddess Venus, associated with the Greek Aphrodite, had a reputation for being the most beautiful among beauties, highly absorbed in the sexuality of everyone she met, and quite "full of herself." Eros, on the other hand, was a most handsome male, known for causing people to abruptly intermingle by shooting them with golden arrows that compelled them to love. Descriptions like these led C. S. Lewis to compare *sex itself* to Venus and *sexual love* to Eros.[3] In the best of times and most fulfilled lives, Eros and Venus dance. Learning that dance and dancing it consistently would constitute twentieth-first-century chastity.

Unfortunately, the single word *chastity* is used to refer to at least three completely different life projects of growing virtue relative to sexual pleasure. Chastity differs substantially in the three traditionally diverse adult life situations— committed sexual loving (marriage), love seeking (single), and vowed celibacy. Experienced lovers, shaped in the crucible of intimacy, may offer life-building advice on all three.

Committed to Intimate Life

A colleague of mine once told me how, the night before, he had ventured where many men fear to tread. In the midst of a heated conversation with his wife he had confronted her in exasperation about their sexual frequency. He told her that for him to feel loved, he needed sex more often than had become their pattern. Experience had told him she was capable, and thus he lamented his observation that she simply wasn't willing as often and as energetically as he needed. Her retort stunned him—and me in his telling of it. "It sounds like you just want me to be your prostitute," she said.

How their views of marital chastity differed! Perhaps to her it meant investing in the relational intimacy so that sex would feel more natural and fun, less obligatory and burdensome. To him chastity meant her sensitivity to what would make him feel loved and intentionally investing, within reason, in whatever that was. No doubt to both of them, chastity in marriage meant fidelity to one another. But it also meant more than that to both of them—and in different directions. According to Kinsey, Ann Landers's readers, and most marriage counselors, their situation is actually quite typical. They simply became open about it that night.

In the light of the growing perspective of partnering spirituality, committed chastity could be redefined as *the persistent adventurous challenge and growing capacity to unite sex with love in everyday living throughout the life cycle.* For virtually all of us, the virtue of chastity is more about intentional loving than about controlling our passions, more about hitting the gas pedal than the brakes. Chastity does not mean prudery. In a weekly column, Andrew Greeley was once reacting to an official church document that warned against "unbridled passion" regarding marriage. The problem is more one of *"bridled* passion," he quipped. John Gottman, David Schnarch, and other marriage theorists continue to develop insight into the morass of emotional muck that builds in relationships, choking off affectionate comments, verbal validation, and gentle touching that make passionate sexual expression possible. Housing architecture of walls and doors evolved largely to promote privacy for the unique love-nurturing processes at home. Chastity for committed lovers is more a grassy field than a restricting barn.

Keeping love and sex together emerges as exponentially more difficult than *getting* them together, as 50 percent of married people discover on the way to divorce. Eros beckons indiscriminately, both to those seeking love and those already committed, and the grass can look quite green on the other side of the fence when you've encountered consistent stonewalling in a mate or made a mess of a treasured love. Chastity inevitably requires expending energy to resolve gnarly personality hurts and a continued learning of how to do so. Intimate chastity thrives on *imagination*, coupled with *courage* to continue engaging the loving mystery despite discouragement and the *generosity* necessary to nurture fun over a long period of time.

Chastity includes failure. Always. The real challenge of chastity is in learning to convey the love one feels, creatively, imaginatively, gently, consistently, expressively, passionately, and generously, in a wide variety of ways that fit the changing tastes of developing lives, simultaneously pleasing the other and oneself in mutual indulgence. No art is developed without failures, and the art of chastity is at least as complex as painting and composing music.

It must be noted that the challenge of chastity for committed lovers increases during times of unavailability of either partner. Mental or physical illness, injury, menopause, necessary absence, and times of conflict-generated learning prompt most lovers to think either of (1) infidelity, (2) violence, or (3) terminating the relationship. While some marriages realistically will not last, the virtue of chastity at those worst times needs to generate fortitude in trying all else before moving in any of those directions.

Single

Chastity for single adults may include more courageous flirting than is found in standard Catholic teaching and advice. The challenge of chastity is to involve yourself in personal relationships with people attractive to you while you continue to develop your personality in your current stage of life. If you are highly hormonally endowed, pleasuring yourself sexually is almost unavoidable. The wisdom that needs to grow in you is to keep that autoerotic aspect of your life from preoccupying you from the joys, challenges, and fulfillment of relational loving. What you learn about spontaneous emotional relating through enjoyable engagement with those who attract you will be far more important in long-term romance than any savvy you gain about specific sexual dynamics you might gain from letting sex get ahead of personally engaging relationships. As you experiment with the freedoms of spontaneous relating and allowing your emotions to have some play among the media plethora of enticing sexual images, reflect frequently on the notion that it is loving you seek, not fleeting pleasure.

And don't let yourself become too despondent if you find yourself attracted to people of your own sex. God loves you every bit as much as anybody else. And all of you, seek counsel from wise and trusted people. It is *your* life, but there truly are others who will offer useful perspectives without imposing them, if you can find them and if you ask. Certified spiritual directors and institutional chaplains are a good bet.

Celibate

Barely ten years after disclosing to a confessor my first experiences of autoeroticism at the age of fifteen, I ministered as a priest confessor at a cathedral parish where many priests came to confession. I soon found that many of my peers masturbated regularly, were somewhat ashamed of it, and had mostly rationalized it as sad failures in attempting to live a celibate life. The "reason" for remaining in an ostensibly celibate lifestyle while routinely failing in it was probably noble—to enable ministry to people for the glory of God. It took ten more years for me to decide at thirty-five that that approach to sexual arousal had no integrity for me.

By then, I had repeatedly seen firsthand what well-known long-term priest-editor Richard Ginder wrote later in his life in *Binding with Birars*, that most priests masturbate at least to some degree and variously either adapt to that practice as necessary human limitation or suffer guilt and pathology over the conflict it represents to a celibacy vow. Studies by priest-psychologists Richard Sipe[4] and Donald Cozzens[5] have further expanded on descriptions of how priests live out the celibate ideal and the price they—and sometimes their parishioners—pay.

If you're a committed celibate, I hope you have become clear on what celibate chastity actually means *to you*. Does it include habitual self-pleasuring to release sexual tension and keep you less relationally entangled for ministry work? Or is that way of living merely rationalized relational reticence, as it was for me? I now believe it is a solemn obligation for you to use consultation to find a healthy celibate expression not only for your own spiritual resilience but for the protection of men, women, and children who may be negatively influenced by repressive sex in would-be spiritual leaders. Learn ways to live a life with the mystery of sexual arousal that has integrity for you or take another path.

Poverty: Sabbath Space for Eros

Poverty is the Evangelical Counsel that is most clearly rooted in the Bible. One of Jesus' favorite themes was suggesting we develop a spiritually healthy attitude toward material acquisition. Stories about people such as Dives (Lk 16:19–31), who regretted never having helped the poor during his lifetime; the unjust debtor (Mt 18:23–35); the generous widow (widow's mite, Mk 12:42–43); and the difficulty of getting a camel through the eye of a needle (Mt 19:24) are sprinkled through his recorded preaching words. He valued teaching that life is about loving, not owning; caring, not acquiring; and community, not convenience. The material world is intended for enrichment of the spiritual rather than the human spirit's being meant to invest in incessant acquisition.

The value of poverty as owning little or nothing to promote openness to the promptings of the Spirit guiding your life emerges from Jesus' apparent love of the "*aniwim*," the "poorest of the poor." Unable to rely on material solidity, He saw the radically poor remaining open day after day to the providence of God in their lives. While a secular capitalistic world sees poverty as a pitied position in life rather than as a virtue, the beatitudes Jesus preached on the Mount laud the hungry and the thirsty as truly blessed and more likely to flourish spiritually than the rich. Well-developed traditions of Catholic history have regarded an attitude of poverty as core to true Christian living.

Among the exceptional champions of owning nothing for the sake of daily openness to the providence of God, a woman born Clare Scifi in 1194 stands tall. Now known as St. Clare of Assisi, foundress of the "Poor Clares" women's religious order, she dedicated herself to God at the age of eighteen under the leadership of St. Francis of Assisi and never left the house in which she did so, even to her death at age fifty-nine. She adamantly refused to own anything despite pressures to do so by bishops, kings, and the pope himself, who wanted her to accept donated property in order to perpetuate her huge religious following. The community of those inspired by her included several of her twenty-two blood siblings and her mother, after the death of her father. The Poor Clares worked for people at no charge, subsisting on what was placed in their opened hands at the end of the day.

Such a view of poverty would, of course, not work for everyone. Nor are many called or gifted for it. What indeed is the virtue of poverty for those finding their spiritual way in the context of sexual loving?

One of the old songs I remember blaring from the radio in my pre-TV childhood sported the refrain, *Oh we ain't got a barrel of money. Maybe we're ragged and funny. But we travel along, singin' a song, side by side.* Those words illustrate as well as any the virtue of partnering poverty—a lighthearted placing of love clearly and consistently above material worth. Often that shared attitude is found to be easy in early romance, making the virtue of poverty mostly a challenge of maturing intimacy.

Maturing sexual lovers, caring deeply about one another's welfare, are constantly learning to share all they have for the good of them both and any family for whom they may be responsible. The sharing requires relative agreement, a basic intuitively shared stance toward money and possessions. Major differences between partners regarding that attitude contribute to the pool of frictions that wear on them, while relative agreement on material ambition smoothes their way together. Couples can collude in greed, and they can sink in tandem material discouragement. But sharing what they have tends to inspire hope, as it does for those engaged in religious community for the good of all members.

I once sat across dinner with an experienced Wall Street broker who was expounding at length about making money on the stock market and the kinds of dedication to detail and intricacies of political maneuvering it requires. At one point I mused aloud about the quality of brokers' love lives, and without hesitation he said, "Terrible. Their *sex lives* maybe are not so bad at times. Money helps with that." But *love lives* eventually suffer and starve where money precedes them in value.

Soulful sharing between lovers about what to do with income and net worth shapes their attitudes and spiritual stance toward material value and the world community. As half material beings ourselves, we cannot escape the ubiquitous questions of how to use limited material resources to enhance enjoyment of one another, promote the welfare of offspring, and contribute to the world of disadvantaged strangers. That is the love-partnering face of the virtue of poverty, which could be redefined as *an ever-evolving attitude, stance, and capacity to make decisions about the material world that enhance our own human spirit, our relationships, and the spirit of the people and communities important to us.*

Besides what a healthy sense of poverty contributes to our own spiritual lives, it also nags us to see ourselves as part of a global community rather than an insular entity focused on "siloed" acquisition. Citizens of the coming world community will need a developed capacity for thrift in order to share a planet of limited resources in peace. Since there aren't enough resources for all to live in opulence, attentiveness to waste in everyday life will be—and already is—crucial.

It is extremely difficult to predict the shape of such thrifty attentiveness. But one can envision the need for habitual attentiveness to the use of water (especially heated water) at home as well as in public places like hotels, schools, and hospitals; preparing no more food than what is needed for this meal; driving small vehicles and only where necessary; recycling clothes that are modestly constructed; and building fuel-efficient homes without excessive luxury. In joyful communal living, thrift and simple comfort will supersede greed and extravagance, as the project of global sharing itself will feed the soul.

Notes

1. *Catechism of the Catholic Church: With Modifications from the Editio Typica*, First Image Books ed. (New York: Doubleday, 1995), no. 1974, 533.

2. *Catechism of the Catholic Church*, 262.

3. C. S. Lewis, *The Four Loves* (New York: Harcourt Brace Jovanovich, 1960), 139–43.

4. A. W. Richard Sipe, *Celibacy in Crisis: A Secret World Revisited* (New York: Brunner-Routledge, 2003).

5. Donald Cozzens, *Sacred Silence: Denial and the Crisis in the Church* (Collegeville, Minn.: Liturgical Press, 2002).

CHAPTER TEN

~

Eros and Social Spirituality

Our entire theological tradition is expressed in terms of mercy, which I define as the willingness to enter into the chaos of others.

—James F. Keenan, S.J.

When Jesus preached that "you will always have the poor with you but you will
not always have me" (Mk 14:7), he seems to have meant that efforts to eradicate poverty are overly optimistic but that what you do for them will benefit
both them and you. Assisting the unfortunate will feed your spirit and in a small
way make a contribution to all of humanity. The Latin root of the word "mercy"
is *merces*, which meant "reward." When mercy is shown, both the giver and the
receiver are naturally rewarded.

A component of Catholic tradition that gradually developed the positive
effect social action could have on individual spirituality was distilled into the
corporal and spiritual works of mercy. Together these fourteen suggestions of
merciful action to assist the pain of others comprise a Catholic "social spirituality." It too can be enhanced by imagining perspectives emergent from
lovers' reflections on how relational mercy grows in the context of their maturing intimate love.

The Corporal Works of Mercy

One of the traditional Catholic reasons for marriage was for the partners to be
"helpmates" to one another. In centuries before anyone but royalty enjoyed
much leisure time, it was especially important to make life a bit easier for each

other, to share the labor, allowing both to rest enough to survive. Can you imagine a Dark Ages life absorbed by incessant drudgery, punctuated with illness, disability, disease, and early death? Simple partnering mercy, born of empathy for one another's fatigue and discouragement, must have been some of the most heroic loving ever experienced.

Excellent lovers do naturally help one another. It is part of getting to know another person deeply. When you are able to tune in to the inner world of somebody because you love her, then you responsively involve yourself at least to some extent in whatever she is doing that is important to her. An energetic and sensitive romantic partner quickly learns to pick up on the words, thoughts, and actions of his "other" and is naturally inclined to assist in whatever projects are currently occupying her reverie, no matter how tiny or enormous. If that relationship continues for more than a few months, the inclination to assist the partner persists as well and moves more deeply into wanting to help with what she values in her core and hopes for in her life as a whole.

Christians have traditionally learned to enhance natural human altruism through such stories as read from the Gospel of Matthew (Mt 25: 31–46) for the feast of Christ the King. Jesus told about the final reckoning in which the criteria for entry into the kingdom was simply caring in basic ways for the "least of my brethren." It is summarized in that memorable phrase, "Whatever you do unto them, that you do unto me."

The preposition "unto," now used only colloquially in English, is key to this part of Matthew. It could be translated either "to" or "for." You either do things "for" them, or you are dong things "to" them. Whether you help or harm these "least," with active assistance, apathetic ignorance, or selfish exploitation, that is what it feels like you have done "to" or "for" Jesus. We go one way or the other regarding the pain of humanity. What we do in response to human suffering forms our attitude toward the cause of Jesus in the world, that is, the growth and evolution of love.

The seven elements of care of the "least of these" in that Matthew story eventually formed the basis for the traditional corporal works of mercy. They were so inspiring that they became the subject of medieval artists who depicted Christians caring in these specific ways for the painful aspects of the human condition. This art eventually found its way onto stained-glass church windows and then into catechisms as a short list of ways to care for humanity as part of the church's essential mission.

The corporal works of mercy survived the great reformation debates over "works versus grace," probably because they so obviously fit what people think of as "Christian"—charitable works performed gracefully or grace manifest through human caring activity. They prod simple actions of providing food, water, shelter, clothing, burial, and companionship during the nasty times of life.

Stated quite simply in their catechism form, they can be enriched in our minds if we think of all people as our lovers, our friends, or our children. Here are a few examples of how these works can be illustrated by noting their parallels in intimate loving and how they can take on a global perspective.

Feed the Hungry

An octogenarian visits his wife's nursing home to feed her every day. He was asked by a staff nurse why he continues to do that since her Alzheimer's disease has progressed to where she hasn't recognized him for almost two years. "She doesn't even know you're here," advised a nurse. "But *I* know," was his quiet reply. He knows he benefits spiritually from the simple act of feeding the one he has loved so long.

The ambivalence many of us feel about giving a dollar to the homeless person pandering near the stop sign comes from the conflict between our natural and Christian inclination to be generous on the one hand and our skepticism of how he'll use that dollar for his own destructive drinking on the other. If we could sit with him at McDonald's and share a "Happy Meal," wouldn't we be clearer on how it would positively affect our human spirit that day? Feeding the hungry in a concrete scenario affects us spiritually far more powerfully that doing so impersonally.

Despite the overorganized drawbacks of an international religious structure such as Catholicism, its priceless value is in its capacity to respond effectively in corporate ways that individuals can't, such as ameliorating major disasters that occur somewhere in the world every year. Catholic Relief Services[1] spends over a half billion dollars annually to feed and care for the hungry in the most difficult communal tragedies on the planet. As a sort of "international soup kitchen," it does what it can to fill major holes in political systems not yet adequately configured to feed the entire race.

But the concrete act of personally feeding someone you care about—stranger, friend, or lover—may remain a more powerful spiritual practice than contributing money, even to worthy causes.

Give Drink to the Thirsty

As a twenty-year-old college student, I watched my mother's last days in a small midwestern hospital. One of only two times I cried during her dying was watching her struggle to respond while my twenty-one-year-old nursing-student sister deftly lifted water to her lips through a glass straw. That scene, decades later, can still moisten my eyes. May I need to do the same for my wife someday?

When somebody you love is so frail that she cannot drink the fundamental fluid of life by herself and her husband does not know how to help with that in this specialized situation, giving drink to the thirsty offers a spiritually memorable reward. Our bodies can live no more than three days without water, and it is plentiful in most of the world. Where it is scarce, a major priority for world justice and charity arises in the need to invest in maintaining availability of at least minimal sources of water.

Clothe the Naked

Students at a South Puget Sound high school were shocked one morning when a teacher arrived to lead the class, clad only in her underwear. In the midst of a psychotic episode of her bipolar disease, she had eluded her husband's supervision in the morning after neglecting to take her medication for weeks. Responses from students ranged from uproarious laughter to dumfounded silence to the action of one boy who offered her his coat. "I sure would have done that for my girlfriend," he said.

There are clearly two fundamental reasons for clothes—to insulate from the elements and to preserve dignity of appearance. Both constitute corporal needs in that they require material resources to meet them. The American garage sale tradition grew up because people could sell for pennies what they couldn't give away because of basic human dignity. Our natural pride resists accepting charity unless we have to.

Today clothing the naked is as easy as contributing discarded clothes to a "goodwill" organization that will enhance the dignity of people poorer than we are. In doing so for people either nearby or distant, we can know we are providing bits of physical warmth to those in colder circumstances and personal warmth to our own souls.

Visit the Imprisoned

The final scene of the poignant movie *American Gigolo* (Paramount, 1979) redeems a self-absorbed, male prostitute. He was being framed for murder because he had so isolated himself in his narcissism that nobody cared what happened to him. In jail with no alibi for the night of the murder, after exhausting all efforts to find somebody to believe his innocence, he is visited by the only woman he's ever allowed himself to even begin loving. In just a few seconds, she manifests her love to him, vowing to abandon her future as a state senator's wife in order to shield him with a fictitious alibi that she was with him the night of the murder. He melts into transforming redemption from a life of exploitation as he genuinely responds to her love.

Estimates of the percentage of the two million incarcerated males in the United States who have been abused as boys run upwards of 80 percent. A history of abuse among the women inmates is frequently estimated at nearly 100 percent. Who knows the nature and the extent of the family and personality-formation deficit of those and even of the other 20 percent who admit to experiencing no such mistreatment as children?

Corrections reform is an enormous need and a low priority for either the funding or the creativity needed to care for prisoners effectively. Who will find ways to augment the personal strengths and fill the holes in the souls of these unfortunate violated violators? Spiritual care of any sophistication is largely unavailable to them. Who will visit the imprisoned, even in this country, let alone abroad? A former student of mine states that his ten years of volunteer jail ministry was some of the most difficult and yet satisfying experience of his life.

Shelter the Homeless

Home is the place for love. In a subplot of the classic movie *Doctor Zhivago* (MGM, 1965), Yuri and his wife suffer their comfortable home being taken over by revolutionaries in the Russian political change from monarchy to socialist republic. Accustomed to live well, they find themselves homeless, although temporarily, as his physician status dissolves. Many viewers remember the encroaching cold that threatens to again overtake the northern-province cabin that becomes their transitory home. Although not comparable to chronic homelessness, even temporary loss of a place to love transforms one's life.

When state hospitals altered their philosophy in the 1950s toward "community mental health" versus near-permanent hospitalization, the number of homeless mentally ill on the streets began to rise and in some places rises still. Disputes continue about how best to serve destitute people who disdain institutionalization yet remain dependent on society for the basic needs of life. Do free food at soup kitchens and lodging at shelters perpetuate the dependence of many who could make better lives for themselves with more focused partnering efforts by savvy and dedicated helpers? Could such exceptional helpers be found? Losing a home is a major grief issue, and it generally nestles among several other major losses that dot the lives and fill the minds of the homeless. These losses typically go ungrieved because of a lack of any appropriate forum for expression and working through the grief, further damaging their spiritual state. Material shelter is a prerequisite to soul care of the homeless. There is no easy way to combine both care of their bodies with care of their spirits, but the task is no less necessary.

The Hospitality Kitchen in Tacoma, Washington, serves nearly twenty thousand meals a month to the homeless and indigent. Other agencies offer temporary sleeping quarters for a night at a time, but The Kitchen, as it is called, provides a chaplain. Funded by a grant from a local foundation, a chaplain resident from the nearby hospital CPE program provides a spiritual presence among the two to three hundred people who gather there at any given time. What that chaplain student learns about life, humanity, and self during the residency year invariably catalyzes permanent changes in him or her, both professionally and personally.

Visit the Sick

The "in sickness and health" segment of the traditional marriage vows is easily passed over by the idealistic commitment attitudes of any wedding couple. It doesn't occur to us on that gloriously happiest day that we will both get sick (and sometimes seriously), eventually to death. On crisis days when the planned schedule instantly dissolves into critical need for sophisticated health care, the one person most adults want present with us is our current lover. Seeing that face, hearing that voice, feeling that hand, and knowing that quiet presence is on our side rivals the best medicine ever invented.

Professional chaplaincy evolved in the United States in the past century as response to the charge of caring for the spiritual needs of hospitalized people in the public institutions of a pluralistic society. There is thus today more professional ministry delivered to patients from a broad spiritual and psychological understanding of people available in North America than in most any other part of the world.

But visiting sick people that you know personally remains a most beautiful endeavor and can form one major strand of almost anyone's interpersonal spirituality. When people are facing the physical limitations of their bodies, their exposed vulnerability changes them for a brief window of time. They often become amenable to care, openly expressive of their emerging deeper values, and briefly willing to conversationally assess their lives differently. Visiting those you care about, with patience and listening interest, even without professional skills for pastoral dialogue, tends to feed the souls of both visitor and patient.

Bury the Dead

Near the end of the Academy Award–winning movie *Brokeback Mountain* (Focus Features, 2005), one gay lover has died, and his partner is disenfranchised from the funeral arrangements because of contemporary rejection of homosexual unions as deranged. He knows that his partner had wanted to have his ashes spread on the strikingly beautiful mountain on which they had managed to celebrate their mystifying and secretive relationship for twenty years. He vows to carry out his lover's last wish and is eventually able to do so only because his partner's oppressed mother comprehends the love that had grown between him and her deceased, rebellious son. Burying his dead lover as he had wanted to be buried becomes a major mission of this man's middle age, and having accomplished it, he can continue his life with a bit more peace and meaning.

The Old Testament credits Tobit with making a major contribution to Judaism through developing the custom of treating dead bodies with reverence by burying them rather than simply letting them rot (Tobit 1:17–20 and 2:7–8). It can require a little work to physically bury a person. There are many people whose hands don't fit that shovel because of age, gender, and physical limitations. Similarly, there are many who do not comprehend the importance of the symbolic specifics of reverential burial that add meaning to the grief of the bereaved.

In most countries there are helpers who make their contribution to the survivors through physically burying the corpse and, in some, actually mourning the dead. Assistance with food and child care for the bereaved are also common in many cultures. Sensitivity to the needs of people immediately after a major loss and offering to assist in creative ways, like all the previously mentioned corporal works, tend to enhance the souls of both griever and helper.

The "Good Samaritan" story, a classic of literature (Lk 10:30–37), teaches that the corporal works of mercy are neither pure charity nor pure justice. They are a combination of both. The spiritual benefit to the worker of these works arises from personally responding to the *spiritual* pains of people who are in concrete *physical* need situations. The question of who was right in the reformation about the true place of "works" in human spirituality is moot. Just as lovers privately care for each other body and soul, so are the public and global arenas places of potential spiritual growth for virtually anyone willing to actively manifest mercy to people when they really need it.

The Spiritual Works of Mercy

It is said that the greatest pains are not physical but felt in the inner world, not bodily but spiritual. If there is a hell, it is not a material place with everlasting fire but a spiritual place filled with regret, loneliness, longing, fear, and rage. Actual charity includes not only material help but also caring for the spiritual pain that life inevitably deals us all. As Muhammad, the Prophet and writer of the Quran, stated, "True charity remembers not only those in need who ask, but also those who are prevented by some reason from asking" (Sura 51:19).

Some of the Catholic traditions that developed over time to prod response to spiritual pain in others as gathered together in Catechisms are called the spiritual works of mercy. Their origin is not as clear as the corporal works in scripture and medieval art, but they have long been catechistically presented in conjunction with the corporal works as parallel.

Inner pain requires significantly more sophisticated helping skills to respond to than it does to "do things" for people materially. Practicing the spiritual works thus has benefited from the developments in psychology, counseling, and teaching that have taken place over the past century. Performing them well can be intricate. They can also be understood more fully by seeing them from perspectives informed by the complexities of intimate love.

Admonish the Sinner

For some people, confronting or correcting a person who is destructive to self or others is quite difficult. For some, it is way too easy.

Some loving partners refrain from even mentioning what disturbs them, annoys them, worries them, or hurts them about their mate's behavior. Thus breeds either quiet contempt or depression. The transactional analysis language of the 1970s called that "peace-at-all-costs" habit "saving stamps." In the days of collecting tiny coupons to be traded for appliances and other gifts, the metaphor implied that one could save up enough hurts for a good "quit," a divorce accompanied by a barrage of well-justified invectives. Instead of bringing attention to a lover's behavior that unsettles you, continuously saying nothing is more likely to wound than maintain a relationship.

Between other couples, however, one partner or the other seems all too ready to mention every flaw, slight, or peccadillo—incessantly. A storm is a beautiful thing, but constant storming would wear out all of us. Indeed, criminal convictions are way too easy in modern societies, where the cynical fad is to condemn people we don't know of major atrocities, at the mere suggestion of guilt. We seem to need only a sound byte of media implication to convict a politician, celebrity, clergyperson, or other public figure in our minds and our gossipy socializing.

Neither a pervasive reticence to address an issue of one's dissatisfaction nor an enthusiastic impulse to constantly criticize is what is meant by admonishing the sinner. Both in love and in the public forum, the need is to learn the art of confronting.

Derived from the Latin *con*, meaning "with," and *frons*, meaning "face," the word's best meaning is "to stand face to face willing to be honest." It is indeed an art, not learned by simply wanting to grasp it. Confronting a person combines insight, self-control, prudence, and fortitude in a moment-fitting expression of wisdom. Loving another over a period of time eventually will require some confrontation, and the better one learns the art, the more likely the love can continue.

One of the most vivid places confrontation can be observed is in excellent chemical dependency treatment programs. There addicted people find out that if everyone is nice to them by ignoring the consequences of their behavior on self and others, then after a wasted life, they will simply die. In such treatment settings you will find frequent confrontational encounters between people guaranteed to bring tears to your eyes. There you will deeply know the veracity of "you will know the truth and the truth will make your free" (Jn 8:32). There are times in all lives, too, when a major truth needs to be spoken in order for us to move ahead in development or comprehension of some aspect of our lives. Love at those times is what has been called "tough love" and what in Catholic tradition was "admonishing the sinner."

The Catholic Church leadership's role in admonishing or confronting globally has been weakened to wimpy by the leadership's centuries-old habit of image management—having to look like it never makes a mistake. Like any human entity, it has obviously made many mistakes that have been excruciatingly harmful to many souls. That is indeed excusable when one considers that what is known now could not be known then. Can we legitimately accuse a woman for not confronting her father of incest when she was six? Can we blame Newton for knowing nothing about quantum mechanics or Freud for missing the oppression of women? Catholic leadership's historic condemnations of receiving interest on money, Galileo's astute science, the hell-damning evil of masturbation, or even perhaps its rigidity on artificial birth regulation could be seen as excusable in the light of evolutionary theory.

Yet learning the art of pastoral confrontation remains a huge project for religious leaders everywhere. To practice the mercy of admonishing the sinner with both solidity and grace would require a bishop to concretely face an accused pedophile, meet personally with an admitted gay priest, and stand with specific women regarding their felt call to ordination rather than deal with these gnarly issues politically and legally. Sorting out who is indeed a "sinner" and who is a lover of God and humanity is too intricate for mere regulatory functioning to be either effective or loving.

Instruct the Ignorant
One good teacher is a treasure in any life, and teaching makes a major contribution to the communal growth of humanity. An excellent teacher is well worth a six-figure annual income. Parker Palmer has written eloquently about the process of teaching as assisting the human growth of students while offering cognitive input that fits their life situation and felt needs.[2] As Dan Rather once said, "The dream begins with a teacher who believes in you, who tugs and pushes and leads you to the next plateau, sometimes poking you with a sharp stick called 'truth.'"[3]

In some Asian cultures the *sense*, or teacher, is the most revered of all professionals. Whether as a psychology professor, an English-as-second-language teacher, a catechist, or merely a grandpa who fishes, engaging in teaching another human being something new that delights and shows him or her a tiny fraction of the beauty of creation is a deeply spiritual endeavor.

How do lovers learn the nitty-gritty aspects of physically and emotionally loving one another? Does it all "come naturally"? Or do partners learn together from experience and mistakes, with gentle honesty, subtle suggestion, and a lighthearted attitude? Do they not teach one another what is pleasing and what they know from autoeroticism, imaginative fantasy, and previous relationships?

The "magisterium" or teaching authority of the Catholic Church could benefit from that loving, teacher-and-learner-learning-together dynamism. Heavy-handed dogmatism is quickly disclosed as obnoxious between lovers and is no more palatable in today's ecclesiastical milieu. Too much feigned certitude that implies there are no mysteries of life will no longer convince anyone. Only collaborative sharing of both thinking and experience will serve to identify best directions in engaging the day's primary manifestations of life's basic mysteries.

What to teach and how to do it as a world mission are questions that need the collective wisdom of the church as a whole, not the narrow judgment of a few ensconced and relatively inexperienced leaders, well meaning as they may be. The first pope recognized this, as seen from his words in the first "encyclical" (1 Pt 2:5): "Let yourselves be built into a spiritual house to be a holy priesthood to offer spiritual sacrifices acceptable to God through Jesus Christ." The idea of the "priesthood of all believers" was picked up and amplified by Vatican II to teach the spiritual mission as a responsibility of the entire believing community.[4]

It seems wise to remember, however, that skirmishing about the political scene will never be as spiritually enriching as actually teaching another human being something that will improve life for that individual or the community as a whole. Concretely teaching another human being is indeed its own reward.

Counsel the Doubtful

As one who grew up with a pervasive habit of self-doubt, I know the balm from a mentor who encourages with solid but gentle assurance that I am either on the right track or veering off into oblivion. My wife has often been that person for me, as many long-term lovers are for one another. Some savvy, mature men I have admired were there at the right time too.

Counseling and psychotherapy have grown into sophisticated professions that assist people with all manner of painful life situations as well as mental illnesses that remain intractable and painfully life-wasteful without it. At the same time, whenever you offer encouragement, support, and even asked-for advice to a sibling or friend, you include yourself in the huge mass of humanity that cares enough to assist one another in difficult times.

As a friend or sibling trying to help with personal issues, the challenge is often to avoid patronizing and pedantic tones while daring enough closeness to actually meet in the place of pain. If you are drowning, do you want somebody yelling instructions from a hilltop on how to swim? Or maybe somebody demonstrating strokes from the shoreline? Or would you not prefer somebody who will enter the water with you, contributing the immediate emergency support you need, perhaps including hauling you to shallow water so you can stand on your own. Maybe you will then learn to swim with new motivation on a calmer day. Helping others personally is indeed an art, not practiced that well even by many professionals.

Pronouncements from on high aren't trusted much anymore, and there is little prospect they ever will be again. We are in a new, partnering age that seeks caring consultation and comment when requested. Religious leadership will need to adapt to that eventuality with new approaches that reverence the astuteness and integrity of ordinary people seeking to fashion the best lives they can for themselves.

Comfort the Sorrowful

Virtually all of us have been devastated by falling hopelessly in love with somebody who never did love us. The perennial popularity of country songs witnesses to the fact that at one time or another we've all had our guts torn out by unrequited love. That is why the lovelorn are a major theme in literature of many cultures. Too unpredictable and fickle to be at all fair, eros invariably causes some of the worst pain we ever know.

Such pain of heart-wrenching rejection is only one occasion for major grief in every life, however. We all hurt deeply from losses. Excellent lovers have learned how to comfort one another on some level regarding the unsettling events of an ordinary day. Yet we can struggle to find the words, sentiments, and patient listening our partners crave after a major life loss such as death of a parent, child, sibling, or friend. When the soul-searing disasters that accost every life occur, love partners seek to be there for one another, to offer comfort rather than advice. While men and women may struggle to be personally communicative of their mutual support in ways that will actually meet the situation, the romantic bond continually invites them to learn the skills it takes.

What was once meant by the spiritual work of mercy of "comforting the sorrowful" may now be called "grief work" or "grief support" of people after a major loss. Here is a need in our society that would boggle the mind if it would show itself physically. Any group taken off the street at any time of day and brought to a well-facilitated grief group would show tears in at least half its members when the reminiscences would be shared and the sad stories told.

If you have ever attended a support group for people who have had one of their own offspring die as children, you have seen the anger and sadness enkindled by how people respond, in well meaning but clueless and insensitive ways, to those who have experienced a child's death. Despite the fact that we all have endured our own painful losses, many of us still tend to treat each other's grief with insipid epithets and cowardly avoidance. Allowing and even facilitating people's grief expression—crying, reminiscing, and sharing of memories—is an art that could be learned by many but currently is comprehended by only a few. Parish funeral committees functioning as servers of funeral dinners are felt by the grieving as wonderfully supportive and caring. One day, however, they will be more, truly assisting the grief process of anyone seeking comfort from loss. In some parishes they are such already today.

On a global level the Catholic Church leadership continues to develop a major presence in the midst of the disasters of the world. It seeks to combine personal presence and acknowledgment of the depth of the pain, with the material support that is organized by many aid organizations. But what is rewarding to individual spiritual lives remains the face-to-face presence, condolences, quiet listening to reminiscence, and honest expressions of sorrow regarding the losses of the sad.

Bear Wrongs Patiently

Love partners gradually learn to put up with a bundle of each other's idiosyncrasies. If we try to correct them all, we find that we do nothing but criticize and eventually nag. Besides, it is frequently embarrassing to find that our partner's foolish way worked better than ours anyway. We similarly accept and make peace with many of the small hurts that have happened between us. Even most true wrongs can rather easily be simply born patiently when the hurt comes from one you deeply love.

The spiritual suggestion that we learn to "bear wrongs patiently" is founded on the underlying belief that very few wrongs done by one human being to another are done intentionally. Other than mentally ill or deeply wounded perpetrators, almost all personal pain inflicted by people to one another is done in the effort to improve something. Reacting to the offense rather than reflectively responding is of little use. The "patience" advised is necessary to reflect on motive, attitude, and your own previous hurts that may be oversensitizing you to this particular wound.

Catholic leadership has traditionally born wrongs to itself patiently— sometimes maybe too patiently. A passive stance gives the impression of insensitivity to the complaint being made. Even though the grievance may be distorted in verbal and emotional attacks against the church leadership, those in power need significant maturity to respond with both patience and cogent attempts to clarify the misunderstanding.

Forgive All Injuries

What man has not been bowled over by his wife's raising, in an argument today, a time that he hurt her years earlier and that he had completely forgotten? Most of us men come to believe that we "let go" of hurts more easily than our women and are mystified by what to make of that. Maybe we don't really forgive more easily, we just don't let the hurts go as deep. But some men too save up their anger that one day erupts in violence.

Resentment is probably as significant a spiritual problem as guilt. The term *resentment* is derived from the Latin *re*, meaning "again," and *sentio*, meaning "to feel." So resentment refers to that human experience in which we "feel again and again and again" hurtful events of the past. While guilt blames self for past stinky actions, resentment blames somebody else for theirs and will not let go. Resentment is "frozen anger" and is related to self-pity. The perverse logic seems to say, "Since anybody treated me that badly back then, I clearly deserve a little sympathy now, even if it keeps me stuck."

On a global level, resentments actually erode the spirits of entire generations of peoples. Huge segments of the world population culturally carry resentments for atrocities of the past that sap their creative and self-development energies— Arabs, Jews, Native Americans, African Americans, women everywhere, colonized Africans, Japanese Americans, crusaded Mohammedans, persecuted Mormons, Palestinians—how long could this list become? Some people habitually enkindle past wrongs, while others learn to "forgive all injuries."

In chemical dependence treatment facilities of excellence, healing resentments is crucial work because they can easily be used to rationalize returning to the addiction. It is the universal experience of counselors skilled at the art of helping resentments heal, that enormous positive energy emerges from the resentful who are able to let go of past hurts. Euphoria almost always follows.

An evolutionary view of the universe allows less resentment and regret. If the world and humanity are evolving, then less blame is appropriate for what was done in previous generations. Evolution is a painful and slow process, moving gradually but relentlessly toward a better world. Apologies and reparations are necessary and can be extremely healing, though they may never feel adequate. Forgiving is an essential path on the way to world community.

Pray for the Living and the Dead

A common successful movie theme or subtheme is the active presence of a lover from "beyond" after he or she has died. *Ghost* (Paramount, 1990), *Signs* (Buena Vista, 2002), and *The Sixth Sense* (Buena Vista, 1999) are fairly recent examples. They convey the heartwarming ideal that intimate love is eternal, continuing to exist after physical death. The notion that lovers can return to help out their still-living partners in beautifully caring ways edifies romance, deepens love, and reduces the fear of losing one another in death.

The Catholic tradition of the "communion of saints" supports this "deceased lover" theme. The basic meaning of that traditional belief is that after death we remain cognizant of the happenings in the lives of the people we have loved.

We pray *for* them because we never know for sure about the reality of the beyond and the possible existence of a "purgatory." We may find ourselves talking *to* them because they may be able to help us here as "spirit guides."

A pastoral student of mine who practiced the Baha'i faith was a semiretired physician seeking late-life fulfillment through clinical supervision and training as a professional chaplain. As I got to know him quite well, he once took me and my three children fishing on an old ramshackle boat he had devised himself. When I met him again some years later, he showed me a dog-eared scrap of paper in his copy of the writings of Baha' Uhla that he read every day. It contained several names, and I noticed that among them were the names of my children. He said he had prayed for them every day since he met them.

Praying soulfully for the living at the very least stirs up love we have for people important to us and at best invites the Spirit to help them both generally and in the specific ways about which we passionately implore. If nothing else, my friend's praying for my children warmed my heart and those of my children when I told them. Indeed, it probably fed him spiritually to strive silently for the improvement of their lives.

Praying for the dead at the least gives expression to our grief and possibly even contributes to their well-being in some way we will only know after our own dying. The monsignor pastor of Sacred Heart Church in Waterloo, Iowa, when I grew up, started all his funeral sermons proclaiming these words based loosely on a passage from the Biblical Book of Maccabees: "It is a holy and a wholesome thought to pray for the souls of the dead" (2 Mc 12:43–46). Although some Christian denominations would dispute the spiritual value of doing so, it is difficult now for me to see harm in endearing prayers for deceased people we truly loved during life, such as my mother, my father, all my grandparents and numerous relatives, friends, colleagues, and mentors. And whether there is a purgatory or not, it is easy to see the spiritual benefit of this spiritual work of mercy for those of us who pray from the soul in their memory.

Notes

1. Compare Catholic Relief Services at www.crs.org.

2. Parker Palmer, *The Courage to Teach: Exploring the Inner Landscape of a Teacher's Life* (Hoboken, N.J.: Jossey-Bass, 1997).

3. Dan Rather, www.quotegarden.com/teachers.html.

4. Austin Flannery, ed., *Vatican Council II: The Conciliar and Post Conciliar Documents, Decree on the Ministry and Life of Priests.* (Northport, N.Y.: Costello, 1975), 864.

~

CHAPTER ELEVEN

Eros and Catholic Social Teaching

It is only by feeling your love that the poor will forgive you for your gifts of bread.

—St. Vincent de Paul

Most of what transpires between people in human communication flows between faces. Despite the "information age" of electronic data exchange, face-to-face and here-and-now experiences continue as what deeply feeds the soul and expands interpersonal connectedness. What matters most to the soul is the intangible beauty of human emotion, most of which is accessible to one another only through the subtle movements of the three hundred muscles of the face. Even the poor aren't satisfied by material gifts. They crave love.

Since the 1950s when television began bringing us easier face-to-face contact with distant strangers, we have been more boldly confronted with the pain of specific people that boldly shows chronic global unfairness. Seeing the faces and life situations of one another on a global scale stabs at our ingrained impersonalization of distant cultures and worldviews far different from ours. It is becoming more difficult to generalize, rationalize, and intellectualize our responses to the enormity of human pain that continues to cover the earth. At the same time, it becomes more difficult to hide our ignoring of it.

The intimate communication of romantic relationships, as they take on a more partnering flavor, can be used as a window into the social inequalities that have always characterized humanity. We learn from the faces of our lovers the sensitivity necessary to fashion and maintain relationships of depth and beauty. We are beginning to learn from the faces of strangers a similar sensitivity to deep-rooted injustice. Outrage at concrete unfairness in our intimate relationships is gradually uncovering an outrage at social injustice that has lain beneath the surface of our consciousness for a long time. Evolution is revealing a new energy toward global equality that is burgeoning and waiting for the leadership it will take to mobilize our resources toward wider communal fairness.

The urge to make a contribution to humanity is a natural phenomenon inherent in human development. Usually before middle age, there arises in people a growing inclination to make some contribution beyond oneself. Developmental psychologist Erik Erikson named this tendency "generativity" as a drive to leave a legacy to the next generation or to the human race as a whole.[1]

Couples too experience an inclination to augment the two-person nature of their partnering to include sharing a child, having a family, involvement in school or church, volunteer work, or some form of social advocacy. Caring well for oneself and a lover catalyzes a next step in spiritual maturity that expands influence beyond the immediate to the communal and even to global evolution.

More recent Catholic tradition includes a specific cluster of teachings that enhances this natural impetus toward broad communal improvement. In spiritual terms, the word *social* in "social justice," "social action," and "social gospel" refers to more than being sociable, as in openly being friendly at parties and around the neighborhood. It means, in effect, *expending some of one's own life energy to improve the lives and living conditions of strangers in need*. Most of what is called Christian social teaching has emerged in the nineteenth and twentieth centuries in response to biblical foundations and a growing cognizance of the world-level needs of the less fortunate, most of whom, through evolving electronic media, we have only recently begun to really see.

What is it that slows to inactivity sixty-five million U.S. Catholics from vigorously voicing social values in a society that appears incognizant of responsibilities to the world community as a whole? Is it our own self-absorbed "acquiring" mode, our skimpy fortitude against being thought idealistic and naive, our lassitude waiting for inspired and energetic altruism in our leaders, or a combination of all three? Could we be energized a bit by looking through the window of our romantic love lives for wisdom about caring beyond ourselves?

Professors of Catholic social teaching have distilled from papal publications and bishops' conferences several concepts that together convey the essence of their message. Each concept makes intuitive sense. But they mean even more when enriched by perspectives from intimate loving. The quotes that follow each section in this chapter—except for the last two—are taken from statements of the U.S. Catholic Bishops.[2] The last two are from the Task Force on Catholic Social Teaching and Catholic Education.[3]

Human Dignity

The classic love story always includes a portrayal of how falling in love immediately distinguishes one human being as profoundly special, from the mass of several billion others. Suddenly one person stands out in our minds forever. We quickly decide beyond logic to invest in whatever relationship might be possible there. Even a feeble octogenarian is likely to be outraged and become physically protective when the dignity of his wife is seriously threatened.

A high school boy or girl who is genuinely in love hurts deeply, though perhaps secretly, when the one that makes his or her heart throb is publicly embarrassed, humiliated, or otherwise treated badly. Nothing energizes the virtue of fortitude in a person more than the need to stand with a treasured partner when human dignity is at stake. Some would even die for that value. Suddenly realizing the immense dignity of one specific person makes it a bit easier to grasp the value of pervasive human dignity beyond the philosophical level.

While it may be easy to agree cognitively that all human beings possess profound dignity, when one person becomes exceptional to one's heart, flesh comes on the skeleton of that concept. The extraordinary beauty of one person can become a model of all people. A lover can reflect personally that "someone possibly loves that stranger as much as I love this woman. I chose this one, or she chose me, or Transcendent Reality chose us both to partner with one another. But indeed all other people are exquisite too and deserve to be treated as nobility. Everybody may be somebody's true love." It was precisely the dignity of human beings that motivated Mother Theresa of Calcutta to begin adding dignity to the dying process of impoverished street people rather than look the other way as they expired in the gutter by the hundreds. She taught by her life, as Jesus did, that we are called to treat them all with profound respect and to fight for any of them to be treated with reverence no matter the circumstances.

Nobody at all deserves to be ignored when in genuine pain. While it continues to be necessary, at this point in evolution, to invest in military forces to protect those we love from potential violent attack, the degree to which that investment is necessary remains a matter of debate. Impersonalizing "the insurgents" and the "terrorists" precludes understanding them and the gnarly question, "What pain has resulted in the character disorder damage that fuels their hate?" Self-protection alone brings nobody closer to collaborative living. Intimate loving combines self-care with interpersonal vulnerability, defenses with openness, softness with assertiveness. Governments and ecclesiastical organizations need more of the "speak softly" to augment the pervasive "carry a big stick" of Harry Truman's famous adage.

> Every human being is created in the image of God and redeemed by Jesus Christ, and therefore is invaluable and worthy of respect as a member of the human family. (*Reflections*, 1)

Respect for Human Life

In Catholic social teaching, respect for all human life is related to human dignity, promoting the belief that people must value what has inherent dignity and dignify what has inherent value. The fact that many of us lovers would die for our partners if necessary (or even if requested) suggests in an experiential way that all human life is invaluable. Watching the love of your life die confirms that belief. Widows, both men and women,[4] are reminded of it by the phenomenon of grief for the rest of their lives.

The Christian conviction that each life has immeasurable worth was consolidated in the fifth commandment of the Decalogue (Dt 5) and reiterated by the words of Jesus (e.g., Lk 12:5–7). Highly valuing all human life doesn't answer all questions about such gnarly ethics issues as euthanasia, abortion, "just wars," and birth regulation. In fact, it complicates them. This is especially true when male theologians without wives have taken the concept of "life" mechanically.

Whose life is to be valued more highly in situations that involve, for example, a mother and a child or her future children? Unfortunately, little if any consultation with lovers in situations that actually face the tough questions in real life has taken place when fashioning regulatory principles. When it has, the wisdom garnered has been ignored and the project abandoned for political purposes rather than honored as movement of the spirit of God among us.[5] As a result, Catholics routinely make their own decisions about issues related to sexuality, believing the leadership has little understanding of the pain, intricacies, and lifelong implications involved. A great deal is left to future developments of "structures of counsel" with those who have been intricately involved in the worst of life situations when applying ethics principles and fashioning the best advice available.

> Every person, from the moment of conception to natural death, has inherent dignity and a right to life consistent with that dignity. (*Reflections*, 1–2)

Association

The principle of association is a somewhat awkward way of saying that people are essentially relational and that aspect of being human should be honored by governments and other leaders. The powerful energy that pulls the individual uniqueness of one person toward that of his lover into an exquisitely intimate "we" confirms that humans are created for togetherness at least as much as for individual excellence. Most of us are wired to be partners and to the continual learning and growth that call implies. Reproduction is creatively arranged so that as many as possible of us will be *born* of loving liaisons, *formed* in the communal context of a family, *inspired* to join lives in intimate loving partnerships, and *moved to procreate* at some point and share ourselves with the next generation in creativity and parenting. The entire life cycle naturally features close relationships. That aspect of our makeup must be honored by leaders, ecclesiastical as well as political.

What then of people of the same sex who constitutionally experience the love of eros for one another? Promiscuous gays that flaunt their orientation in flamboyant ways disgust many of us by making public what is sacredly private. But are they more disturbing than those obnoxious heterosexuals who similarly act out in nonverbal rebellious display of their freedom to love where and when they wish? Where does the right to choose one's associates end? Eventually, societies will decide in structures of authentic consultation who deserves discrimination for their relationships, if anyone, and who does not and what, if any, values are worth that discrimination. This principle of association ought to be a partial guide to what is just among members of a race that is essentially relational.

> [O]ur tradition proclaims that the person is not only sacred but also social. How we organize our society—in economics and politics, in law and policy—directly affects human dignity and the capacity of individuals to grow in community. (*Reflections*, 4)

Participation

Only in the twentieth century did the notion of egalitarian love relationships begin to flourish. In partnering, which is becoming an intimacy ideal, both parties are understood to have equal rights to participate in any significant decision made regarding the relationship between them. What once was taken for granted as a male's right to decide now is immediately disclosed as oppressive (pressured against), suppressive (pressured from above), unfair, obnoxious, and ultimately depressive (pressed down) of both sides. Not only is it unfair for one so-called partner to make all major decisions for both, but it also stunts the growth of the one with power. Those who dominate miss the natural human development available in engaging the mystery of intimate partnering. Even if one member refuses to participate in joint responsibilities, she does not by that act nullify her right to participate in them in the future. The principle of participation teaches that she cannot, in justice, be prevented from doing so.

Just as maturing lovers know they each have a right to participate in major decisions regarding their relationship as well as a right to hold separate opinions, so too societies need to take shape in negotiating dissent without oppression. If we don't participate in the messiness of cooking with various foods and spices, we don't benefit fully from the exquisite diversity of human cultures. Fully participative partners will be the leaders in the unforeseeable models of preserving the beauty of distinct ethnic cultures while gradually building collaboration between them.

Democracy is not the only form of participative governance, but some of us believe it is the best known and most successful so far. It proposes that decisions that seriously affect the common good be made by a wide selection of qualified representatives while all people are freely able to participate in making them. The idealism of that statement blares to the point of disgust, however, in face of the reality of democratic leaders' everywhere jousting, maneuvering, bullying, and otherwise acting for their own good rather than the benefit of the community. A preponderance of political leaders that will sustain a global view beyond nationalism and addictions to power, money, and the limelight is yet to assemble.

Can any form of *ecclesiastical* governance refuse to honor this principle of participation as well? While the Catholic Church is not a democracy and democracy may not lend itself well to organizations with a spiritual mission, *participation* in any form of governance is essential. Unfortunately, established leaders can so easily interpret participation to mean enthusiastic validation of the party line or status quo. As between lovers, so in governance, protest and violence arise when participation has not been adequate in decision making.

As women have begun to find their voices in the past fifty years, insisting on greater and equal participation in intimate, regulatory, and organizational decision making, are they being included fairly in church decisions? The Catholic bishops have applied the principle of participation mostly to employment situations. Does it not equally apply to ecclesial leadership? This principle applies in a special way to conditions associated with work.

> Work is more than a way to make a living; it is a form of continuing participation in God's creation. If the dignity of work is to be protected, then the basic rights of workers must be respected—the right to productive work, to decent and fair wages, to organize and join unions, to private property, and to economic initiative. (*Reflections*, 5)

Preferential Treatment of the Poor and Vulnerable

When my wife needed knee surgery, we were fortunate enough to have good health insurance. Eventually, three trips to the operating table cost in excess of $140,000, and our policy paid most of that. Does everyone receive that kind of care? What happens to the homeless person and those millions without insurance who exhibit the same diagnosis with gnarly complications?

On the other hand, the wide strain of dependence in society does not serve the communal health of society well. We've known for decades what it takes to give ourselves the best chances at health—diet, exercise, rest, hygiene, moderating alcohol, and above all refraining from nicotine. Is it fair to society to ignore your own responsibility for health maintenance and then expect to be taken care of when the body fails? My wife and I had the insurance partially because we had both made contributions to health care over several decades. Should a person who could have worked but never did be allowed to reap the benefits of society without contributing to them?

This social principle assumes that it is likely that such an unfortunate person has been impoverished from causes beyond his control. Society has an obligation over the course of evolutionary progress, to develop structures that discern carefully who can receive resources that are not plentiful enough for all to consume. At the same time, all individuals have an obligation to contribute to society and not merely benefit from it. Decision makers need to consider as one component of the mix that the poor are indeed disadvantaged and deserve breaks despite any past or projected future failures to contribute.

When one love partner is sick, lives with a debilitating condition, or otherwise develops special financial needs, that person commands special attention. Similarly, the needs of a person in a particularly vulnerable life situation call for particular care that pushes him or her ahead in the line for resources. It may be awkward, annoying, and discouraging to deal with special circumstances of health care or employment debilitation, but lovers almost routinely find the tolerance and flexibility to identify the best solutions despite negative emotions. This is done only because a primary focus in the decision making is the soul and the eminent worth of the partner, mixed with the consideration of material resources.

Similarly, the "needy" of society require special consideration. Pervasive dependence of some people ought not to be fostered because it is actually damaging to both individual and communal wellness. Distinguishing true need from exploitation ought never to be taken for granted, and "structures of counsel" are already gaining acceptance in hospital ethics committees that are forced to make such complex decisions daily. The open and authentic consultation that characterizes their decision making constitutes a leading force in teaching and continually learning how to implement the principle of preferential treatment of the poor.

> In a society marred by deepening divisions between rich and poor, our tradition recalls the story of the last judgment (Mt. 25:31–46) and instructs us to put the needs of the poor and vulnerable first. (*Sharing Catholic Social Teaching*)

Solidarity

Could one lover eat while his partner had no food? Could a couple who are in love share a sumptuous meal while watching two other lovers languish from three days without eating? That is difficult to picture. Even in the idealistic, otherworld of their romantic infatuation, the almost immediate identification of the fortunate pair of lovers with the unfortunate would generate empathy that would not allow them to sit in full view of such outrageous inequality.

As electronic media and population growth bring humanity ever closer together, we will become increasingly unable to simply "not see" brothers and sisters in dire need. The principle of solidarity suggests that we bring that day forward to intentionally see them more clearly now for our own spiritual good as well as for the sake of basic justice. As twentieth-century union activist Eugene Debs once wrote,

> "Am I my brother's keeper?" . . . Yes, I am my brother's keeper. I am under a moral obligation to him that is inspired, not by any maudlin sentimentality but by the higher duty I owe myself. What would you think me if I were capable of seating myself at a table and gorging myself with food and saw about me the children of my fellow beings starving to death.[6]

The principle of solidarity refers to the fact that all humans are related by blood and have a natural inclination to unite in supportive collaboration so that all have enough. This principle will not allow some to cling, either stubbornly or cluelessly, to excessive comfort and the power needed to maintain it. The globalization of love progresses, century after century, toward a communal inclusion of agape love that we can now only vaguely envision. Our cooperation with the loving energy that is slowly producing that widespread unity is a component of virtually everyone's spirituality.

Catholic social teaching proclaims that we are our brothers' and sisters' keepers, wherever they live. We are one human family. . . . Learning to practice the virtue of solidarity means learning that "loving our neighbor" has global dimensions in an interdependent world. (*Reflections*, 5)

Stewardship

My first purchase of life insurance took place only when I was thirty-eight, recently married, and finding that my wife was pregnant with our daughter. However well we have managed material resources before we fall in love, doing so becomes more complicated and more realistic after. Caring for one another in the concreteness of everyday living casts new light on how lovers manage resources. Being challenged daily by *sharing* a checkbook, a home, a vehicle, a child, bodily health, and a shared future makes our spirituality more practical. Early in a relationship the concern of material assets recedes into the background like everything else as the romantic emotions rage. Then a re-visioning of the future begins to form in lovers' minds, a mixture of dreaming and strategizing how their combined potential resources can support a rich partnered life. In relationships of domination, exploitation, or manipulative "gold digging," that fantasy is eventually disclosed as decidedly more one-sided. Stewardship becomes skewed.

Stewardship of creation as a whole can become more real, too, on reflection of our spiritual role in it. Collectively we know we are responsible for the environment—croplands, grasslands, woodlands, air, water, minerals, petroleum, and other natural resources. But our own behavior in such simple daily decisions as turning off unused lights, minimizing waste, recycling, and curtailing water use is a basic spiritual issue. Even though the actual saving in a single such decision is minuscule, caring frugally for our own living space helps internalize the principle of stewardship of creation. The ways we use our natural endowment in sexual partnering and our material resources in the nesting that supports it remind us how we've been given gifts from which the human community can benefit and are thus charged with responsibility to invest in caring for them wisely.

The Catholic tradition insists that we show our respect for the Creator by our stewardship of creation. (*Reflections*, 6)

Subsidiary Justice

This Catholic social teaching says in effect that no higher level of organization should perform any function that can be handled efficiently and effectively at a lower level of organization by persons who, individually or in groups, are closer to the problems as they are lived out in daily life. Nobody, including the state, for example, has a right to regulate how a couple intimately communicates or makes love, except when the good of society is obviously at risk, as in situations of domestic violence. Organizations have a duty to strive to protect society from destructive individual behavior but also the obligation to honor boundary limitations on how organizational forces influence intimate relationships.

When applied to ecclesiastical corporations, this principle, as the documents of Vatican II stated, is confusing. It states that the bottom line of decisions on family size belongs to a couple and their consciences while continuing to insist that those consciences must be conformed to the teaching authority of the Church,[7] a corporate group who has admittedly not experienced the concrete spiritual struggle about which it is teaching. Has the Church's magisterium violated the principle of subsidiary justice in so vigorously condemning some forms of birth regulation without authentic input from those living intimately close to the conundrum? Isn't that decision an intimate one to be made by the people involved, optimally in consultation with other similarly affected couples? Is there really communal danger that justifies the corporate prohibition? Where is the spiritual perspective that honors intimate loving as a primary component of the decision?

Similarly, does disallowing gays and lesbians the benefits of matrimony violate the principle of subsidiary justice? Who can say that gay people living together for extended periods of time are not in love? Who can justly assume that their marriage would damage society more than failed heterosexual marriages do? The practice of proclaiming teachings void of consultation with maturing lovers on official teachings that bind those lovers in their intimate relationships calls for careful examination relative to the principle of subsidiary justice.

> This principle deals chiefly with "the responsibilities and limits of government, and the essential roles of voluntary associations. ("Summary")

Human Equality

Alfred Adler noted about love relationships that

> if each partner is to be more interested in the other partner than in himself there must be equality. If there is to be so intimate a devotion, neither partner can feel subdued nor over-shadowed. Equality is only possible if both partners have this attitude. It should be the effort of each to ease and enrich the life of the other. In this way each is safe. Each feels that he is worthwhile; each feels that he is needed.[8]

Can a chatty woman and a pondering man partner in enduring intimate love? Did the marriage last between the protesting social activist wife and the Minneapolis police chief husband whose employees had to arrest her? Or, much closer to home, can romance between a high-testosterone man and a low-libido woman transmute into life partnership? All three answers are "of course." Differences are the very grist of the intimate loving mill. Dealing with the myriad ways in which partners differ when the romantic blindness recedes, as it inevitably must, challenges people to see the richness of diversity above the inherent conflicts it causes. Even the way males and females are naturally configured bodily is quite convincing that differences among people are Creator-intended as a component of the immensely diverse spiritual milieu in which we mature.

Treating equals equally is one way of defining justice, which was understood classically as "rendering to all persons their due." Underlying the notion of equality is the simple principle of fairness. One of the earliest ethical stirrings felt in a developing toddler is gaining a sense of what is "fair" and what is not. But that intuitive impression of justice is about "me." The new awareness of justice born of intimate engagement is about equality between me and others. All of us lovers bring with us into romance the habitual focus on our own getting our due. Sometimes that self-absorption condemns the relationship to resentful feelings of having been duped into believing this was love "for me." At other times it pulls lovers into a maturing sense of the equality of all people everywhere.

> Equality of all persons comes from their essential dignity. . . . While differences in talents are a part of God's plan, social and cultural discrimination in fundamental rights . . . are not compatible with God's design. ("Summary," 23–24)

Common Good

When a punky college senior sits at your kitchen table touting anarchy "because I can," renouncing allegiance to the country that birthed and supports him, it is difficult to remain silent in respect of your daughter who is his friend. Blatant self-absorbed adolescence turns ugly when it endures into adulthood. The quieter, more slickly rationalized and surreptitious self-interest of wealthy corporate exploiters has lasted longer, found more success, and caused much more damage to the common good than a self-absorbed twenty-something pseudoanarchist.

In the 2004 presidential election, one minor candidate, John Kucinich, was suggesting that a single member be added to the presidential cabinet whose responsibility would be to consider and advocate for every issue from the point of view of its implications for world peace. That member's job would be to lead efforts at promoting the conditions of world societies necessary for all individual humans to reach their unique, full potential and to realize their enormous dignity. What an idea! Bring on the day when that is the bottom-line job of *every* member of the cabinet.

If lovers don't naturally consider their decisions based on the common good of both of them, something is askew in their partnering. "Two shall become one flesh" (Gn 2:24; Mk 10:8; Eph 5:31) clearly trumpets the birth of a uniquely sacred "we." Catholic social teaching extends that "we-ness" to the broader society with reference to the individual's responsibility to consider the good of society when deciding to litter, waste, "shoot up," steal, or foster dependence. When one man's ox is gored, we all go a little more hungry. As William J. Byron, S.J., has written,

> Today, in an age of global interdependence, the principle of the common good points to the need for international structures that can promote the just development of the human family across regional and national lines.[9]

> The common good is understood as the social conditions that allow people to reach their full human potential and to realize their human dignity. ("Summary," 25)

Notes

1. Erik Erikson, "Childhood and Society," in *Eight Ages of Man* (New York: Norton, 1963), 266–68.

2. U.S. Catholic Bishops, *Sharing Catholic Social Teaching: Challenges and Directions, Reflections of the U.S. Catholic Bishops*, June 19, 1998, www.usccb.org/sdwp/projects/socialteaching/socialteaching.htm.

3. "Summary Report of the Task Force on Catholic Social Teaching and Catholic Education," U.S. Catholic Conference, Washington, DC. http://www.usccb.org/sdwp/projects/socialteaching/socialteaching.htm.

4. The Latin roots of "widow," *di-videre*, means "to divide," and *viduus* means "bereft, void," without reference to gender.

5. Op. cit., Ginder, pp. 105–114. Cf. also Garry Wills, op. cit. pp. 86–103.

6. Eugene Debs, *The Appeal to Reason* (speech delivered in Girard, Kansas, May 23, 1908).

7. Austin Flannery, ed., *Vatican Council II: The Conciliar and Post Conciliar Documents. Gaudium et Spes* (Northport, N.Y.: Costello, 1975), 954.

8. Op. cit., Adler, p. 125.

9. William J. Byron, S.J., "Ten Building Blocks of Catholic Social Teaching," *America*, October 31, 1998.

CHAPTER TWELVE

~

Intimate Love and the Leader's Own Spirituality

> . . . the presiding elder must have an impeccable character . . . a man who manages his own family well, and brings his children up to be well behaved: how can a man who does not understand how to manage his own family have responsibility for the church of God?
>
> —1 Timothy 3:2–5

Any of the ten thousand professional hospital chaplains across the United States and Canada could recount from a given day's work at least two or three stories of patients who, sometime during their lives, have been deeply hurt by the religious organizations intended to spiritually help them. The structures of a faith group failed them at a point in their lives when they needed it most. The resultant buried mixture of festering hurt, buried resentment, nagging confusion, unasked questions, and sometimes desperation during crisis could be called *religious wounding*. It surfaces during the most challenging times of life, and it is responsible in large part for the disenchantment of millions of "former Catholics" as well as for the splintering of Christianity into hundreds of denominations over at least nine centuries.

Much of this exacerbation of the human individual struggle with mystery is due to the confusion between *spiritual* leadership and *corporate* leadership. Few people are gifted as both *priests* and *kings*, called to spiritual leadership as well as administrative leadership excellence. Fewer still exhibit the capacity to vision as *prophets* while at the same time being administrators and helping to sanctify people's lives. A new kind of collaboration among variously gifted individual leaders needs to develop and can benefit from a closer look at the cooperative intimacy of lovers.

What people seek from churches is a source of effective spiritual experience that is grounded in coherent wisdom on meeting the complexities of life's primary mysteries. We want insight and practice that will bolster our engagement of life, love, illness, tragedy, death, parenting, and all the other confounding issues that shape our most significant days. Confidence that somebody appreciates the intricacies of coping with and enjoying the greatest life questions and is leading from a place of integrated wisdom and authentic integrity compels us to join a religious community and involve ourselves for the sake of ultimate values.

Many corporate leaders, however, tend to *assume* the entire meaning-oriented missions of their organizations and limit themselves to the work of making an organization thrive by observable standards. Designing and maintaining management structures, administrating funds, satisfying regulatory frameworks, and negotiating personnel issues are enough to occupy any chief executive officer. Integrating values into an organization's culture may fly high on a few corporate flagpoles, but it seldom occupies much strategizing time in the top leadership boardroom.

When the organization that is being administrated is a religious one, however, unique challenges fill managers' days. Spiritual growth, the very aspect of management that is generally neglected by administration, is what the religious organization is about. If churches are intended to promote the spiritual enrichment of individuals and communities, then ecclesiastical leaders need to be experts in the spiritual life as well as skilled in corporate administration. At one point early in the U.S. Catholic Church's 2002 pedophile tempests, Boston's Cardinal Bernard Law was quoted as publicly complaining that the media were treating him as a corporate official rather than a spiritual leader. He seemed unaware that diocesan Catholics and outside observers alike expect him to be both and had seen him function mostly as skilled at administration and law.

From this point of view, the personal spirituality of religious leaders becomes crucial. Like any aspect of the spiritual life, the maturity, excellence, and resilience of a person's human spirit are only partially visible. But they *are* partially visible. Public figures, such as potential leaders of the world's most powerful nations and the world's largest religions, ought to be scrutinized not only for their policies, plans, and promises but also for the unique flavor with which they demonstrate their own acquisition of virtue. Too many people depend too much on their influence on the quality of our lives for us to neglect our impressions of the souls of our primary leaders. Can they lead the planet toward world community unless they comprehend unity as their mission and demonstrate significant progress on their own, acquiring the basic virtues that will allow that mission to succeed?

What are those essential virtues? Who will decide what developed capacities for meeting life's mysteries ought to be central in the evaluation of potential leaders? Some answers to those questions have already been found. They were etched and hewn during Christianity's first thousand years. Distilled from historical wrangling during the second thousand years, for Catechism students of the twentieth century, they have been the substance of the early chapters of this book.

While the decision making that takes place in intimate loving relationships differs significantly from that of ecclesiastical administration, still they are similar in that they exist to promote human love, individual spiritual growth, and communal unity. Clearly there are ways to acquire the virtues of Christian spiritual excellence other than engaging the natural intimate loving crucible. Integrative endeavors such as personal psychotherapy, facilitated grief work, spiritual direction, and the traditional methods of Catholic practice can be successful.

But we have shown how reflection on the intimacy arena can illuminate many of those Catholic traditions. What can be learned by ecclesiologists, bishops, and other Catholic leaders from looking at the parallels between corporate leadership of a religious organization and the intimate loving arena inherent in sexual humanity? What personal characteristics or Christian virtues should be visible on close examination in assessing the quality of spiritual leadership that a potential official might provide an organization? What does the spiritual perspective on intimate love have to contribute to forming partial answers to these questions?

Leaders' Personal Spirituality

In intimate relationships, logic recedes in favor of the senses and intuition. In sorting potential romantic partners, making a checklist of what a person wants or needs in a lover may be useful but only if she is willing to ignore it when her heart begins to throb. We go about romantic sorting by allowing ourselves to be affected by our emotional impressions and only then employing the mind with prudence and temperance. The heart leads, and the mind guides. The heart of a leader needs to be reasonably well integrated with his or her mind.

Since we are part body and part spirit, the characteristics of lovers that will enable relational development are all partially observable. In love-seeking, the natural inclination is to operate first on the impressions enkindled inside us by being in the presence of any potential lover. In romantic relationships we can "make sure" of nothing and "control" nothing, but we engage this mystery from the perspective of how any given prospective partner affects us first emotionally and then reflectively. We can ask ourselves, "How do I feel in her presence?" and only then, "What do I think about her?"

Likewise, we need to take our intuitive impressions of spiritual leaders very seriously, using both heart and head, wondering about the ways they include their emotions in their thinking and deciding. How do they talk about the way an issue affects them personally? Since they are people first and leaders second, how we regard them to be as spiritual people becomes a central question. Such intuitive apprehension does not do well through electronic media, which seek mostly sensational sound bytes.

Consider, for example, a group of potential spiritual leaders. How do they stand in terms of the fruits of the Spirit? Since it is not likely that they can lead other people spiritually without having at least begun to engage life's primary mysteries, the impressions one receives when in their presence can be partially measured by the yardstick of traditionally identified virtues: joy, charity, peace, and so on.

Regarding joy, for example, is there joie de vivre that shows in their approach to life? Or do they seem just short of overwhelmed by the seriousness of life and heaviness of religious values? Does their positive attitude feel contrived for the press? What actually delights them? Does that delight show publicly at times, or is it always hidden away? What makes them laugh? Do their followers ever see them articulating their life fulfillment in ways that don't feel like public relations hype?

These questions will seem overly personal to leaders who have hidden themselves from the human intimacy with which most people invest a significant portion of their spiritual lives. Yet aren't they necessary?

Isn't it also necessary that they exhibit charity, kindness, gentleness, benignity, and patience in ways that seem genuine? Is there a graciousness of generosity in the way they relationally spend their time with people amidst administrative demands. Or does one sense a time-stinginess that seems intent on conserving energy for esoteric matters that are always "more important"?

In carefully observing them, can one see a general kindness and attentiveness to what others need in the here and now of everyday life? Do they convey a personal peacefulness despite what seem to be constant interruptions? Have they mastered a capacity to adapt to the slower or more rapid pace of another person? Do they maintain a basic simplicity of goodness in their life outlook and work? Is there a gentleness about their words and movements that dispels impressions of cynicism, hostility, or resentment, festering underneath a political facade?

Regarding trustfulness, is there discernable a deep and pervasive belief in the goodness of humanity and the world *as it is* that supersedes habits of grave suspicion that life and religion are basically quite grim and even scary? Can they articulate their own values fairly clearly? Are they generally able to exhibit restraint and personal disclosure in openly balancing their own passionate beliefs and convictions with the diversity of values of the people around them?

Using traditional Catholic concepts of spiritual excellence can be a first step in evaluating potential corporate leaders of religious organizations. Those leading the spiritual growth of populations diverse in gender, culture, ethnic heritage, and sexual orientation will need to be thoroughly familiar with their own spiritual strengths and weaknesses and be articulate about them without feeling like they are "blowing their own horn" or exhibiting contrived modesty.

Further assessment efforts could be designed around the cardinal virtues and even the seven deadly lifestyles. But since spiritual maturity is naturally required of spiritual leaders, the gifts of the Spirit may provide the best windows from which to view the quality of spirit and soul of those selected to guide us.

Genuine *Counsel*: The Conviction, the Skill, and the Use

One of the most difficult aspects of raising children as a single parent is lack of a confidant with whom to discuss vexing parental decisions as they arise. The natural inclination to swap experiences and opinions with at least one other person when facing the uncontrollable aspects of life prods use of the gift of counsel. Ordinary issues include "Are we doing the best we can with the checkbook?" "What should we do about Jimmy's math avoidance?" Should we have somebody assess Ginni's pronunciation?" "How do we artfully address Kim's thievery?" and "Why do you think Jen was crying on her way home from school today?"

Partners in whom intimate love is flourishing use each other for sounding boards as well as for deciding many things together. Openly discussing decisions on such natural issues as nesting, financial pressures, career development, friendships, and extended family relationships are excellent examples of using the gift of counsel. As a regular practice, it lends a sliver of confidence in arriving at the best way to handle the daily questions that beset us all.

Leaders, especially in spiritual organizations, need this kind of open discussion about their own best decisions regarding complicated and pivotal issues. But the skills of using counsel with integrity do not come easy. They are learned with courage in an arena of rich personal feedback that requires trust and open vulnerability in order to actually benefit from the insight of others. One never learns the art of consultation simply by speaking positively about it. Having a diocesan committee of "counselors" whose role is to confirm the leaders own inclinations—an "old boys' club" of sorts—will not promote growth of the gift of counsel. In the 2000 book *Papal Sin: Structures of Deceit*,[1] active Catholic history professor Garry Wills has outlined in very scholarly ways how political agendas, consistently refusing widespread consultative input, have badly influenced Catholic Church organization and doctrine over much of its life.

In the past century, however, a great deal of progress has been made in exploring people's inner processes and interpersonal dynamics. Some of that learning, if it were embraced by leaders, could be helpful in healing the results of endemic political maneuvering. It could thus improve the ways Catholic leadership functions.

As an essential component of professional practice, consultation has been highly developed in such circles as *clinical pastoral education*, in which the clinical method of learning is designed to take a close look at the functional effectiveness of ministry efforts. Using a small group of peer ministers diverse in age, faith group, gender, and ethnicity, it facilitates open peer validation and critique among the group members. In a concentrated process over a few months, pastoral caregivers learn a great deal about how to consult each other with integrity as well as some ways they have habitually tended to avoid such practical honesty.[2]

In the mid-1920s when Freud was the rage and his methods were changing the ways society looked at relationships, groups of clergy familiarizing themselves with depth psychology began forming to collaborate intimately in looking clinically at the personal aspects of their ministry. Forty years later those groups organized themselves into the Association for Clinical Pastoral Education, formally committing themselves to the mission of combining theology and the behavioral sciences in continually improving pastoral care. Essentially they had devised a small group use of the gift of counsel, laying aside the pursuit of dogmatic, absolute truth for the sake of asking what specific hurting people actually need and how best to provide it.

That group of academically and clinically trained educators continues practicing and teaching skills for consultation in clinical settings through some three hundred programs across the United States and Canada. They commit themselves to a professional life of continual counsel and dedication to looking closely at one's personal reverie as it influences helping relationships. They have developed what is probably the finest arena for the learning of the gift of counsel ever devised.

Organizational leaders desperately need to acquire the skill of counsel and a measure of dedication to it as a way of life in order to assist them in monitoring their own ego processes and political pressures—the internal and external distortions that tend to derail their objectivity and inclusiveness in spiritual leadership. The way in which autoeroticism continues to be officially forbidden and yet informally condoned, for example, twists the minds of preachers and teachers to present facades when authenticity is crucial to spiritual care effectiveness. Such indirect operations as partially hidden agendas, rationalized actions, indirect maneuvering, and coercive pressures of overcontrol are not spiritually healthy for either leaders or members. All person-oriented ministers need a forum for close examination in processes of open consultation.

The word "consultation" is derived from the Latin *con*, meaning "with," and *sultare*, meaning "to strike." Those who openly consult "strike together" on a question or issue that needs addressing and has no obvious best solution. Hospital ethics committees are an example of the professional use of consultation. They began to develop in the 1980s for consultation by physicians regarding complex medical situations that have no obvious best intervention. Usually including experienced professionals such as nurses, a social worker, a chaplain, and sometimes family members, they proceed with commonly accepted principles in a consultative way that imposes no decision beforehand. The process requires openness to the power of what Christians might call the working of the Spirit of God among them as they authentically ask good questions with the intent of finding the direction that best fits the patient and the situation.

As a second example, I have been involved a few times in a Quaker tradition called the "Clearness Committee." Several Friends members are all invited by the seeker, who organizes the event for his or her own benefit. They sit in a circle and agree to treat the seeker with the persistent gentle attitude they might maintain toward a wounded bird lying in their palms. The seeker puts to them the current question of his or her life for which he or she has requested the meeting. The group members then only ask questions, offering no advice and confronting one another gently if they sense attempts to steer the seeker in a particular direction. I found the power of such groups to be incredible and challenging to the core. The seeker makes his or her own decision in his or her own time, and the members may or may not ever hear the resolution.

Structures of consultation are desperately needed by the Catholic Church leadership. No doubt bishops talk over their organizational decisions with one another and with well-chosen diocesan "consultors." But some focused training in the art of including one's deeper reverie in the consultative process, using professional, confidential clinical supervisors, would benefit the leadership skills of most Catholic spiritual leaders. In addition, in a world church filled with gifted, educated, dedicated, and faithful members, a much broader and deeper practice of consultation is necessary now than in centuries when the education level of laypersons was limited. Theologically expanded and deepened use of consultation would respect the Vatican II theme that the Spirit guides the entire Church, not merely its leadership.[3]

The secret and infamous Pontifical Commission on birth control formed by Pope Paul VI in the mid-1960s invited a variety of key experienced people to seriously discuss the question and write a report for his consideration. But when the decisions seemed to be going counter to the conclusions he sought, apparently for political image, he rejected their report and recommendations. Catholic Church leadership needs to find the courage and humility to gain competence in using consultation broadly, authentically, skillfully, and effectively, and then do so comprehensively and consistently.

The results would be astounding. The spiritual discernment power of consultation is truly awesome. The phrases "two heads are better than one" and Jesus' words "Wherever two or more are gathered together in my name, there am I in the midst of them" (Mt 18:20) emerge not merely as high-sounding phrases but also as functionally true. Consultation could form the backbone of a "political compass" for making decisions on a global level that take seriously the spiritual nature of ecclesiastical leadership work rather than imprisoning it in a mere political view.

Dominican ecclesiologist John Markey, O.P., has suggested a model of church that would indeed use communal consultation on a regular basis in every diocese as well as in Rome.[4] There would be a "Vatican Council" annually and a diocesan synod meeting under every bishop seeking to effectively use the gifts and charisms of people in the diocese and parish rather than blithely ignoring, merely controlling, and fearfully regulating them.

Meanwhile, we can live to develop the humility, prudence, courage, and articulation of our own opinions and spiritual needs in preparation for the coming time when faith of leaders will grow to allow their trusting the Spirit of God that continually and tirelessly wafts among us.

Understanding and Organizing Individual Charisms

The old phrase "well endowed" said with a gleam in the eye refers more to physical attributes of a young woman than the financial resources of a university. Recognizing the primary features of one's body, having it validated by others in ways that are personal rather than insulting, coming to cherish it as it is rather than how one wishes it to be, and learning to use it in sharing love constitutes a path toward loving excellence. Maturing intimate love is based on learning to discover and use one's natural endowment to love another human being as much as oneself.

The teaching of Catholic tradition is that the gifts we all receive from the Creator, physical and personal, are intended to enrich our lives, enhance the life of others, and make a contribution to society as a whole. As Thoreau once quipped, "The gifts of Heaven are never quite gratuitous."[5] St. Paul enthusiastically honored the particularity of human gifts given for the good of community in Ephesians: "The gifts he gave were that some would be apostles, some prophets, some evangelists, some pastors and teachers, to equip the saints for the work of ministry, for building up the body of Christ, until all of us come to the unity of the faith and of the knowledge of the Son of God, to maturity, to the measure of the full stature of Christ" (Eph 4:10–12). That these diverse gifts were to work together for the same communal purposes he made clear in First Corinthians: "Now there are varieties of gifts, but the same Spirit; and there are varieties of services, but the same Lord; and there are varieties of activities, but it is the same God who activates all of them in everyone" (1 Cor 12:4–6).

The Spirit of God seems to activate our gifts through a combination of factors. Diverse gifts need leadership to organize them communally. In the best of cases, a *call* from within combines with *intentional effort* to develop the gift, *validation* of it by at least one elder who recognizes and communicates delight in it, and an organizational leader who *authorizes its use* in communal care. If any element of that scenario is missing, the gift languishes in disuse.

It will never be known how many greatly gifted lectors, singers, teachers, and youth role models never find their gifts or have them recognized by key leaders who are preoccupied with management, finances, and regulation. One of the greatest gifts any leader can possess is the motivated ability to recognize personal gifts and prod them into communal use. That ability requires a clear understanding of Christianity's global mission, the maturity to work with the messiness of orchestrating charisms rather than managing for neatness, and the capacity to convey understanding in the moment of an individual's gift, honoring it into spiritual care use. That process doesn't progress far without the leader's significant demonstration of the spiritual gift of understanding.

Knowledge: Of Oneself and of Humanity's Unfolding Discoveries

There are two kinds of knowledge a spiritual leader must constantly seek: significant discoveries humanity makes about the world and increasing familiarity with the ever-unfolding mystery of that leader's own person. Knowledge, as the gift of the Spirit that compels us to courageously "encounter the new," prompts us all to continually learn. For leaders it also calls for that growing knowledge to be used for the benefit of humankind.

The powerful concept of the "natural law" in Catholic tradition created and maintained the illusion that the world is "set." It implied that one can determine from an established understanding of "how people are" clear notions of what the Creator intended in a given creation or process. In reference to sexuality, for example, observation of anatomy indicated to the men in positions of academic and ecclesiastical leadership that simultaneous orgasm with the penis in the vagina was natural and therefore mandated as standard. If conception was not possible, there was sin. They were thinking only with penis experience in an age when that was all they could know.

But human understanding is evolving, even if one concludes that the universe is not. Can a realistic understanding of "natural law" ignore new knowledge of women's experience and its implications for human love? Will Pope Benedict XVI's first encyclical, *Deus Caritas Est*, show the way to bringing unfolding understandings of psychology, anatomy, and physiology into deliberations on issues of sexual morality?

Lovers everywhere already wonder why Catholic leadership can honor artificial human influence on all other natural processes and exclude them regarding sexual love. Artificial alimentation, hydration, breathing, and augmentation of sight, hearing, and mobility are promoted as enhancing human living, while limiting birth for the sake of loving relationships must be seen as sinful. Including the spirituality of intimate loving as a major component in discussions about such issues would likely have considerable healing effect on people's confidence in Catholic spiritual leadership, if not on improved regulation.

While history can be a great teacher, leaders preoccupied with it are like drivers looking only through the rearview mirror. The only responsible way for spiritual leaders to function is to take humanity's constant flow of new discoveries into consideration as they make key decisions about how to nurture the human spirit, including the flourishing of intimate love. As Jerome Bruner, twentieth-century psychologist and educator, wrote, "Surely knowledge of the natural world, knowledge of the human condition, knowledge of the nature and dynamics of society, knowledge of the past so that one may use it in experiencing the present and aspiring to the future—all of these, it would seem reasonable to suppose, are essential to an educated man."[6]

The spiritual gift of knowledge would also include ever-increasing self knowledge too. Lovers who mature learn about themselves anew over and over again. Who we are as our lives unfold—as persons, as lovers, as spouses, as parents, as midlifers, as menopausal partners, as retirees, and as disabled aged—is intimately discovered together through the continual renewing personal exchange of intimate sharing. Leaders of all kinds are likewise called to continually learn more about their own person as they proceed through the life cycle. That will not happen in isolation.

Devotion to Partnering Piety

While increasing knowledge and understanding, gained partly through the practice of open counsel, are essential to potential ecclesiastical leaders, devotion to loving relationships stands underneath them all. As St. Paul wrote, "Knowledge puffs up, but love builds up" (1 Cor 8:1). Loving specific people in personal ways is indispensable for anyone leading a spiritual organization, especially one built on the primacy of love.

In a thriving suburban Seattle parish, a series of pastoral leaders, over a period of twenty-two years, had developed a marriage and family ministry that included twenty-one different programs to enhance intimate loving and parenting relationships. Hundreds of couples were involved in leading and benefiting from that ministry, clearly one of the finest in the country. The fact that a new pastor was able to fire the longtime developer of that ministry in a matter of weeks could not detract from the numbers of families that had grown and flourished in the communal education, healing, and nurturing that took place there over those two decades.

If intimate relationships hold a primary place in the spiritual lives of most people worldwide, then leaders who recognize that fact and work to foster partnering spirituality are heroic at this stage of evolution. Authentic consultation that included parish couples would likely have taught that new pastor a great deal about everyday spirituality if he had allowed it. As the contemporary hymn suggests, when called to be leaders, we commit ourselves to hold God's people in our hearts.[7] That hymn could continue, "I will not hold the organizational structure as primary in my heart, nor keep the intimate loving people merely on my mind. I will allow my heart to be affected by what seems to be feeding people spiritually, and invest in the Spirit of God that is moving there."

Leadership styles based on control no longer promote spiritual growth in people any more than intimate loving can stand a controlling partner. Spirituality by its nature features vulnerability and humility in the face of mystery. Controlling efforts are as effective in the spiritual realm as they are in facing the wind, the sea, and the sky. As partnering becomes more and more the way of progress in the world, leaders will need to embrace that new paradigm and promote it.

Perhaps the days of powerful emphasis on overly specific dogma as the leading force in providing the direction of religious organizations are nearing their end. To the "common person" those days are virtually over already. It is clear by now to many Catholics that accurately defining the ultimate truth in detail is as likely as analyzing a smile, measuring the antics of a son, or regulating tears of a grandma. In a hospital ministry there are increasingly more patients who express the attitude that "well, we all worship the same God anyway" because overpondering the complexities of doctrinal jousting beleaguers their souls at a time when they need concrete spiritual help.

As a theology student in the 1960s, I knew that courses called "aesthetic theology" and "spiritual theology" were quite minor, even peripheral, as branches of the master's degree curriculum. They were low-credit courses taught in a final year, outlining the Christian virtues, some saints' lives, and an overview of traditional monastic methods of spiritual practice.

With the rise of functional spirituality, however, that is, *paying attention to the unique ways human beings effectively feed their souls*, spiritual and aesthetic theology are gaining ground. Perhaps they will one day stand tall beside systematic, sacramental, and biblical theology. Isn't the purpose of religion to feed the human spirit, using whatever perspectives and practices are effective in edifying and developing human souls while honoring and promoting community in diversity? Integration of these theological perspectives is only beginning.

A basic artistic principle asserts that "form follows function." In essence, in designing and decorating homes, it teaches, "Figure out what you want a room to be and what you hope it will do for you and then fashion, decorate, and furnish it accordingly." Aesthetic theology emphasizes what is beautiful in human personality and unfolding lives, transcending the moral view of what is evil in human living. Spiritual theology, along with pastoral theology, teaches historical and creative suggestions about how to actively aspire to those ideals. Indeed, isn't that the practical spiritual wisdom the majority of maturing persons seek in order to care for their own souls? Sincere seekers emphasize what gives us meaning, purpose, and life satisfaction and de-emphasize the rest. Scary as it may be to systematic theologians, it is time the richness of the spiritual view of the sexual mystery is taken seriously by all of Catholic theology.

Intimate loving can provide some insight into both the spiritual and the systematic branches of theology and some hints at how leadership can fashion a usable religious organization to foster human excellence. The elusiveness of absolute truth along with the human need to impose it on everyone else has caused enough wars, confusion, and splintering of Christianity. Whatever regulatory framework eventually emerges to guide committed Catholics' life decisions and daily practice will need to make sense to practitioners and be experienced as reasonably effective by members. If intimate loving offers any indication, it will need to highly honor the unique gifts and limitations, wide diversity, natural altruism, autonomy, erotic energy, need for trusted consultation, and hunger for meaning inherent in the human person.

Regulatory Wisdom

Enormous knowledge on most any topic, available in libraries and on the Internet, can be incorporated by anyone who earnestly seeks it. Wisdom, however, is much more elusive and rare. What to do with knowledge, even when one understands it, is a matter of wise application to actual situations, problems, and planning. As William Cowper wrote,

> Knowledge, a rude unprofitable mass,
> The mere materials with which wisdom builds,
> Till smoothed and squared and fitted to its place,
> Does but encumber whom it seems to enrich.

Knowledge is proud that he has learned so much;
Wisdom is humble that he knows no more.[8]

—William Cowper (1731–1800), British poet

Mystery does not do well under expressions of excessive certainty, heavy-handed management, and regulation in general. Intimate love, for example, recedes in the face of coercion. As a man cannot write a play with a pistol aimed at his head or a woman cannot become sexually aroused in the face of violence, so too spiritual excellence does not flourish in the face of fear-provoking regulatory threats. Making abstinence from meat on Fridays a mortal sin never made much sense to the spiritually mature, though some of us still practice it today as a weekly spiritual discipline and communal symbol of the sufferings of Christ. Current regulations on the permanence of marriage do little or nothing to feed the love between partners. Any regulatory action regarding the spiritual life needs considerable wisdom to not exceed the limits of certainty about what actually feeds the soul.

Finding a balance of law that will on the one hand protect from the chaos of unmanageable erotic energy while on the other hand allow the play of intimate loving to flourish has been a challenge since the first efforts at devising legal frameworks around the eighteenth century B.C. Hammurabi and Moses were two legal geniuses who struggled with making laws strong enough to provide guidance and protection, while Jesus and Luther were two priests who suffered from overregulation of life's mysteries. The answer to the need for this balance is not in the perfection of legal systems. It lies in the wise application of legal principles and the oversight that sees law always in service of love and the human spirit.

Lovers know this intuitively. Overcontrol of a partner may be possible in some relationships but only at the expense of intimacy. Control by rules in romance works about as well as drawing that line down the middle of the car seat shared with your brother when you were eight. So too the ministry work of leaders in societies made up of people of sophisticated intelligence and persistent spiritual thirst is not so much to regulate and administrate but to preach, inspire, consult, counsel, console, and lead spiritual practices that inform, sustain, and guide excellence of decisions for the good of individuals and the community as a whole.

In the comprehensive consultative dialogue that is ahead for the Catholic Church, one consideration will be whether use of the term "law" regarding spiritual matters is appropriate at all. When the budding Alcoholics Anonymous movement was struggling to define itself in the mid-1930s, somebody (anonymous!) came up with a phrase to help protect from poor leadership arising in the form of overregulation: "We make no spiritual laws. We only make spiritual suggestions." While a legal framework will be necessary to guide functioning of an organizational structure relative to secular establishments, won't wise leaders always remember Jesus' teaching that the law is there only to serve humanity rather than vice versa?[9]

From the New Testament recorded misuse of the Hebrew Decalogue to the lifeless 1983 version of the Code of Canon Law to the unspoken political norms that now often govern without counsel, law has always failed to promote love. Only uncommon wisdom that knows the primacy of love deeply in the soul can keep its place as protecting the boundaries of relationships rather than micromanaging their play. A broad range of committed, experienced, informed, and intimately loving people need to consult intensively and extensively in order to find a contemporary form of ecclesiastical law. It will honor charism over correctness, feature protective general statements rather than arid definitions, and value spiritual growth over organizational neatness. And it will be a thin book.

Deft Fortitude

Serving as a leader has become far more difficult since hippies, Richard Nixon, *Humanae Vitae*, and Vatican II. Criticizing religious leaders has become more common than ever before. No leader, secular or ecclesiastical, can function well now without considerable fortitude.

The virtue of fortitude must be distinguished carefully from excessive stubbornness, however. While being stubborn can provide virtuous strength to standing your ground in solidity, fortitude finds greater courage to move ahead rather than merely holding on. There are world bishops calling for another global council, a "Vatican III" if you will, banding together to seek signatures of others who will join them. There are other bishops who avert their eyes from members of their clergy who secretly maintain sexual relationships while ostensibly living celibate lives. There are many priests who will not hazard preaching their own deep spiritual convictions for fear of losing their positions of church leadership. There are leaders of all levels who know and appreciate gay and lesbian people actively living in committed love with one another and see them as loved by God like anyone else, gifted for ministry, and some called to ordination. And there are ordaining prelates who personally know women they believe are called by God to be ordained priests and remain silent about their right to ordain them. When will individual and communal fortitude grow so great that silence will no longer serve our integrity? It is then that we will join voices and stand for what we believe in the depth of our souls. It is then that true counsel will begin.

Finally, Awe

In the historical drama movie *The New World* (New Line Cinema, 2005), set in the early seventeenth century, Captain Smith falls in love with Native American girl Pocahontas, woos her, and then leaves her in the middle of the night, without a good-bye, to pursue his grand world exploration career. Years later, returning to England, where she now resides, he meets with her, presumably to assess any future for their relationship. She knows she still loves him and has even told her husband so. Looking at her intently, Smith reflects the depth of his recent pondering with the words, "I thought it was a dream, what we had in the forest. But it's the only truth." "Perfect love casts out fear" (1 Jn 4:18) but not the awe that mystery will always evoke. The intimate loving mystery is there to remind us in daily ways that partnering with the Beyond is the only worthwhile spiritual path.

Notes

1. Garry Wills, *The Papal Sin: Structures of Deceit* (New York, Doubleday, 2000).

2. See the Association for Clinical Pastoral Education website at www.ACPE.edu. See also books such as Charles Hall, *Head and Heart: The Story of the Clinical Pastoral Education Movement* (Decatur, Ga.: Journal of Pastoral Care Publications, 1992), and Joan E. Hemenway, *Inside the Circle: A Historical and Practical Inquiry concerning Process Groups in Clinical Pastoral Education* (Decatur, Ga.: Journal of Pastoral Care Publications, 1996).

3. Op. cit., Flannery.

4. John Markey, *Creating Communion: The Theology of the Constitutions of the Church* (Hyde Park, N.Y.: New City Press, 2003).

5. Henry David Thoreau, *A Week on the Concord and Merrimack Rivers* (Princeton, N.J.: Princeton University Press, 2004), Friday chapter.

6. Jerome S. Bruner, *After John Dewey, What?* (New York: Bank Street College of Education Publications, 1961).

7. Dan Schutte, *Here I Am Lord* (www.danschutte.com/works.htm).

8. William Cowper, *The Poems of William Cowper, The Task, Book VI, The Winter Walk at Noon* (London: Oxford University Press, 1905), 221.

9. Mark 2:27. Then he said to them, "The Sabbath was made for man, not man for the Sabbath."

Index

addiction recovery, spiritual insight from, xiii, 7, 41, 43, 51, 73–75, 98, 151. See also alcoholism; Alcoholics Anonymous; Al-Anon

Adler, Alfred: and discouragement, 8; and education for partnership, xv; and true partnership, 162

adolescence as a new spiritual arena, xi, xiv, 18, 23, 25, 26, 31, 55–56, 61, 64, 89, 92, 99, 121, 130, 163. See also arousal

agape, xiv, 16, 101–102, 104, 107; and communing, 108–111; and leaders, 125–128; and matrimony, 114; and the principle of solidarity, 160–161; and reconciliation, 117. See also love, selfless

Al-Anon, spiritual insight from, 73–74

Alcoholics Anonymous and spirituality, 6, 12, 73, 78

alcoholism: and counsel, 40–43; and gluttony, 72–75; and temperance, 98–99

anger, 26, 30, 31, 48, 62, 80–82, 111, 149, 151. See also wrath

anointing of the sick (Last Rites), 123–124

arousal, xvi, 21, 55, 56, 63, 64, 135

Arrupe, Pedro, S.J., 11

Augustine of Hippo, 60, 69, 99

autoeroticism, 59, 63, 64, 135, 148. See also masturbation

avarice, 71. See also greed

awe: in counsel, 172; and dying, 122; of intimacy (fear of the Lord), 5, 10, 12, 23, 30, 44–46, 79; in leadership, 179; in parenting, 78; in worship, 104, 107–110

baptism and belonging, 104–107

benignity (simple goodness): in leadership, 168; in romance, 22–23

birth control, 63, 66, 80, 171

capital sins (seven deadly sins), 53–85, 54, 81

cardinal virtues, 87–99. See also fortitude; justice; prudence; temperance

care: altruistic, xiv, 78, 101–102, 148,159; anger and, 80–82; communal, 159, 173; intimate 18, 19, 24–25, 31, 33, 35, 36–40, 56, 63, 73, 76, 77, 98, 108, 116, 144, 159; ministerial or pastoral, xiii, 12, 46, 47, 79, 91, 101–102, 107, 121, 124, 125, 126, 129–130, 132, 140, 139–152, 143, 144, 145, 170; parental, 25, 93; self, 48, 82, 121, 156, 176; therapeutic, 9. See also fortitude caress, 16, 19, 20, 23, 24–25, 26, 33, 63, 98, 110, 119

Catholic social principle (Catholic social teaching), 153–164; of association, 156; of the common good, 163–164; of human dignity, 155–156; of human equality, 162–163; of participation, 157–158; of preferential treatment, 159–160; of respect for human life, 156; of solidarity, 160; of stewardship, 161; of subsidiary justice, 161–162

de Chardin, Pierre Teilhard, 101

charity: antithesis of greed, 71; and the corporal works of mercy, 139–45, 142, 145; as fruit of the Spirit, 15, 18–20; as grounding the evangelical counsels, 101, 130; as sexual generosity, 18–20; and spiritual leadership, 168; and the spiritual works of mercy, 145–152; as theological virtue, 4, 10–12, 101. *See also* love

charisms (gifts for life and ministry), 112, 127, 172–173, 178

chastity: as committed celibate, 135–36; as Evangelical counsel, 129, 132–136; and lust, 56; as married, 133–34; as single, 135

Code of Canon Law, 178

commitment: to celibacy, 64; to intimate relationship, xv, 16, 43, 47, 50, 63, 65, 72, 77, 83, 113, 114, 133, 144, 178; to spiritual excellence, 37, 95, 105, 170, 175, 176, 178

communing, 104, 107–112

communion of saints, 151

community: charisms and, 173; Christian, 106, 107, 112, 120, 121, 125, 148, 151, 166; and dying, 122; and eros, xiv, 101–181, 111; and the Evangelical Counsels, 129–130, 137; global, xv, 34, 72, 97, 102, 105, 154, 158, 161; and leaders, 125, 176, 177; and partnering, xv, 40, 42

compulsion, 109–110

corporal works of mercy, 139–145; bury the dead, 144–145; clothe the naked, 142; feed the hungry, 141; give drink to the thirsty, 141–142; shelter the homeless, 143–144; visit the imprisoned, 142–143; visit the sick, 144

Confession, 116, 117–120

Confirmation, 104, 105, 120–122

confrontation in love, 43, 74, 81, 113, 126, 133, 146–147

consultation, 42, 52, 56, 63, 65, 66, 117, 125, 136, 145, 156, 157, 160, 162, 169–172, 177, 178. *See also* the gift of counsel

counsel: as developed skill and virtue, 42, 135; as an Evangelical Counsel, 129–138; as Gift of the Spirit, 30, 40–42

counseling, 52, 81, 117, 133, 146, 148

counter transference, 35

Decalogue, The, 156, 178

Dante (Alighieri), 61; greed in *The Inferno*, 70; lust in *The Inferno*, 61

Debs, Eugene, 160

Deus Caritas Est, 174

Divine Law, 62

divorce, 9, 12, 47–52, 48, 52, 82, 116, 126, 134, 146

domestic violence, 52, 81, 82, 92–94, 162

dying, xiii, 5, 49, 50, 122–124, 141, 152, 155

envy, 54, 69, 75–77

Eucharist, xvi, 40, 45, 105, 107–112, 123. *See also* communing; communion

eros: and Catholic social teaching (principles), 153–164; and chastity, 132–136; and communing, 108–112; and Confirmation, 120–122; defined, xv, 29; and global community, 20, 101; and greed, 70–72; and intimacy, 23; and justice 91–95; as love, xiv, 5, 10, 20, 29, 32, 36, 56, 102; and matrimony, 112–115; and poverty, 136–138; and pride, 77–80; and reconciliation, 115–119; and sloth, 84–85; as spiritual, 1, 20, 23, 33, 47, 69, 103–104; and spiritual leaders, 124–128, 165–179; and temperance, 91–95; and the works of mercy, 139–152

faith, 4, 4–7, 46, 47, 48, 49–50, 58, 96, 113, 127, 171, 172, 173
fornication, 27, 61–65
fortitude, 21, 42–44, 95–99; and care, 96; defined, 42, 96; etymology of, 42
Fox, Matthew, 16
Freud, Sigmund, 11, 35
fruit of the Spirit, 15–27; benignity (simple goodness), 22–23; charity (sexual generosity), 18–19; gentleness, 24–25; joy, 16–18; kindness, 23–24; patience, 21–22; peace, 20–21; self-control ("long suffering"), 27; St. Paul and the, 15; trustfulness, 25–27

gay, 12, 60, 114, 115, 127, 144, 147, 157, 162, 178. See also homosexuals; lesbians
gentleness, 24–25. See also caress; kiss
gifts of the Spirit, 29–46; awe (fear of the Lord), 44–46; counsel, 40–42; fortitude, 42–44; knowledge, 31–34; piety, 36–40; understanding, 30–31; wisdom, 34–36
Ginder, Richard, 66
global community. See community, global
gluttony, 72–75. See also addiction
von Goethe, Johann Wolfgang 15
Gottman, John, 11, 111
Grafenberg spot, 19, 63
greed, 44, 54, 70–72, 137, 139. See also avarice
grief, 9, 47–52, 123–124, 149, 150, 152, 156, 167
G spot, 19, 63
guilt, ix, 22, 23, 48, 50, 82, 94, 115–120, 135, 146, 151

healing, vii, viii, ix, 9, 15, 25, 26; power of love for, 58–59; of sexual misconceptions, 61–66
Holy Orders, 105; and leadership, 124–128
homosexuals, 114, 115, 144. See also gay
hope: and addiction, 7, 72; and belonging, 104–107, 137; and communing, 109; and depression, 9; and despair 9; failures of, 9, 58, 81, 94, 112; and fortitude, 95; and leaders, 127; levels of, 8; and romantic love, 3, 4, 7–10, 11,

26, 42, 43, 49, 50, 140 ; and soul-flow 6, 9, 10, 132
Hosea, 5–6
Humanae Vitae, 61

incest, spiritual damage from, xii, 58, 59, 62, 89, 147
indulge, indulgence: and chastity, 132–136; excessive, 27, 54–55, 73, 74 75, 88; loving, 58; mutual, 15, 16, 33, 54; self, 9, 27, 54, 64
intimate, intimacy, xi-xvi; and adolescence, 130; and Confirmation, 121; defined, 16, 29, 98, 131; failure of, 47–52, 53–68, 69–85; and faith, 4–7; and friendship, 15; and fruits of the Spirit, 15–28; and hope, 7–10; intentionality and, 17, 18–20, 56, 60, 89; and justice, 92–95; and law, 10; and leaders, 91, 117–119, 124–128; and lust, 57, 59, 61; maturing influence of, 1, 29–46, 58, 65; as mystery, 3–4, 6, 58; and pain, 47–53, 58, 59, 62, 65; and sacraments, 103–128; as spiritual, 11, 53, 54, 102, 103; and the virtue of chastity, 133–134

Janus, Roman god, 53
Joel, Billy, 9, 58, 121
joy; and anger, 81; of belonging, 104, 107; of communing, 112, 128; of early romance, 87, 16–18, 97, 104, 111, 135; versus excess, 74, 75, 76; and mild excess, 87, 97, 99; as fruit of the Spirit, 15, 16–18, 78; and leaders, 168; versus lust, 60, 61, 64; of maturing love, 97, 111, 118, 121, 127, 138; as spiritual, 4, 10, 11, 26, 38, 44, 54; of women, 19, 59
justice, 5, 91–95; as cardinal virtue, 87, 91–95; and Catholic social principles, 154, 158, 160, 161–162; defined, 92, 163; and fortitude, 96; and gay lovers, 114, 158; global, 94; learned from intimate loving, 92–95; and reconciliation, 116; and sloth, 83; subsidiary, 161–162; and the works of mercy, 142, 145

Kama Sutra, 17
Kennedy, Eugene C., 80
kindness, 23–24
Kinsey, Albert, 11, 62
kiss, (see also caress) xiv, 18, 104, 119
knowledge, 31–34
Kucinich, John, 164

lesbians, 12, 114, 162, 178. See also gay; homosexuals
Lewis, C.S., 48; The Four Loves, 53, 56; A Grief Observed, 45
loneliness, 41, 48, 65, 81, 82, 104, 106–107, 145
love: barriers to, 69–85; and belonging, 104–107; and Catholic social teaching, 153–164; and chastity, 132–136; and communing, 107–112; and Confirmation, 120–122; and dying, 122–124; end of, 47–53; and faith, 4–7; and fear, 12; and hope, 7–10; intimate, xi, xii, xiii, xiv, xv, xvi; and leaders, 124–128, 166–178; and lust, 53–67; and matrimony, 112–115; maturing, viii, 6; and mercy, 139–152; and obedience, 130–132; and pain, 5, 47–53; and poverty, 136–138; primacy of, 10–12; and reconciling, 115–120; and regulation, 12; romantic, 3, 4, 5; types of, 101–102; and virtue, 1, 15–28, 29–46, 87–99; and vulnerability, 5. See also agape; eros; intimate love
love-seeking, xiii, 15, 62, 63, 64, 66, 89, 91, 114, 121, 133, 167
loving Spirit (or loving mystery), 3–4
lust, lusty, 53–67; in Dante's Inferno, 61; as Deadly (Capital) Sin, 54; as loving, 62, 89; original meanings, 57; as personally destructive, 55, 58, 61, 62, 114, 115; and prudence, 91; traditional meanings, 60; versus eros, 58, 64

Masters and Johnson, 62
masturbation, 20, 59–60, 61, 63, 135, 136; and celibacy, 136. See also autoeroticism
matrimony, 112–115; of gays, 114–115
maturing eros, 1, 29–46, 58, 65, 97, 111, 118, 121, 127, 138; defined, 29

Mill, John Stewart, and the contribution of marriage to morality, 94
ministry, 38, 52, 64, 91, 101, 127, 129, 136, 143, 144; and Clinical Pastoral Education, 170; gifts for, 107, 178; and regulation, 177; and spiritual leaders, 107, 170, 173, 175; training for, 91, 118, 170
morals, morality: and the Capital Sins, 87, 88; and pastoral, 119, 174, 176; and spiritual, xii, xiv, 17, 53–54, 53–67, 114; teaching of 12, 61, 65, 73, 81, 83; theology, 27, 53, 54, 60, 62, 63
Muhammad, 145
mutual pleasuring 4, 16
mutual vulnerability 4
mystery, 3

narcissism, (as destructive pride), 77–80
Narcissus, 77
Natural Law, 63

obedience, 130–132; erotic obedience defined, 131
obesity, 74
obsession, 109–110
ordination, 124–128
orgasm, orgasmic: 16, 19, 20, 44, 45, 56, 58, 62, 63, 64, 84, 132, 173
oxytocin, 19, 62, 63

pain, of romance, 5, 16, 17, 24, 30, 33, 34, 36, 44, 47–53, 72, 73, 75, 116, 117, 149
St. Paul, 4, 6, 12, 15, 27, 54, 93, 172, 174
partnering, elements of, 40
Paschal Mystery, 47–52
Patience, 20–21
Peace: after breakup, 49; as fruit of the Spirit, 15, 18, 20–21; of grief healing, 144; kiss of, xiv; and leaders, 168; of sharing, 132; world, 138, 164
piety: as gift of the Spirit, 30, 36–40; leaders and, 174–176; partnering, 36–40
Pinkola-Estes, Clarissa 19
pleasure: and anger, 81; and awe, 44; and eros, 102, 126, 132; and fortitude, 43; and hurt, 116; influence of, 16, 45, 131, 133; and justice, 92; and lust, 57, 58, 59; and lusty love, 57, 58; and mercy, 82;

and morality, xi, 53–67, 58, 59, 60, 73;
mutual, xii, 4, 5, 12, 16, 18–20, 21, 29,
34, 46, 75, 90, 105, 111; oneself, 135,
136; and sloth, 83, 84; as spiritual, xi,
xii, xiv, xvi, 1, 15, 18, 29, 66, 87; and
temperance, 97; women's, 63. *See also*
arousal; autoeroticism; masturbation
poverty (as a virtue), 136–138; defined,
137; as evangelical counsel, 136–138;
versus greed, 70–72
power-over, 111, 126
presumption (as failure of hope), 8–9, 112
pride (as capital sin), 54, 69, 77–80
priest (as spiritual leader), xvi, 64, 66, 103,
111–12, 112, 124–128, 177; and
anointing, 123; and celibacy, 135–136;
and fortitude, 178; giftedness for
priesthood, 165; priesthood of all
believers, 107, 148; and reconciliation,
115–120
prudence (as cardinal virtue), 87, 88–91; as
component of loving confrontation, 146;
and drunkenness, 73; defined, 89; and
justice, 103; and leaders, 167

Rahner, Karl, 112
rape, xii, 58, 59, 89, 115
reconciliation (Confession), 104; intimate,
104; and leaders, 125; as sacramental
ministry, 104, 115–120
respect for human life, 156
ritual, 39, 104, 105, 108, 109, 110, 112,
113, 117, 119, 123, 124, 125, 127
romance, romantic love: defined, 16; and
joy, 16–18. *See also* eros
Rumi, Jalaludin, 1, 115

sacrament, xiii, xvi, 102, 103–104,
104–128, 176; of Anointing the Sick,
122–124; of Baptism (belonging),
104–107; of Confirmation (maturing),
120–122; of Eucharist (communing),
107–112; of Holy Orders (leading),
124–128; of Matrimony, xii, xvi,
112–115; of Reconciliation, 115–120
sacramental, 50
sacred: anger and the, 81, 111; awe and the,
45; intimate love as, xvi, 77, 157, 164;

joy as, 18; leaders, 112; marriage as, 114;
person as, 157; Vatican Constitution on
the Liturgy as, 107
Schnarch, David, 29
Schulz, Charles, 18
seduction, 57–58; as loving, 57
self-control: as fruit of the Spirit, 15, 27;
and patience, 21; in confrontation, 146
seven deadly sins (capital sins), 1, 69,
54–85; defined and named, 54
sexual continuum, 62
sin, xi, 9, 54, 71, 73; anger as, 81–82;
laziness as, 82–83; mortal or serious, 60;
primal, 77–80; venial or minor, 60;
sexual, 61, 63, 65
sloth (laziness), 82–84
social action, xi, 139, 139–152, 153–164.
See also Catholic social teaching;
corporal works of mercy; spiritual works
of mercy
social gospel, 154
social justice, 154. *See also* social action
soul, xi, xvi, 1, 3, 5, 7, 8, 9, 10, 11, 15, 17,
18, 19, 20, 21, 22, 24, 25, 29, 31, 32, 36,
56, 70, 103, 176, 177; and awe, 44, 79;
and belonging, 104–107; and
communing, 108–112; and dying, 123;
etymology of, 26; flow between souls, 8,
9, 10, 21, 26, 34, 37, 38, 46, 51, 52, 63,
70, 98, 99, 132; and fortitude, 44, 96;
and joy, 18, 39; of leaders, 166, 169,
178; and matrimony, 112–115; and
prudence, 87; and maturing love, 29, 30,
31, 32, 36, 93, 132; and pain, 47, 49, 58,
71, 73, 75, 77, 81, 147, 149, 175; and
piety, 37; and reconciliation, 117; sex
and, 55; sharing of, 21, 26, 137; and
social spirituality, 142, 143, 144, 145,
152, 153, 159. *See also* soul-flow
spirit: etymology of, 26
spirituality, vii, xii; and anger, 80;
communal, xii, 102, 125, 127; and
communing, 107–112; defined, xv, 4, 54;
functional, 4, 103, 176; and humility,
78; individual, 1, 37, 144, 160, 166;
intimate, xii, xvi, 3, 38, 54, 161, 174; of
leaders, xiii, 165–179, 112, 125, 128,
165–178; and morality, 12, 53–67;

partnership, xv, 75, 125, 128 , 134, 175;
religious, 108; social, 130–152; women
and, xiii, 60, 62
spiritual works of mercy, 145–152;
admonish the sinner, 146; bear wrongs
patiently, 150–151; comfort the
sorrowful, 149–150; counsel the
doubtful, 148–149; instruct the ignorant,
147–148; pray for the living and the
dead, 151–152
spiritual life, xi, xii, 1, 4, 6, 7, 39, 46, 64,
70, 87, 105, 125, 130, 166, 177
stewardship of resources, individual, 161

Teilhard de Chardin, Pierre, 101
temperance, 97–99; defined, 97
theological virtues, 1, 4. See also faith;
hope; charity
Thurman, Howard, 34
Tobit (Tobias), 144
transference, 35
Trinity, 45
trustfulness, 25–27; defined, 26

understanding, 30–31

Vatican II, vii, 105, 107, 115, 119, 123,
162, 172, 178
Vatican III, 178

Wills, Garry, The Papal Sin, 66, 80
widow, 47, 122, 123, 136, 156
wisdom, 10, 17, 34–36, 33, 44, 166; and
awe, 44; collective, 148; and
confrontation, 146; defined, 34; as gift of
the Spirit, 30; and leaders, 91, 118, 125,
166, 176, 176–178; of lovers, 154, 156;
and morality, 53, 54, 88, 89; and
obedience, 130–32; and pain, 47–49;
and single chastity, 135; of women, 133
women's sexual and intimate experience,
xiii, 17, 18–20, 21, 27, 33, 51, 56, 57,
58, 60, 61, 62–63, 65, 66, 76, 78, 80,
81–82, 84, 88, 89, 90, 93, 102, 118, 126,
133, 142, 147, 151, 158, 174, 178
wrath, viii, 94; as capital sin, 54, 62, 80–82.
See also anger

~

About the Author

Gordon Hilsman, D.Min., is a lifelong Catholic. He currently directs the Pastoral Care Education programs for the Franciscan Health System in Tacoma, Washington.